The British Commandos

Winston Churchill, instigator, protagonist and champion of the Commandos, with one of the first Tommy guns procured from USA and issued to the Commandos in 1940. (Photograph by courtesy of the Imperial War Museum.)

The British Commandos

The Origins and Special Training of an Elite Unit

James Dunning

PALADIN PRESS · BOULDER, COLORADO

The British Commandos:
The Origins and Special Training of an Elite Unit
by James Dunning

Copyright © 2000, 2007 by James Dunning

ISBN 13: 978-1-58160-612-6

Printed in the United States of America

Published by Paladin Press, a division of
Paladin Enterprises, Inc.,
Gunbarrel Tech Center
7077 Winchester Circle
Boulder, Colorado 80301 USA
+1.303.443.7250

Direct inquiries and/or orders to the above address.

Originally published in the United Kingdom under the title
It Had to Be Tough: The Fascinating Story of the Origins
of the Commandos and Their Special Training in World War II.

PALADIN, PALADIN PRESS, and the "horse head" design
are trademarks belonging to Paladin Enterprises and
registered in United States Patent and Trademark Office.

Visit our Web site at www.paladin-press.com

This book, commemorating the
60th anniversary of the founding of
the Commandos, is dedicated to all those
who served in the Commandos in the
Second World War and, in particular, to
those 1,706 members killed in action.

'We will remember them . . .'

Contents

List of Illustrations ix

Introduction xi

Chapter I   'A Bold Step' – Churchill's Commandos 1

Chapter II   Setting Up – Billets and Organization 23

Chapter III   Making a Start – Initial Training and Tribulations 33

Chapter IV   On the Water – Small Boats and Landing Craft 54

Chapter V   Weapon Training – Shoot to Kill 69

Chapter VI   Training Centres – Lochailort and Achnacarry 88

Chapter VII   Special Operational Training –
The St Nazaire and Dieppe Raids 126

Chapter VIII   Small Canoes and Thick Jungles – SBS and Burma 149

Chapter IX   Snow, Mountains and Surf 163

Chapter X   Parachuting Pioneers 181

Chapter XI   And Finally... 193

Bibliography 207

Index 209

Illustrations

Winston Churchill . . . . Frontispiece
An assault landing led by Major Jack Churchill 15
Photograph from Troop Diary, September 1940 49
No 4 Commando act as 'Fifth Columnists' 50
'Out Troops' – disembarking from a landing craft (LCA) 56
Commando Bren gunner 71
Tackling barbed wire – 'Me and My Pal' style (2) 72
In action from Goatley folding boats 79
Unarmed combat (2) 96
Natural obstacle courses in Scotland (2) 98
The parade ground at Achnacarry 99
Lord Lovat and Lieutenant Colonel Charles Vaughan 100
The 'cemetery' at Achnacarry 104
The Toggle Bridge 112
Ropes used for crossing obstacles 115
The Achnacarry fleet 119
A mock-up used for street fighting 122
Boxing on board the Ulster Monarch, 1941 124
Logs used for PT 136
Canoeists of 101 Troop 151
C Troop climbing in North Wales (3) 165
Snow and mountain warfare in the Cairngorms 172
Commando Ridge, Cornwall 174
The Death Slide, Cornwall 175
Parachute pioneer 183
Parachute training – the 'hole exit' 184
And Finally. 205

Introduction

The seeds of this story were sown some years ago after I had given a talk at the National Army Museum on 'Commando Training in World War 2'. Several of the audience wanted to know more and suggested that it warranted a book devoted to the origins of the 'Green Berets', the types who volunteered and how they, building on the best of the past, initiated and developed a whole range of new-style and demanding forms of military training that became universally known as 'Commando Training'.

I accepted the challenge and this book, now appearing to mark the 60th anniversary of the founding of the Commandos, is the outcome.

There is an old military maxim, 'Train hard, fight easy', and this was undoubtedly the guiding philosophy of the Commandos from the onset. Those who couldn't make the grade were 'returned to unit' (RTU).

But it wasn't straightforward or easy, the enthusiastic and eager-for-action volunteers were beset by many difficulties, problems and frustrations. Ironically this, in effect, helped to weed out those who couldn't take it.

However, within months the exploits of this new force of Commandos had captured the imagination of Allied servicemen and civilians alike.

Although there was some ill-advised newspaper publicity which presented Commandos as hard and mean gangster-like thugs, nothing was further from the truth – as is explained in the story – and success in action came as a result of adhering to such well-tested and tried military principles as sound leadership, thorough and rigorous training, discipline and high morale.

The potential offensive operations visualized by Churchill for his Commandos involved both seaborne and airborne landings on enemy-held territory, but in 1940 there was neither the means nor the training experience to immediately carry out these operations. A couple of seaborne raids were made within weeks of the Commandos being formed but they were disappointing failures, inadequate training being a major cause.

As a result new methods, skills, drills and techniques had to be developed, too frequently from scratch, to meet the demands of intended offensive operations.

The list of subjects to be covered was formidable, including such innovations as cliff climbing, mountaineering and parachuting. Fortunately within the ranks of the original Commando volunteers were leaders with the drive and imagination to initiate and develop the necessary regime of training adequate for the tasks ahead. How they achieved success is told in the story that follows, and, of course, in the impressive list of thirty-eight Battle Honours and the numerous awards, including no less than eight Victoria Crosses, for bravery in action.

But that's not all. 'Commando Training' became an accepted military model that set standards and targets for the rest of the Allied armies including the US Rangers. Furthermore, two of the original Commando volunteers, David Stirling and Roger Courtney, founded the Special Air Service (SAS) and the Special Boat Section (SBS) whilst the original No 2 Commando, Britain's first parachute unit, became the predecessor of the Parachute Regiment. It is, therefore, a salutory thought to reflect that today all of these four Special Forces owe their origins to the Commandos of 1940 and have continued to base their training on the principles, patterns and standards of Commando Training pioneered sixty years ago.

So much then by way of an introduction. I must now take this opportunity to acknowledge and thank all those old comrades, friends and others who have helped in the writing of this book, making contributions or lending pictures; in addition some authors have kindly allowed me to quote from their books. Instead of listing all these people here I decided to acknowledge their help by naming them in the context of their contribution in the narrative itself. I thought this would be more appropriate.

However, having said that, there are exceptions. First I must pay tribute to the help and encouragement of my wife, Jane. She has prompted and prodded me over the years to complete the book in time for the anniversary – and bearing in mind my advancing years, 'before it's too late!' I must thank my son, Graham, too, for his generous help and support, but I would be amiss if I didn't acknowledge the advice and help of our stalwart, Henry Brown, Secretary and Treasurer for forty years and currently President of the Commando Association; also his successor, as Secretary and Treasurer, Ron Youngman.

Finally, but by no means least, I am very grateful to those individuals and organizations who have kindly made donations towards the costs of production of this book.

To one and all, named and unnamed, I offer my sincere thanks.

Romsey, January 2000   James Dunning

CHAPTER I

'A Bold Step' –
Churchill's Commandos

The Commandos were formed at a time in the Second World War when Britain's fortunes were at their lowest ebb. It was the summer of 1940. Within three weeks in that June the armies of France, Britain and the Lowland Countries were defeated and routed by Hitler's forces, who then swept on to the Channel ports forcing the withdrawal from Europe of the British Expeditionary Force (BEF). Their successful evacuation via Dunkirk was hailed as a miracle, but it incurred the loss, apart from personal weapons, of practically all the considerable remaining weapons, stores and equipment.

It was a tragic military disaster leaving Britain standing alone and ill-equipped, whilst the Germans, now masters of Europe from the Arctic to the Pyrenees stood poised ready to invade these islands. The Nazis had an invasion plan (Operation Sea Lion) and indeed made a start with a series of daylight raids by the Luftwaffe on targets in the south of England.

Winston Churchill had only taken over as Prime Minister and Minister of Defence in the May, and, thus, his first few weeks in office were witness to a catalogue of defeats and disasters merely outlined above.

By July the threat of invasion was real and it completely dominated the thoughts and lives of all in these islands. They were grim days. To meet this dire threat our first lines of defence were on the sea and in the air.

Fortunately the two services involved, the Royal Navy and the Royal Air Force were in better shape to meet the threat than the Army, which was frantically reorganising and re-equipping after the 'deliverance of Dunkirk'. A new volunteer force, the Local Defence Volunteers (LDV), later retitled the Home Guard, was also in the process of being formed to bolster the regular land forces available to meet the invasion threat, but they as yet had few weapons.

The main priority for everyone whether in the Forces, Civil Defence, munitions or industry was clear and undisputed – the defence of Britain. Churchill recalled the mood of those momentous days, 'This was a time when all Britain worked and strove to the utmost limit and was united as never before ... the sense of fear seemed entirely lacking in the people ... Nothing moves an Englishman so much as the threat of invasion, the reality unknown for a thousand years ...'

It was then in this awesome atmosphere, with daily fears of German tanks coming ashore and German parachutists descending from the skies, that Churchill took the bold decision to look ahead beyond the immediate bleak future and propose the raising of an elite military force to take the initiative and carry the fight to the enemy with some forms of offensive action.

In the short term, and raised immediately, they would be available for defence, 'to spring at the throat of any small landings or descents'. But the main purpose of these storm troops, or Commandos as they soon became known, was to wage a continuous campaign of tip-and-run raids on the enemy's extended European coastline, thereby establishing a reign of terror prior to the eventual invasion of Europe. For even in those dark days Churchill was confident of ultimate victory and the liberation of Europe from Nazi tyranny.

Some special forces had already been formed and had been sent to Norway soon after being formed without having time to train and settle down as units. When they returned to Britain after that doomed expedition they were deployed on anti-invasion duties. Known as Independent Companies, they had been recruited mainly from Territorial Army (TA) infantry battalions. Later they were integrated into the Commandos.

In spite of the existence of the Independent Companies Churchill wanted his own corps of shock troops and to start afresh. In a typical Churchillian memorandum he outlined his proposals to the Chiefs of Staff. In all the books written on Commandos and dealing with the subject of their origins credit is rightly afforded to Lieutenant Colonel Dudley Clarke, Military Assistant to the Chief of the Imperial General Staff for the initial outline plan for their formation. Clarke, who had served in Palestine at the time of the Arab Rebellion, had made a study of guerilla warfare, and so was admirably placed to set out his ideas with a plan. This was duly approved as was the name 'Commandos'.

However, it was a memorandum written by the then Director of Military Operations, Major General R.H. Dewing, which is fully quoted in Charles Messenger's definitive history of the deeds and actions of the Commandos, 1940-1945, that clearly sets out the 'nitty-gritty' details of how the units of this elite force would be recruited and also the means of organizing the unorthodox subsistence arrangements and administration.

One restriction on recruiting was imposed from the onset, namely, that no single existing unit should be diverted from its paramount task – the defence of Britain – to set up these forces. Instead, volunteers would be sought from all units within all the Commands (regional concentrations of troops) of Great Britain.

Furthermore volunteers were sought, not just from the 'teeth' arms, i.e. infantry, tank regiments and the artillery, but also from the 'services' such as the Royal Army Service Corps. Indeed, several outstanding early Commando volunteers came from the latter units.

To make a start, after calling for volunteers – officers, NCOs and other ranks – in each Army Command, a suitable volunteer officer would be selected as a Commando Leader/Commanding Officer with the rank of Lieutenant Colonel.

These COs would choose their own ten Troop (sub-unit) Leaders and they could be captains already, or if not, promoted to that rank. They in turn would select their own two subordinate Section officers and the remaining 40-odd NCOs and men to make up the full Troop of 50 all ranks. This would provide in total, with a handful of administrative officers and other ranks (details later in Chapter II) just over 500 altogether in each Commando.

Having settled the basic organization General Dewing outlined the general principles governing administration, training and the pattern for operations.

Although it was intended that the Commandos would be self-sufficient and operate with a minimum amount of administrative chores, it was recognized that there would be a need for an administrative officer 'to relieve the Commanding Officer of paper work and carry out fundamental administration'. He would set up a permanent HQ in the Commando's 'Home Town'.

General Dewing's directive concluded with this summary:

The main characteristics of a Commando are:

(a) Capable only of operating independently for 24 hours.
(b) Capable of very wide dispersion and individual action.
(c) Not capable of resisting an attack or overcoming a defence of formed troops, i.e. (Commandos will be) specialising in tip and run tactics dependent on success and upon speed, ingenuity and dispersion.

The history of the Commandos from 1940 to 1945 records how the original concept of tip-and-run raids was extended so that they were increasingly used for sustained operations for which they were neither organized nor equipped. It due course these drastic changes in the roles of the Commandos affected the organization because the scale of weapons had to be increased, whilst transport and wireless sets were but two other additions needed to meet the extensions to the role of Commandos. Consequently from early 1942 these changes naturally affected and increased the range of subjects to be covered in Commando training.

However, for the moment it is intended to show how the original proposals for the recruiting and formation of the Commandos materialized.

Fortunately, it can be followed, in the case of a Troop in No 4 Commando, from a surviving diary of those days. Its story is typical of the other Troops in all Commandos.

For forty-five years the 'F' Troop diary had been preserved by ex-Sgt Vic (Tich) Garnett who, as one of the original members of that Troop, kindly lent it to me.

The cover of the diary is battered and worn, but inside the contents are as legible as on the day they were penned – in ink – in those pre-Biro days. The introduction captures the atmosphere of the post-Dunkirk and invasion-threatened period: 'A True Record of the trials and adventures of F Troop of No 4 Commando during the years when Great Britain alone fought for the freedom of nations'.

Written by our Troop Leader, Capt L.C. Young (The Bedfordshire and Hertfordshire Regiment) it follows the above introduction with a description of the recruiting of his Troop:

> It was Tuesday 8th July 1940 when I was stationed at Bognor Regis that I was interviewed by Colonel Legard, commanding No 4 Commando and invited to command F Troop.
>
> I accepted his invitation . . . and went to the Salisbury Plain area to choose the men for my Troop . . . I established my Headquarters in the George Hotel, Amesbury, and from there set out each morning on the important task of finding the right men . . .

He interviewed me in nearby Bulford camp where I was serving as a sergeant in a Royal Armoured Corps (RAC) training establishment.

Here it is relevant to explain that the officers and men being interviewed were volunteers who, through notices in their unit orders had applied to serve in 'Special Service Forces'. There was a paucity of details about the nature of these forces, but for many it seemed implicit in the short list of qualifications required. In my case the unit orders had specified, 'able to swim, not prone to sea-sickness, prepared to parachute or travel in a submarine and able to drive a motor car and ride a motor cycle'.

The names of all the volunteers were forwarded from units to the local District Headquarters and made available to the interviewing Commando officers. Although each Commando Leader had provided guidelines for these interviews to each of his ten Troop Leaders, they, in turn, interpreted them with a bias dependent on their own beliefs and the priority they gave to the various factors involved, plus of course, their own arm of service background, i.e. infantry, tanks, artillery, Brigade of Guards etc. To this extent the selection was subjective, reflecting personal preferences – as the following three examples, taken at random, show.

Peter Young (a formidable Commando Leader introduced later in this chapter), writing on the subject and his method, had this to say: 'To pick them? You look at them, don't you? You talk to them a bit, make up your mind if he's a bull-shitter or has something to contribute . . . you can tell. Young soldiers are good. They have no wives or children to consider . . . A good old soldier is a good soldier, but a bad old soldier is worse than useless . . . '

Another Commando Leader, Roger Courtney – more about him later too – wrote: 'My first choice was any Boy Scout, especially ex-Rover Scouts, they need no explanation.' He also favoured any army bandsmen because 'they were universally known as good shots on account of their particular training, playing an instrument, reading the music and marching, all at the same time. This makes them excellent marksmen, because they have to do three things at once – aligning foresight, backsight and target at the same time, at any range and with any weapon.' In addition he went for studious and artistic types because they were super sensitive which he reckoned was essential for his own specialized Commando sub-unit, the Special Boat Section (SBS).

Another famous Commander Leader, Bob Laycock, had a couple of pertinent suggestions: 'Choose your other ranks more carefully than you choose your wife . . . tolerate no creepers.'

Whatever their priorities all agreed there was one undesirable type none wanted, 'the swaggering tough type, whose toughness was mostly displayed in pubs under the influence of alcohol'.

We all have our tales to tell about the interviews. But in all instances it was clear that there was no shortage of volunteers. It appeared that the acceptance rate was in the order of about 1 to 6 volunteers.

What many will find extraordinary is that there were no tests of any kind, physical, medical, musketry or any other sort. Many of the early volunteers readily admit that had there been they would probably have failed. The weeding out came later in the training.

Commenting on his results, our Captain Young, having selected his two section officers and the forty-seven other ranks, wrote: 'I feel that we have got off to a flying start . . .'

Before listing all the volunteers, he added an appropriate rider: 'All of them have volunteered not only out of a sincere desire to serve this country, but also for the fun and adventure.' These last two factors were certainly prominent in the minds of the younger – rather naive – soldiers like myself.

Having been selected, we all then duly arrived from our various units at Weymouth – our appointed 'Home Town' – and were installed in civilian billets. Next day we all attended our first full Commando parade, held in the Pavilion of that Dorset resort.

There, on 22 July, some 500 officers and men, all volunteers, drawn from a wide range of famous infantry, armoured, artillery and engineer regiments, plus those from service corps, were eagerly, and apprehensively, awaiting the 'welcome' speech from our new Commanding Officer.

The Colonel wasted no time in outlining the purpose and role of our new unit, emphasizing the urgent need to settle down, and start to get fighting fit and prepare to strike back at the enemy. There was a murmur of approval.

He told us that in spite of the grave and imminent dangers of an enemy invasion we were going to take offensive action. Not for us the job of waiting for Jerry to land before we struck. No, we would go out across the Channel in small boats to carry out raids on the enemy's coastline and start a reign of terror on the Nazis. We would hit first, hard and often.

He warned the training would be demanding and tough. Those unable to meet the standards required would be returned to their unit (RTU). This method of military action was an innovation, but was to be, without any shadow of doubt, one of the fundamental factors attributing to the success of the Army Commandos. There would be no right of appeal against the CO's decision to RTU any officer or other rank; by the same token any volunteer could, in his turn, request to leave the Commando at any time. Albeit in my six years in Commandos I cannot recall any man being retained against his wish, but the number of RTUs was countless. This system of selective culling was a prerequisite to the maintenance of the highest standards of military efficiency and morale.

The Colonel went on to tell us of the origin of the unit's unfamiliar name – 'Commando'. Most of us had no idea that it belonged to an old enemy, the Boer guerillas who had wrought some humiliating defeats on Queen Victoria's redcoats in the South African War of 1899-1902.

Finally, the Colonel reiterated the urgent need to be ready for action in a matter of days and weeks, rather than months. There was no time to lose. We must all be ready as soon as possible. So with high hopes of almost immediate action, we were dismissed, excited, to start training straightaway.

In the event we, in No 4, had to wait several months before we went into action. Meanwhile we trained and trained; we even rehearsed and prepared for operations, but they were cancelled resulting in frustrations and temporary lapses in our usually high morale.

Before describing the initial organization and early training it may be of interest to look at some of the main reasons that prompted so many to volunteer for special service in the Commandos.

Basically, without going into individual cases, I contend there were three main groups of volunteers. All, in these groups, had one common and dominating reason to volunteer – 'to have a go at the Jerry'. Whatever other reason or reasons they had this was the crucial and fundamental one.

To understand the other main reason of my first group it is necessary to cast one's mind back, not just to 1940 and the then current war situation, but to before the War, to the inter-war years, when the young men were growing up. Because they did so in an era when patriotism was generally and genuinely accepted by all it was not regarded as a 'dirty' word . . .

Britons had been brought up and nurtured on beliefs in the merits, virtues and invincibility of the British Empire.

Suffice it here to provide just one example of how such patriotism was fostered. Every school, annually on 24 May, celebrated Empire Day. The day usually started with a special assembly in the school hall, at which patriotic fervour featured in hymns, songs, poems and readings. At the conclusion the school was generally dismissed for a half-day holiday or had a school outing or a sports meeting. It was a special day with significance and meaning, a day that was part of our heritage.

With this kind of background in mind, in the summer of 1940 the Fall of France, the defeat of the BEF, the threatened invasion and the growing number of enemy air raids invoked many to express their defiance and patriotism in a definite and positive way. They did so not with noisy jingoism, but with a quiet and reserved determination to strike back and restore the honour of their wounded Britain. They did not need other specific causes or ideologies; these they left to latter-day historians and commentators to expound. They refuted the age-old axiom of the old sweats, 'never volunteer for anything', but did just that. They were sure it was the right and patriotic thing to do.

The second group of volunteers consisted of the regulars, reservists, pre-War Territorials and conscripts who had survived Dunkirk and Norway. They had felt, most strongly, they had been 'let down' and were humiliated. Furthermore, the professional pride of the regulars, in particular, had been badly wounded, and that hurt. These soldiers knew they were as good as 'Jerry'. No! They were better and needed the chance to prove it. They wanted revenge, and preferably, wanted that chance quickly, as soon as possible. Volunteering for the Commandos would seem to offer this chance.

Thirdly, and finally, there were the those officers and men, some from the service corps who would not normally have been involved in offensive operations, who welcomed and cherished the prospects offered by Special Service. For them the chance 'to have a go' at the enemy – and the inherent training and methods involved – would undoubtedly provide the 'fun and adventure' mentioned in Captain Young's diary. In this group of volunteers were those intrepid Commando characters – and what 'characters' some were – who pioneered parachuting and adapted civilian mountaineering, cliff climbing and canoeing techniques for military operations, plus those leaders who founded the Special Air Service (SAS) and the Special Boat Section (SBS). Many in this group were young soldiers with little military experience, but all saw in that brief description of qualifications needed for Special Service the possibilities of excitement, fun and adventure. They were not to be disappointed . . .

So much for some of the main reasons for volunteering, but from whence did they come and exactly what manner of men were they? Briefly, as intended, they came from all the many regiments and corps in the British Army. At one time in No 4 Commando we had officers and men from over ninety different regiments and corps; all wore the cap badges of their parent unit, initially in their normal headdress, be it a forage ('fore and aft') cap, a Service Dress cap, beret or Tam'o Shanter etc., until in 1942 the green beret was introduced for all Commandos, but even then we all continued to wear our own regimental badges in the beret.

Not only did the volunteers come from all units, but they were of all ages and of all different types and backgrounds.

Although the majority were in their twenties there were some youngsters under twenty – I was just twenty. At the other end of the range were 'old sweats' nearing forty years; the latter tended to keep quiet about their age for fear of being rejected. There was a handful of exceptional officers, who as youngsters had seen active service in the First World War. In No 4 Commando examples of both types spring to mind. Two youngsters, both ex-boy soldiers and barely on 'man' service, were original members at Weymouth, Gunners Halliday and Pike were promoted in stages to Sergeant in No 4 before both were commissioned. 'Spike' Pike became a post-war officer in the Glosters and was with them when they made that glorious stand against overwhelming Chinese forces on the Imjin river in Korea.

Two 'oldies' in No 4 who developed into outstanding Commando characters were 'Chalky' Blunden and 'Private' Donkin. Both were hardened pre-war regulars, well into their thirties when they volunteered. Normally quiet and well-disciplined soldiers they were virtual tigers when roused, and most outspoken if they reckoned the task in hand was pointless, unprofessional or just 'a load of bull . . . ' On such occasions they didn't mince their words and the fact that they had not been promoted beyond acting unpaid lance corporal was evidence of their refusal to be 'Yes' men or 'creepers'. Notwithstanding in a tight corner or desperate situation they didn't question or flinch, they 'got stuck in . . .'

'Chalky' Blunden, a regular in the Rifle Brigade, became a stalwart of B Troop. He never faltered on training, speed marches or the assault courses in spite of having to carry the cumbersome, heavy and unpopular Boys anti-tank rifle. He had plenty of guts, set a good example to the younger soldiers in the Troop, and went on to win a Military Medal at Dieppe in 1942.

Arguably, most outstanding was 'Private' Donkin, an ex-miner, ex-regular and reservist of the Loyal Regiment. With his regimental mate, McVeigh (who won the Distinguished Conduct Medal, yet consistently refused promotion until late in the War) they trained – and trained – together and fought together until the death of Donkin outside a concrete bunker in the assault on Flushing in November 1944 separated them. Donkin, at forty-one years, was the oldest man in No 4 when they landed on 'D'-Day. Father of nine children, his wife was expecting 'Number ten' when he was killed. Murdoch McDougal, a section officer in No 4, in his book, *Swiftly They Struck*, recalls Donkin's end:

> Both feet planted firm, stocky body balanced on slightly bandy legs, he methodically started his tommy gun from left to right among the fifteen or so Germans visible to him by the bunker. He reached the right-hand end of his swing and was starting the return, when one man on the left, whom he

9

had missed at the start, got in a quick shot. It took him straight through the throat, killing him at once. McVeigh, who was beside him with his rifle made no mistake with his return shot . . .

So ended tragically a great comradeship that began in Weymouth in July 1940.

These men exemplified the type of 'good old soldiers' Peter Young had in mind when he set out his ideas on recruiting volunteers for the Commandos mentioned earlier.

Campaign ribbons, a rarity in 1940, on the battledress blouses of the regulars and reservists provided evidence of active service, and in our Troop were those tank men who had served on the North-West Frontier. In the other Troops were infantrymen and gunners who had also seen action in India plus others who had been involved in the Arab Revolt in Palestine. All wore the ribbons of those campaigns.

In every Commando there appeared the odd soldier – or two – who had fought against Franco in the Spanish Civil War. Youthful-looking Lew Chattaway was one of these veterans. He joined B Troop at Weymouth as a private soldier and had progressed up through the ranks to Sergeant Major in the troop by the time they stormed the beaches on D-Day. Like the others of the Spanish Civil War, Lew wore no campaign ribbons.

On the other hand there were amongst the officers a few who proudly wore their First World War ribbons. Included in this category were Lieutenant Colonel Dudley Lister MC, Major Charles Vaughan MBE, and Major J.E. Martin. I will say more about the first two later, dealing with just 'Slinger' Martin here. He, like the other two, was an original volunteer for Commandos; in his case he joined No 8 as their Administrative Officer. After the First World War he, like Vaughan, had risen through the ranks to Regimental Sergeant Major (Martin in the 16th Lancers and Vaughan in the Brigade of Guards) before being commissioned.

During the inter-war years 'Slinger' distinguished himself as an Army champion in both shooting and riding. Together with the above two, and others, Martin brought to the Commandos examples of all that was best in a formidable and experienced professional soldier of the 'old school'.

When in early 1941 No 8 Commando was posted to the Middle East Martin, much to his annoyance, was reckoned too old to accompany them and was subsequently posted to No 3. Ironically, with them he later saw action in Sicily, Italy and North-West Europe as their Admin Officer.

Among other founder members were those officers and men who were destined to become Commando heroes, a few to rate as legends within the short five years lifespan of the wartime Army Commandos. Of the original COs, four, in particular, were in this class. Pride of place must go to a young pre-war regular, Bob Laycock, of the Royal Horse Guards. He was promoted to Lieutenant Colonel on appointment to command No 8. Of average height, Laycock had a good physique, always looked fit and gave the impression of a 'strong, silent' type, who knew what he wanted and how to get it. Stationed in London District he recruited his volunteers from troops in and around the capital. Because of the high numbers of socialities in No 8, it was often called the 'Blue (blood) Commando'. Among those he recruited were the son of Winston Churchill, Randolph, and the author, Evelyn Waugh. The latter based his novel, *Officers and Gentlemen*, the second of a trilogy on the War, on his spell in No 8 Commando. Reading it one has to bear in mind it is a novel written by a satirist, and much has to be taken with a large pinch of salt. Neither Waugh nor Churchill were proven suitable as Troop Leaders in that Commando, although they were employed as staff and liaison officers.

In January 1941, after nearly six months of initial training, a spell on the Isle of Arran and a couple of disappointing raids, the scene changed dramatically when Colonel Laycock was appointed commander of a special force, Layforce (consisting of Nos 7, 8 and 11 Commandos, the newly formed canoe section – destined to become the SBS – and a Troop from No 3), and dispatched to carry out a mission in the Middle East, namely, the capture of the enemy-held island of Rhodes. Shortly after arriving in the Middle East the Rhodes operation was called off and subsequently Layforce was employed on operations in North Africa, covering the withdrawal from Crete and a raid in Syria.

Laycock, himself, took part in one of the final raids of his force, on Rommel's Headquarters in North Africa, where Colonel Keyes won the Victoria Cross. After the raid Laycock and Sergeant Terry, their planned pick-up by submarine failing to materialize, made their way back through enemy-held territory to the British lines. Their trek took forty-one days, a figure that gave rise to the nickname 'lucky' Laycock and the claim that the two had exceeded the famous Biblical fast in the desert by one day.

Shortly afterwards Layforce, sadly depleted, was disbanded. However not all the surviving Commandos were returned to field force units, two of them, both original volunteers and both outstanding junior officers, strongly convinced in the need to continue the concept of Commando operations in the Middle East, were able to persuade GHQ to allow them to develop these concepts. Captain Roger Courtney continued and expanded his Special Boat Section, which was officially recognized as such, whilst Lieutenant David Stirling (ex-No 8 Commando) was allowed to develop a special raiding force, which under his daring leadership became the famous Special Air Service (SAS). Among those he recruited from the disbanded Commandos was Paddy Mayne, who had been an original volunteer in No 11. Both Stirling and Mayne were exceptional 'big men' in every sense. Stirling stood 6ft 6ins tall; fit and lean, he had boundless energy and thrived on physical and exciting challenges. Mayne was a mountain of a man, very strong and very powerful as befitted a pre-war international rugby player.

Stirling, later nicknamed the 'Phantom Major' by the Germans, was eventually captured, through a betrayal by Arabs, in North Africa, but not before his SAS had accounted for some 150 enemy aircraft, countless vehicles and dozens of store dumps behind enemy lines.

Mayne carried on Stirling's work with further SAS operations in Sicily, Italy, France and Germany, exploits which resulted in him being awarded the DSO and three bars.

It is, surely, a salutary thought that but for the demise of Layforce neither of these famous elitist forces, the SBS and SAS, might have developed as they did during the Second World War, and subsequently become valued units of our peacetime armed forces. It's an ill wind . . .

Bob Laycock returned to Britain and took command of all the Commandos, then grouped together under the banner of the Special Service Brigade. Later in 1943 he was promoted Major General to succeed Lord Mountbatten as Chief of Combined Operations (CCO), a post he held until final victory in 1945.

Admired and respected by all who served under his command as CCO, Laycock showed unstinting regard and support for 'his Commandos'. Knowing, at first-hand, their characteristics and capabilities, he was always anxious that they should only be employed for tasks for which they were specially organized and trained to undertake. Yet in spite of his voice at the top level, the Commandos were often mis-employed, much to Laycock's chagrin.

The Commanding Officer of No 3 Commando, John Durnford-Slater, was one of the original COs who was still serving with Commandos when the War ended. By that time he had been promoted to Brigadier and was the Deputy Commander of the whole Special Service Group.

In spite of his Dickensian appearance John Durnford-Slater was a seasoned sportsman. A good horseman, he had excelled at pigsticking in India; in addition he was a useful rugby player. There was no doubting – despite his outward appearance – he was a man of action. This he demonstrated as a Commando Leader by always wanting to lead from the front, keen to be the first ashore and the last away. He did just that on No 3's first raid on one of the Channel Islands and again on the Vaagso Raid, before successfully leading his Commando on operations in Sicily and Italy, earning a well-deserved DSO and bar on route to promotion to Brigadier.

Another successful commanding officer, although not a regular peacetime soldier, was Charles Newman. He had joined the 4th Bn, the Essex Regiment of the Territorial Army in the mid-1920s. He enjoyed the comradeship and friendly attitude engendered in the TA towards soldiering. For him it made an ideal apprenticeship in man-management for his Commando days when command and discipline tended to thrive more on mutual respect rather than authoritative obedience.

Thirty-five years old at the outbreak of the War, married with a family of small children, the successful building contractor had been an early volunteer for the Independent Companies. This genial pipe-smoking, almost father-like figure, in the introduction to a book on the St Nazaire raid, provides the apparent reasons for his volunteering for the Commandos, when he wrote: 'We had been through a period of every-thing going wrong for Britain . . . and as we all loved Britain we had an earnest desire to do something about it, to strike back . . .' And strike back he and his men of No 2 Commando did in March 1942 with the St Nazaire raid.

Finally, in this quartet of original commanding officers who distinguished themselves and led their Commandos to fame and glory was Lieutenant Colonel Ronnie Tod, of the Argyll and Sutherland High-landers. Like Newman he had originally volunteered for the Independent Companies and commanded No 6 Company, but when these Companies were absorbed into the Commandos he commanded No 9. Apart from a small raid in late 1941 No 9 had to wait for some time before seeing plenty of action in Italy and in the Balkans, including the liberation of Athens, under the bold leadership of Tod. Not only was he awarded the DSO and bar for this leadership, but was also promoted to Brigadier to take charge of 2 Commando Brigade for the crucial – and successful – amphibious assault on Lake Comacchio.

Among the original Troop Leaders and junior officers were several who were destined to become Commanding Officers of their own, or another Commando. They included regular, TA and Emergency Commission officers with differing backgrounds, personalities and physical attributes, yet regardless of such differences they all shared one common quality –

leadership. And it was the application of this priceless intangible quality that made them outstanding and inspiring Commando leaders.

Peter Young was one such officer. At the outbreak of the War he was a subaltern in the Bedfordshire and Hertfordshire Regiment. Frustration and exasperation at the lack of opportunities in his battalion led Peter, after Dunkirk, to volunteer.

By the end of the War this subaltern of 1939 was a Brigadier, commanding a Commando Brigade. His record of service in the Commandos demonstrates how a capable young officer with leadership, initiative, courage and elan, rather than seniority justified meteoric promotion in the Commandos.

A maverick of strong and solid physique, Peter possessed self-assuredness and tremendous confidence, traits he seemed to instill in his subordinates who would follow him anywhere. Cavalier in his attitude to war, Peter wanted to be where the action was and eagerly sought it. That he safely survived raids – Lofotens, Vaagso and Dieppe – plus protracted action in Sicily, Italy, Normandy and Burma he dismissed as 'being lucky', but a DSO and MC with bars testified to his leadership and bravery.

Another outstanding volunteer was Jack Churchill, 'Mad Jack' as he was known, a flamboyant and colourful Commando character. A pre-war regular officer in the Manchester Regiment, he had served in India and Burma, but had resigned, disappointed and disillusioned with peacetime soldiering. Being on the Reserve of Officers he was recalled to the Colours on mobilization just prior to the outbreak of the War and so rejoined his regiment; he went with the BEF to France and saw action against the Germans; in fact, he was awarded the Military Cross for his part in the fighting at L'Epinette, in which he was reported as accounting for at least one of the enemy with his beloved and favourite weapon – the bow and arrow.

After Dunkirk and back in England he did not relish the prospects of being in an infantry battalion 'denuded in weapons and condemned to watch the coast in expectation of an invasion...' For him the chance to volunteer for Special Service was a heaven-sent opportunity to strike back in retaliation.

Jack soon became well known throughout the Commandos with his bow and arrow, his claymore and his bagpipes, accoutrements he took on all the early training and exercises, and later into action. There is the lovely story of how Jack, when second-in-command of No 3, and Peter Young, then a Troop Leader in the same Commando, competed against each other to be the first in the fray on the Vaagso raid.

Major Jack Churchill, claymore in hand, leads his Commando troops ashore from an 'Eureka' craft on an early amphibious training exercise in Scotland.

Jack was playing 'The March of the Cameron Men' on his 'pipes' as his landing craft made its approach, then leaving them behind in the care of the coxswain and brandishing his claymore, as his men leapt ashore, he was initially behind Peter Young. But not for long because as Young paused to reform his men before pushing on, Jack, both claymore and pistol ready, and shouting fearsome oaths and cries, overtook the stationary Young to win. Shortly afterwards Jack was wounded; fortunately it wasn't serious. However that race between these two officers provided plenty of competitive motivation, not only between them, but between the troops they were leading too. It was typical of their resolve to be in the thick of the fray and to lead from the front.

Later Churchill took over the daunting task of reforming and training No 2 Commando when, as a result of the heavy casualties on the St Nazaire raid, it was reduced to just a handful of survivors and a few others who hadn't gone on the raid. It was a case of almost starting from scratch, but he succeeded to lead that Commando to gain battle honours in Italy and the Adriatic. In the latter, particularly in raids on the Dalmatian Islands and in cooperation with Tito's partisans, they carried out operations more akin to the original and intended roles of the Commandos. Suddenly Jack's Commando exploits ended in June 1944 whilst leading a combined force, including No 2, on an assault on the island of Brac, his position was overrun in an enemy counter attack and he was captured. Happily he survived to continue his distinguished military career after the War.

Robert Dawson was an Emergency Commission (hostilities only) officer, commissioned in the Loyal Regiment. He was rather shy and retiring.

In No 4 his promotion from a Section Officer, to Troop Leader, and ultimately to Commanding Officer came as a result of his outstanding ability to incorporate imaginative and purposeful training into pragmatic preparations for Commando operations. His fluency in French and his understanding of the Gallic traits and characteristics made him the obvious choice to have under command the Free French Commandos for the Normandy invasion.

Dawson's courageous leadership in Normandy and later in the assault and capture of Flushing earned him the awards of the DSO, the French Legion D'Honneur and the Croix de Guerre.

Finally, there was Ken Trevor, a pre-War regular in the Cheshire Regiment. He had served in India and West Africa before joining No 1 as a Troop Leader, and was nicknamed 'Junior', because at the time his cousin, Tom Trevor, was commanding. He was second-in-command when No 1 went to North Africa and later on return to England was appointed CO and in command throughout the Commando's time in the Far East. Ken was one of those unflappable and stoic commanders who refused to be ruffled, and with his dry sense of humour would always see the funny side of even the most dismal and desperate situation. Nowhere were these qualities more clearly demonstrated than in Burma in operations at Akyab, Myebon, Kangaw and in their final bloody battle on Hill 170. It was there Ken won his DSO, 'standing in the middle of the forward troops directing the action with courage and coolness', as one eye witness recorded.

I too can vouch for these commendable qualities of Ken, as I saw them displayed when we served together in the Korean War during 1950-1.

So far all the Commandos mentioned were among those recruited solely in Britain during 1940, but they were not the only original Commandos. By July 1940 plans began to materialize in the Middle East to raise a couple of Commandos – Nos 50 and 51 – out there, shortly to be followed by a third, No 52.

The task of forming No 50 was delegated to a Royal Engineer officer, Major George Young. He was assisted by another regular officer, Captain

Fox-Hunter of the Durham Light Infantry. Both had made studies of irregular warfare and were now anxious to put their theories to the test. George Young had also been involved in a clandestine military intelligence project in Romania, initiated in 1939, which was called off after the fall of France. Fox-Hunter had persuaded General Wavell as early as 1936 to let him try out some guerilla-type activities during the army manoeuvres that year. They were successful too, but not followed up. Now in 1940 he had another chance – this time for real.

When the call for volunteers went out in the Middle East, as in the UK, there was no shortage. In addition to those from the British forces, No 50 Commando had a sprinkling of volunteers from both the South African and Rhodesian forces, plus a contingent of some sixty Spanish troops, veterans who had fought against Franco, but had fled Spain when he came to power.

No 51 Commando was raised by Major 'Kid' Cator MC, and although most of the officers and senior NCOs were volunteers from regular and TA units, the majority of the other ranks were from his old command, a unique and unlikely unit, No 1 Palestine Company, Auxiliary Military Pioneer Corps. In his diary Major Cator described them as a 'Foreign Legion, three quarters of them were Jews (Poles, Czechs, Russians, Bulgarians, Austrians, Germans and Spaniards), the other quarter were Arabs, including Egyptians, Iraqis, Palestinians and Sudanese'.

Unfortunately, the Middle East Commandos had a short lifespan. After much hard training, many 'false starts' and the cancellation of proposed operations they went into action in raids along the North African coast, saw protracted action in Eritrea and Abyssinia, took part (as part of Layforce) in the battle for Crete and an abortive raid on Castelorizzo, an enemy-held island off the coast of Turkey. Much depleted they were disbanded in late 1942. However, as in the case of the other Commandos of Layforce, many of the officers and other ranks found their way into other special forces units, SAS, SBS and SOE in the Middle East, whilst others went to the Far East to join Wingate and his Chindits.

That the ME Commandos had such a short and frustrating history was very sad. Winston Churchill was most annoyed at the way they had been mishandled and misemployed; he told the Chiefs of Staff that they 'had been frittered away'.

In all military formations, but particularly in Special Forces, operational success frequently depends on the quality of the junior officers and NCOs who invariably find themselves left in charge of the situation because of casualties among their superiors, or at short notice have to undertake special missions. They must be leaders, be dependable, respected and trusted, well trained and, probably, above all else be capable of reacting with calmness, confidence and initiative in a tight corner.

Each of the original Commandos had these types in abundance. Training made them physically – and mentally – fit for action, subsequent action made them seasoned campaigners ready for higher appointments.

Gordon Webb of No 4 was a typical example. A fit, exuberant and energetic young wartime officer in the Royal Artillery, he won a MC and bar on raids before leading his beloved B Troop over the fire-swept beaches of Normandy on D-Day. The War over, he returned to business in Sussex.

Dennis O'Flaherty, had a small, slight and almost boyish physique, which belied his 'guts' and bravery. He had plenty of 'elan'. He, too, was a 'gunner', in No 3. As a subaltern (Section Officer) he took part in the Vaagso raid and although badly wounded won the DSO for 'outstanding bravery under fire'. Such a high award for a junior officer was rare. On recovery and release from hospital Dennis returned to Commandos as an instructor.

Not all the junior officers were of the same ilk, many were quiet and very reserved, some with academic backgrounds. Gerard Brett epitomized this group. He was a museum curator pre-War, was then commissioned as an Emergency Officer in the Royal Ulster Rifles and had joined No 12, but was 'lent' to No 2 for their raid on St Nazaire. There he won the Military Cross, but was captured. After release he joined us at St Ives as a climbing instructor before returning, on demobilization, to the Victoria and Albert Museum – a far cry from the Commando scene.

Lieutenant Anthony Deane-Drummond was a volunteer who joined No 2 Commando in 1940. This was the Commando originally designated as the parachute Commando.

Tony Deane-Drummond, like many of his Commando comrades, was involved in the humiliation of Dunkirk, and so volunteered, joining the rest of the original No 2 at Knutsford, near Manchester, to start parachuting. With them he took part in Britain's first parachute raid of the War on an aqueduct in the heart of southern Italy in February 1941. Although he, along with others, was captured he did, later, manage to escape and travelling through France, finally got back to Britain. By this time his old unit was fully incorporated into the newly formed Airborne Forces and it was with them that he next saw action at Arnhem. There he was again captured, but after an amazing thirteen days hiding in the cupboard of a house occupied by the enemy, managed to escape yet again.

After the War, as a regular officer, he commanded the SAS in Malaya and South Arabia. He retired as a Major General having been associated with Airborne Forces for a considerable amount of his service, and incidentally was at one time the national solo gliding champion, but all his 'airborne' activities started in No 2 Commando in that summer of 1940.

Most of the early volunteers whose Commando backgrounds have been mentioned saw action on operations at the Commando level or in detachments of their parent Commando. However some managed to see action in specialized 'private armies' – offshoots of the Commandos.

A notable example of this type of private army was the Small Scale Raiding Force (SSRF) formed by two original volunteers from No 7 Commando, namely Captain Gus March-Phillips and Lieutenant Geoffrey Appleyard, Their unique little force of Commandos initially operated in a Brixham trawler and was based in Poole and trained along the Dorset coastline before going off on the 'Maid of Honour' to operate off the coast of West Africa. On return to Britain they switched to more conventional craft to continue their clandestine raids. A few of their operations were carried out under the special secret orders of the Special Operations Executive and to this day details of these exploits have been withheld – or destroyed. Unfortunately few of SSRF survived the War. Some were killed in action, or some, as in the case of March-Phillips, tragically drowned; even more tragic, a few, including a founder member, Captain Graham Hayes, were 'executed' by the Nazis after capture in accordance with Hitler's infamous, shameful and secret order that all Commando soldiers, whether 'they are in uniform, armed or unarmed, in battle or in flight are to be slaughtered to the last man . . . ' The order went on to direct that even those captured for interrogation were 'to be shot immediately after this is completed'.

Mention of these executions by the Nazis brings to mind a most daring raid, Operation Musketoon, on the hydro-electric power station at Glomfjord in Norway in September 1942. The raiding party of twelve was led by two more of the original volunteer officers, Captains Black (a Canadian, who had won a MC on the Vaagso raid) and Houghton (a survivor of the St Nazaire raid, who had been employed in Norway pre-War, knew the country well and was an expert skier). Their hazardous mission succeeded, but at a cost. Two of the party were killed; both the officers – who were wounded – and four others were captured, just two got away. The six captured were taken to Germany and were the first to be executed in accordance with Hitler's wicked directive.

The two members of this raid who managed to escape and make their way back to Britain, Sergeant O'Brien and Guardsman Fairclough, were interviewed by the author Stephen Schofield, who wrote a book on the raid. He expressed his surprise that 'such quiet and pleasant men could achieve so stupendous a task'.

There were many quiet, unassuming and seemingly ordinary 'chaps' such as these two survivors from 'Musketoon'. Commandos were not the 'Rambo', swaggering and cut-throat desperadoes too often portrayed in the popular press at the time – much to the annoyance and embarrassment of the men in green berets.

From the onset there were in all Commandos NCOs and men capable of holding higher rank; later many volunteers relinquished 'pips and stripes' to join, such was the prestige and appeal of this new fighting force. These two factors meant that at any time there was within the ranks of the Commandos a wealth of potential officers and senior NCOs.

Accordingly from 1941 onwards a fair number of NCOs in Commandos were recommended for commissions. Some continued to serve in their original Commandos, others became instructors in Commando warfare. Not a few won awards and decorations in action. Outstanding among these were two who gained commissions and as officers won two of the Commandos' Victoria Crosses – both posthumous awards.

George Knowland had been a NCO in No 3, but on commissioning was posted to No 1. He was an officer in No 4 Troop at the time of that unit's bloody stand at Hill 170 in Burma. His offensive-defensive action must surely rank as one of the most heroic in the War. Knowland's section of just twenty-four men held a key position against 'platoon after platoon of Japs who came in waves for two hours'. Knowland was everywhere in that section position, hurling grenades, firing his rifle, later a Bren, then a tommy gun and finally a 2-in mortar before he fell mortally wounded. His action saved the day.

Anders Lassen was a Dane who enlisted in the British Army and became a NCO member of SSRF in operations aboard the *Maid of Honour*. Subsequently his 'talent for killing Germans' was recognized and he was commissioned as a subaltern on the General List (of officers) of the British Army. He continued to serve with the SSRF, winning the Military Cross plus two bars, then the Victoria Cross at Comacchio where he was operating with No 9 Commando. Accompanying a fighting patrol, which was held up by a machine-gun post, Lassen continued to advance. Single-handed he silenced that post, then went on to knock out four more pill boxes with grenades before he was shot at close range when advancing to accept the surrender of the fifth pill box. Gravely wounded, he died shortly afterwards, but not before the rest of the patrol had finished off the job he had nearly done single-handed.

Among the regular warrant officers and senior NCOs who initially volunteered in 1940 were the likes of RSM 'Jumbo' Bill Morris and 'Timber' Woodcock. Morris, Royal Tank Regiment, was in his thirties when he joined No 4. Of medium height and thick set, he was tough, but never athletic, nor was he the archetypal, bawling, bullying, barrack-square regimental sergeant major. He had a quiet but decisive manner – 'firm, but fair' summed up his philosophy as a RSM. Men knew where they stood with him and he gained the respect of all ranks by providing a good example of guts and determination. No one sweated and struggled more than RSM Morris on the gruelling speed and cross-country marches that he hated, but never dodged. He served with No 4 until the last stages of the War in North-West Europe gaining the award of a Military Cross, a rare distinction to other than a commissioned officer. It was well earned.

'Timber' Woodcock was a regular sergeant in the South Staffordshire Regiment, but was promoted to TSM in No 4. After the Dieppe Raid he was recommended for a commission, but declined, preferring to go on to what he considered greater things – a top-class RSM. It was in this rank he became Colonel Vaughan's first RSM at the Commando Depot at Achnacarry in 1942; wanting further action he later joined Col Mills-Roberts' No 6 as RSM, where he became greatly respected by all. Landing on D-Day he was reputed to be seen, after the Commandos had taken up a defensive position beyond the river Orne, in the thick of the action, carrying his pace stick which he used to measure the length of the slit trenches, just six feet long, equal, near enough, to two regulation paces!

Finally mention must be made of the largest group of volunteers – the private soldiers. Whether they were gunners, sappers, troopers or drivers, those who survived the initial testing training soon acquired the necessary skills and experiences for promotion. Indeed in No 4 alone, by D-Day many of the senior NCOs who rushed up the beaches on that fateful morning had joined us at Weymouth in 1940 as private soldiers – 'Tich' Garnett, Frank Major, John Skerry, Hughie Lindley, Ken Phillot, 'Darky' Woodward, 'Ken' Kennett and Ernie Brooks, to mention just a few whom I knew well. Others had become warrant officers like Bill Portman, Lew Chattaway and Les Heaynes. Every Commando had comparable lists.

To sum up, within a few weeks in the summer of 1940 a formidable mixture of officers and other ranks had been recruited both in Great Britain and the Middle East to become our first corps of 'shock troops'.

Churchill's 'bold step', taken against the awesome background of a threatened invasion, had materialized. A start had been made. How this mixture of volunteers developed, in spite of many shortages and set-backs, to become a very successful fighting force follows.

CHAPTER 11

Setting Up –
Billets and Organization

One of the unique features of the original Army Commandos was the prerequisite that each individual – officers and other ranks alike – would be responsible for his own quartering and feeding. This was an innovation for the British Army.

There were operational and administrative reasons for this decision. However, from the outset the advantages of this arrangement were most apparent in the matter of training. It enabled the Commandos to overcome at a stroke one of the inherent problems of other fighting units who were stationed in barracks or camps, namely the ubiquitous and querulous deployment of combatant troops on domestic chores and the inevitable, but equally obligatory, guard duties. Such commitments made heavy and wholesale demands on manpower. These daily tasks, seemingly never-ending, drastically curtailed the numbers available for training. It is fair to say that as many as 20 per cent of an infantry battalion could be employed daily on these non-combatant duties. Quite clearly this situation imposed considerable limitations on training and progress towards optimum fighting efficiency. But worse still, these irksome and tedious 'necessities' not only sapped morale they also stifled initiative. For example in the new Commando set-up there was no Orderly Sergeant, as there was in barracks, to chase soldiers to be punctual and properly prepared. Every man was on his own, independent and responsible – yet part of a team.

To make this system work was simplicity itself. All ranks were paid a daily subsistence allowance and, equally important in wartime Britain, everyone was issued with a ration card. Without this important piece of paper none of the basic foods such as meat, tea, butter, cheese or sugar could be purchased from food shops by either the Commando soldiers or their landladies. The daily subsistence allowance was 13 shillings and 4 pence (66p) for all officers, and 6 shillings and 8 pence (33p) for all other ranks. In both cases it was a flat rate throughout, the same for the

Commanding Officer as the junior subaltern, likewise a private soldier got the same rate as the Regimental Sergeant Major. Introduced in 1940 these daily rates stayed unchanged until the disbandment of Commandos in 1946, and such were the effects of wartime price controls, food subsidies, rationing arrangements and the almost total absence of inflation they were always adequate.

The payment of this allowance gave rise to the mistaken belief by other servicemen that Commando soldiers were paid extra 'danger money'. It was never so. They received just the same basic rate they would have received in their parent unit. Indeed, those who relinquished rank to join the Commandos were, in fact, worse off because by so doing they received only the pay of the lower rank they had elected to accept.

The subsistence allowance was withdrawn whenever Commandos went into barracks, military hospital, transit camp, boarded one of HM ships and went overseas or at any other time when they were quartered and fed from service sources.

How and where each Commando soldier organized his accommodation was his own responsibility. There was just one proviso, every soldier had to be on parade in good order and fully prepared for the task in hand at the right place and at the right time as detailed. Failure to comply with this fundamental requirement usually had only one recourse – Return to Unit (RTU).

The finding of civilian billets, the normal and popular solution to the problem of quartering and feeding, was seldom a problem.

For many landladies and housewives, denied of normal incomes from letting or because a breadwinner had been called up, the opportunity was most welcome. The going rate for full board for other ranks was '30 bob' or one pound ten shillings (£1.50) per week, seemingly a pitiful amount, but at a time when the average weekly wage for a skilled manual worker was in the order of £5 per week, the prospects of having a soldier or two at these rates were most attractive.

With their larger daily allowances the officers were able to billet themselves in a hotel or local pub with all the in-built advantages of a bar as a substitute 'mess'. Frequently, however, the officers opted for accommodation with local families. Officers and other ranks alike often succumbed to likely possibilities where there was an attractive daughter or lonely young landlady in the offering.

At all times the Commando soldiers seemed to strike a happy relationship with their landladies no matter where they were billeted, and the list of locations read like a Tourist Board brochure for Britain.

Residents of the seaside towns of Salcombe, Falmouth, Dartmouth, St Ives, Paignton, Tenby, the Scilly Isles, Weymouth, Brighton, Bexhill, Seaford, Worthing and Bridlington in England; Largs, Ayr, Girvan, Troon and the Isle of Arran in Scotland, whilst mountain resorts in North Wales, the Lake District, the Cairngorms and the Isle of Skye, and the boating havens on the Beaulieu and Hamble Rivers on the Solent – to mention only those that readily spring to mind – all accommodated 'the lads' in their homes, with generous hospitality.

Quite a number of Commando soldiers made permanent love-matches and married the girl of their dreams whom they met in the town or village where they were billeted. Indeed, one of the largest concentrations of ex-Commandos was in Ayrshire, where No 4 was stationed in 1941-2 and several lads took local lassies for brides; so that is where they returned after the War to settle down.

Such was the homely relationship and atmosphere in the billets that many of the soldiers were able to organize the family to undertake some of their military chores and the 'dhobi' (Army slang, based on Hindustani, for washing/ironing). It is on record that a Commando soldier reprimanded for dirty brasses on parade promptly blamed his landlady! Certainly where there were youngsters in the billet many of them earned the 'odd copper' for polishing boots and brasses, or going down to Troop Headquarters to find out the details for next day's parade. This, the beneficiaries maintained, came under the heading of 'organisation and initiative training'. Although the landladies mothered their 'boys' they were not amiss to reprimanding them if they were wayward. More than once a portly middle-aged 'Mum' castigated her tough Commando lad for daring to traipse through the house and upstairs – 'upstairs, of all places' – in muddy boots. It would be hard to have imagined a comparative scene in wartime Germany involving the billeting of their Special Service Troops – a simple but significant reminder of the humility of our Commando comrades.

Every Commando veteran has his fund of stories about billets.

On the question of food, the weekly rations of meat, bacon, butter, tea and cheese were meagre. Today they would look mean for a day's ration let alone for a week. Fortunately, staple items such as bread, milk, potatoes, fresh seasonal home-produced vegetables and fruit, and cereals were not rationed, whilst the rarer 'luxuries' such as eggs, poultry, rabbits, sausages, offal, whale-meat and pies were off-ration, but, in such short supply, they were, in effect, rationed by retailers on a rota basis or sold 'under the counter' as depicted by L/Cpl 'Butcher' Jones in the popular TV series *Dad's Army*.

It was ironic that the men in the Commandos, reputedly undergoing the toughest physical training, had to subsist on the bare civilian rations whilst other servicemen in barracks, many of them on sedentary jobs, received the larger Services rations. This did not unduly worry the Commandos, as most reckoned the shortages were a small price to pay for the freedom from unnecessary 'bull' and the impositions of authoritarian soldiering. It certainly did not affect their stamina or physical prowess, nor did it lower their morale – just the opposite.

Living in civvy billets meant that personal weapons had to be kept in the billets, and ammunition too, during the invasion threat. As responsible soldiers, all were expected to observe the basic rules of safety. It worked well, but there was the occasional hiccup. One happened during the winter of 1940 when some of No 5 Commando were billeted in a guest house in Salcombe, Devon. They were due to go off to practice-fire their Colts .45, but snow delayed their departure. One of the lads took his mate's Colt, not knowing it was loaded. Absent-minded, he pulled back the actuator and went to pull the trigger, too late the cry went up, 'It's loaded'. Luckily, as a well-trained soldier, he had the weapon pointing to the floor and the bullet sped through it. They were on the first floor and the landlady was downstairs in the kitchen below. She was about to make a cake and had climbed onto a chair to reach a cake tin on the top shelf just as the bullet crashed through the ceiling. It hit the tin, knocked it clean out of her hand and sent it ricocheting round and round the kitchen. It left a hole in the ceiling and a flabbergasted landlady sprawling on the floor; astounded but unhurt.

In spite of this isolated incident landladies were soon accustomed to having an armoury of weapons in their homes and some even took an interest in the cleaning of them, although this was usually done in the privacy of the soldier's bedroom. Often Mills (36) hand grenades – unprimed, of course – ornamented the mantelpiece of bedroom fireplaces, and canvas bandoliers, each containing 50 rounds of .303 ball ammunition, hung on coat hooks. Albeit, they were never left unattended.

Right from the beginning the combination of the subsistence allowance and the encouragement for all ranks to use their initiative provided opportunities to resolve the commissariat problem in a variety of ways. Not everyone automatically – or even regularly – chose 'civvy billets'. Take the example of Captain March-Phillips and his subaltern, Geoffrey Appleyard, introduced in Chapter I as the founders of SSRF. Prior to the establishment of their little 'private army' whilst they were still in No 7, they had the whole of their Troop accommodated in a large empty house in Newmarket. They managed to persuade a local unit to lend them a couple of cooks and supply them with army rations so that they could get all their own men out daily for training. The furniture in the house was non-existent except for some tables, benches and other oddments which they managed to acquire. They did have a bathroom, lavatory and running water, so with these bare administrative essentials they got down to their initial training, and, concluded Geoffrey Appleyard in a letter written home at this time, 'when we finally move from here to a new location on the coast, we shall walk – 60 or 70 miles – in two or three days, bivouacking at night in barns and haylofts and living off our ration allowance of 6s 8d per day'.

Being paid this allowance, meagre as it may seem today, also provided the chance for some officers and other ranks as well to capitalize on it, so that by living rough they could save some money to spend on other needs. Probably the best-known case is that of Lieutenant Colonel Dudley Lister, who raised No 7 Commando, then following a reshuffle and reorganization of Commandos after Nos 7, 8 and 11 left for the Middle East, became our CO in No 4.

A veteran of the First World War, he was nevertheless an imposing figure on parade and 'looked the part'. He had won a Military Cross with his regiment, the Buffs, in the First World War, whilst during the inter-war years had established a great reputation as an amateur heavyweight boxer. He was not only an Army champion, but a national one too, representing Great Britain in the 'Golden Gloves' contest in Maddison Square Gardens in New York. His fanaticism for physical fitness was reflected in his training of No 4. However, to return to the point of mentioning him here, he was one who decided for personal reasons to save some of his allowances for other purposes. He had, shall we say, marital problems. So with this aim in mind he pitched a tent on the sand dunes at Troon (where we were stationed at the time) and with the help of his batman, a primus stove, sleeping bag and a hurricane lamp stuck out the winter of 1941/42 in Spartan fashion. But to see him on parade no one would have believed how he was living at the time, not only was he well turned out but he was very fit, living off a simple diet in which baked beans and sausages must have featured often and regularly.

There were other cases, similar in purpose, but different in detail. However it is fair to contend that for the majority of Commando soldiers, 'Home from Home' is how they remember their civvy billets. They invariably became part of the family, and in those days of the blackout spent many hours with the rest of the family in the evenings, when not on duty or training, listening to the wireless (TV was not on the scene until some years after the War). Popular amongst the wartime shows was Tommy Handley's *ITMA*, Vera Lynn (the Forces' sweetheart), Garrison Theatre (with Jack Warner, Elsie and Doris Water), the Big Band Shows, among which were such bandleaders as Billy Cotton and Joe Loss, or on a more serious note listening to Winston Churchill's rousing broadcasts; they were classical examples of inspiring oratory which did much to raise morale on the Home Front. Those who heard him will never forget his words as at the height of the invasion threat: 'we shall fight on the beaches . . . we shall fight on the landing grounds . . . we shall fight in the fields and in the streets . . . we shall fight in the hills. We shall never surrender.' They were stirring words, growled out with his typical bulldog determination. Also too there was his memorable tribute to the fighter pilots of the Battle of Britain: 'never in the field of human conflict was so much owed by so many to so few'.

The subsistence arrangement did succeed in meeting all the administrative and operational purposes it was meant to cover, and although it was retained until the Army Commandos were finally disbanded in 1946, there was initially a time, in November 1940, when it was being queried as necessary. The debate was led by no less than Sir John Dill (Chief of the Imperial General Staff), who was an antagonist of Special Forces. Fortunately at a War Office conference convened to discuss this matter, the merits of the allowance were upheld. There were many good reasons for its continuance and high on the list was the accepted opinion that it did greatly help to develop self-reliance and initiative. And in the context of this particular point it is interesting to compare the Commandos raised in the UK with those formed in the Middle East.

The author of the book *Middle East Commandos*, Charles Messenger (he had the assistance of the ME Commandos Historical Research Group when writing) in comparing the organization of the ME viz-a-viz UK Commandos had this to say re billets:

> Another significant difference from their UK-based counterparts was that it was not possible (in the ME Commandos) to foster individual self-discipline and self-reliance by paying each man ration and lodging allowances and making him find his own accommodation. Suitable civilian billets simply did not exist in Egypt and hence the ME Commandos were forced to live in a conventional camp.

Finally, on this issue of subsistence and billeting it is interesting and pertinent to give the last word to the famous American leader of the US

Rangers (the equivalent of our Commandos), Colonel Darby. He recalls that in 1942 his Battalion, after their training at the Commando Basic Training Centre, Achnacarry arrived in Dundee in Scotland to team up with No 1 Commando for joint training in preparation for Operation Torch, the landings in North Africa. He writes: 'There were no barracks or camps at Dundee, so the troops had to be billeted in the people's homes (in the same way as No 1 Commando). It was a system unknown in the Rangers.' Posters announcing their arrival and requesting billets were displayed in the city, but only sufficient homes with furnished rooms and board could be found for four of his six companies. The others had to sleep rough in the city hall for the first night.

> On the following morning we were prepared to seek a government building for barracks. As we were about to set out in search, an excited group of women swarmed around the city hall. The first night had gone well as the men talked their way into the hearts of their hosts. The word spread so rapidly that by midmorning all my Rangers had homes.

Colonel Darby went on to explain that when 'the soldiers lined up for the battalion's day's training they had their homemade lunches with them'. If there was an all-day exercise or an even longer one, they all took food, supplied by their new-found homes, for the entire period of the manoeuvre.

> It was during this time that the cooks, first-aid men and other administrative personnel generally required to maintain a combat unit became actual members of the Ranger team, equipped and trained for action. The cooks became real fighting men, and in later amphibious landings were often sent ashore in the first wave as tommy-gunners.
>
> I did my best to exert tight discipline despite this extraordinary billeting arrangement and let every Ranger know just where he stood concerning his personal deportment. I found, as expected, that these men thrown on their responsibility reacted almost perfectly. Furthermore, it was excellent training for the men, since the Rangers later were often to act as independent small groups on their own initiative .. The Rangers were pleasantly excited about this billeting and I found that with this arrangement, they acted as guests with their new families. They didn't have the heart to get drunk, rowdy or disorderly as might be the case in barracks, where at a late hour, they would only disturb other soldiers.

Darby went on to record that the cases of ill-discipline and rowdiness, so common in barracks, were greatly reduced. He was undoubtedly impressed by the advantages of the Commando billeting system and his Rangers obviously benefited from it too.

So much then, for billeting – now to briefly describe the organization of the Commandos.

Initially, in the summer of 1940, Commandos raised in the United Kingdom consisted of Headquarters and ten Troops. Those formed in the Middle East had a different organization as will be outlined later. It will be noted that the ten fighting sub-units were designated with the cavalry title 'Troop' and not with the infantry 'company/platoon' title.

Headquarters consisted of Commanding Officer (Lieutenant Colonel), Second-in-Command (Major), Adjutant (Captain), Medical Officer (Captain, Royal Army Medical Corps), Intelligence Officer (Lieutenant) and the Administrative Officer (Captain).

Details of how the Medical and Intelligence sections were organised and trained follow in a later chapter. The Adjutant and Administrative Officer, each with a small staff, were responsible to the CO for the efficient and smooth running of all general and personnel matters within the Commando.

Brigadier Peter Young in his *Short History of the Commandos* commented that all Commando units 'were notably fortunate with their administrative staffs, who were Commando soldiers first and foremost, and as such not only gave their all in the planning and organising of raids or the sustaining of long campaigns with remarkable imagination, ingenuity and perseverance, but were prepared to take their place alongside their comrades in action. And they frequently did.' There is nothing one need add to that tribute, coming as it did from one of the most distinguished Commando leaders.

Initially there was neither Motor Transport nor Signals sections, which were added in late 1941.

Although the number of Troops in a Commando was reduced from ten to six in 1941, the basic set-up of a Troop, as described below, remained basically the same for the rest of the War.

Each Troop was commanded by a captain, the Troop Leader. His little HQ consisted of a Troop Sergeant Major (originally this appointment was just a senior sergeant, but it was soon recognized that the job warranted a higher rank, so that of TSM was introduced, but even then it was unpaid at first – as I know from personal experience!), a batman/runner and a clerk/runner. When the handy 2-inch mortar was introduced, the operators Nos. 1 and 2 also became part of Troop HQ.

Each Troop consisted of two sections, both being commanded by subalterns (2nd or full lieutenants). In Section HQ was the officer's right-hand man and deputy, the section sergeant, and a batman/runner.

The section was sub-divided into the Commando's smallest fighting entities, two sub-sections. Each was commanded by a lance-sergeant and consisted of a Bren group (lance corporal and numbers 1 and 2 on the gun) and two rifle groups, each led by a lance corporal, usually armed with a sub-machine gun, and two riflemen.

To sum up, each Troop consisted of 3 officers, one warrant officer (TSM), 6 sergeants, some 12 junior NCOs and 28 privates, making a grand total of 50 all ranks.

It will not go unnoticed that the proportion of officers and NCOs to private soldiers was seemingly high. This reflected the intended independent roles envisaged for the small sub-units and also the high calibre of soldiers sought as volunteers. Even so as time went by many officers and NCOs accepted reductions to their rank in order to get into the Commandos, especially as the Commanding Officers preferred to promote from within their Commandos rather than bring in officers and NCOs from outside to fill vacancies caused by casualties.

The outline given above applied to those Commandos formed in the United Kingdom; those raised in the Middle East had a different set-up. They were also recruited under different conditions and circumstances. To start with, in the UK there was no bar on the source of the volunteers, recruitment was open to all arms and corps, but in the Middle East there was no such leniency.

The Middle East Commandos were organized on the basis of a small HQ and only three Troops. The HQ was similar to the UK set-up, except that it included Arabic interpreters. Like the UK Commandos, the ME ones had no Motor Transport or Signals sections, although initially there was some training on camels.

Although the ME Commandos had only three Troops compared to the original ten Troops in the UK, each of the ME Troops had double the number of men, in four sections, with a total of five officers and 100 ORs.

The overall strength of the ME Commando was in the order of 350 all ranks.

So much for the organization of the original UK and ME Commandos. Unfortunately, as mentioned in Chapter I, by early 1942 the ME Commandos as such had ceased to exist; meanwhile back in the UK the Commandos underwent changes. Firstly, in the autumn of 1940 the Commandos and the Independent Companies were organized into Special Service Battalions – 'SS Bns'. After a couple of months or so, however, there was another change, when because the SS Bns were reckoned to be unwieldy and top heavy, plus the fact that the title 'SS' had an undesirable likeness to the odious Nazi SS, there was a reversion back to the original Commando organization as already outlined, but instead of ten Troops there were from thereafter only six Troops.

Now it is time to look at the training, in detail, of the Commandos from the time they were formed in July 1940.

CHAPTER III

Making a Start –
Initial Training and Tribulations

From the onset all Commanding Officers were fired by two main aims: to prepare their fledglings for the first mission, and to make their Commando the best one.

Understandably, to succeed and achieve these aims, there was only room for the keenest, fittest, most efficient and self-disciplined soldiers.

With this in mind, it was obvious that any officer or other rank failing to live up to these requirements would have to be RTU'd.

There was, especially in the early days, a steady stream of rejected men, who for one reason or another, were considered unsuitable or undesirable for service in Commandos. Fortunately, there was never a lack of forthcoming volunteers to replace them. So at no time were standards lowered.

Among the several problems facing the COs in the initial fulfilment of their aims was the very wide range of subjects expected to be covered in training and the serious lack of experience and knowledge of amphibious operations – plus, of course, the shortage of suitable landing craft.

These problems were exacerbated by the impossibility of having a progressive timetable for the training. The Commandos were raised with the purpose – and hope – of immediately sending them off on raids across the Channel, and this short-term intention precluded a thorough and systematic build-up from individual training to collective and amphibious training. Events were soon to expose the inadequacy of the initial training and 'half-baked' preparations ill-served by unsuitable craft for such offensive operations.

Notwithstanding, the prospect of imminent action dominated the first weeks of training. So it was that within a month of being raised a force of No 3 Commando accompanied by men from an Independent Company carried out a raid on Guernsey. Only those from No 3 Commando got ashore, the others failed to find suitable landing beaches. The whole operation turned out to be a disappointing failure. Militarily it achieved nothing. Durnford-Slater, who commanded No 3, aptly summed up the reasons for the failure: 'Looking back, I can see that under such rushed conditions, with no experience, no proper landing craft and inadequate training, this first operation was foredoomed to failure. Later, the word "Commando" became synonymous with perfectly trained, tough, hard-fighting and skilled specialists. You don't achieve that overnight...' How right he was.

All concerned with that abortive raid were understandably very disappointed, none less that Winston Churchill, who called it 'a silly fiasco'. But the lessons learnt – and there were many – were taken to heart and incorporated in the already long list of training subjects.

In those early days all COs had to draw up their own lists, as there didn't seem to be a single common directive. So COs set their own standards and decided on priorities. As a result each Commando ran its own show, but there were exchanges of ideas when Commandos were based near to one another and when Admiral of the Fleet Sir Roger Keyes took over as Director of Combined Operations; he had more than a passing interest in the Commandos and made frequent visits to each of them to watch the progress of training. He was a great favourite with all ranks and although there was a 'generation gap' (he was sixty-eight years old), between him and his young Commandos there were unmistakable bonds of mutual trust, respect and admiration. 'Old Sir Roger', as he was fondly known to us, set a splendid example of single-mindedness and purpose as he turned up in all types of weather to watch our training.

Lord Lovat, pays a warm tribute to this doughty old salt and warrior:

> The admiral believed in leading from the front... I've seen him wet to the skin, struggle to the wrong beach in a high running sea, and then call for a repeat performance... nor did he quit until the last man was back aboard his ship. time spent in his company made us feel twice our size; and that, of course, is what leadership is all about...

But back to those lengthy lists of training subjects... I have only seen one survivor of any such list drawn up by the COs and that was compiled by Colonel Newman, just after he had taken command of a newly formed No 2 Commando following the renaming of the original No 2 to 11 Special Air Service Battalion. This fresh new No 2 was made up from men who had been members of the Independent Companies. The list, therefore, was written some months after the formation of the other Commandos. Nonetheless, from personal experience, it would have been typical and provides an excellent example of the wide range of subjects it was hoped to cover and the standards to be aimed for.

No. 2 Commando

SERVICE IN A COMMANDO   by Lt. Col. Newman

1. The object of Special Service is to have available a fully trained body of first class soldiers, ready for active offensive operations against an enemy in any part of the world.
2. Irregular warfare demands the highest standards of initiative, mental alertness and physical fitness, together with the maximum skill at arms. No Commando can feel confident of success unless all ranks are capable of thinking for themselves; of thinking quickly and of acting independently, and with sound tactical sense, when faced by circumstances which may be entirely different to those which were anticipated.
3. Mentally. The offensive spirit must be the outlook of all ranks of a Commando at all times.
4. Physically. The highest state of physical fitness must at all times be maintained. All ranks are trained to cover at great speed any type of ground for distances of five to seven miles in fighting order.

Examples:
(a) Fighting Order (seven miles in one hour (march and run)).

(b) F.S.M.O. (Full Service Marching Order)
5 miles in one hour (marching)
9 miles in two hours (marching)
15 miles in 4^1/4 hours
25 miles in 8 hours
35 miles in 14 hours

After all these distances and times, troops must be ready, in para (a) to fight, and in para (b) to fight after two hours rest.

5. Cliff and mountain climbing and really difficult slopes climbed quickly form a part of Commando training.
6. A high degree of skill in all branches of unarmed combat will be attained.
7. Seamanship and Boatwork. All ranks must be skilled in all forms of boatwork and landing craft whether by day or by night, as a result of which training the sea comes to be regarded as a natural working ground for a Commando.
8. Night sense and night confidence are essential. All ranks will be highly trained in the use of the compass.
9. Map reading and route memorising form an important part of Commando training.
10. All ranks of a Commando will be trained in semaphore, morse and the use of W/T.

11. All ranks will have elementary knowledge of demolitions and sabotage. All ranks will be confident in the handling of all types of high explosive, Bangalore torpedoes, and be able to set up all types of booby traps.

12. A high standard of training will be maintained in all forms of street fighting, occupation of towns, putting towns into a state of defence and the overcoming of all types of obstacles, wire, rivers, high walls, etc.

13. All ranks in a Commando should be able to drive motor cycles, cars, lorries, tracked vehicles, trains and motor boats.

14. A high degree of efficiency in all forms of fieldcraft will be attained. Every man in a Commando must be able to forage for himself, cook and live under a bivouac for a considerable period.

15. All ranks are trained in first aid and will be capable of dealing with the dressing of gun-shot wounds and the carrying of the wounded.

16. These are few among the many standards of training that must be attained during service in a Commando. At all times a high standard of discipline is essential, and the constant desire by all ranks to be fitter and better trained than anyone else.

17. The normal mode of living is that the Special Service Soldier will live in a billet found by himself and fed by the billet for which he will receive 6s 8d per day to pay all his expenses.

18. Any falling short of the standards of training and behaviour on the part of a Special Service Soldier will render him liable to be returned to his unit.

Detailed examination and explanation of what was entailed in this comprehensive syllabus will follow, but from the outset it will be noted that marching played a prominent part in all training. As a result marches with full loads along roads and across all types of terrain was a fundamental part of all training at all times (with the notable exception of the special Boat Section).

It was so much an essential feature of Commando training and life that it became second nature. Nowhere is this more aptly illustrated than in the following story which concerns the legendary Captain Anders Lassen VC. When in Italy reorganizing after a period of action he was asked what type of training he intended to give his men; he briefly retorted in his heavy continental accent: 'Zey vill marsch... And when they have finished their marsch? Zey will marsch again...'

Marching, especially speed-marching, became a recognized and accepted means of keeping 'battle-fit and fit for battle'.

One captures a glimpse of this from the letters of Geoffrey Keyes, the son of Sir Roger Keyes, who was another of those pre-war regular officers so disappointed and frustrated after Dunkirk.

He was a cavalry officer in the Scots Greys and on volunteering joined No 11 Commando, often referred to as the 'Scottish' Commando, and went with them to the Middle East as part of Layforce. Following the death of his Commanding Officer, Lieutenant Colonel P.R.N. Pedder, on the Litani River raid in Syria, in early June 1941, Geoffrey was promoted to command. Some months later in November he too was killed whilst leading the Commando raid on Rommel's Headquarters in North Africa. For his heroic leadership on this raid he was awarded a posthumous Victoria Cross – the first of the eight VCs awarded to Commando soldiers.

Of his early training he had written: 'We march and swim and do other violent things. I go to bed very weary and sleep like a dog...' and later recalled in another letter a Commando 'walking tour' on the Isle of Arran. 'The first day was a shocker, as we started off from scratch with eleven miles cross-country, non-stop in three hours, twenty minutes halt for lunch, then on again. It was no joke. I finished rather lame as did most of my cavalrymen...' But he had to continue next day, then spend a bitterly cold night under the stars.

Paddy Mayne wrote of similar experiences. He too was in No 11 Commando on the Isle of Arran at the same time as Geoffrey Keyes and recorded, in a letter, the first day of an early scheme. They had left in the early afternoon and for the first four or so miles they had only 'odd showers'. These didn't hinder them much since they quickly dried, but then for the next thirteen miles it not only poured, but there was a gale blowing off the sea so that the rain pelted into their faces. To add to their discomfort the night march included a river crossing, but even that water hazard didn't really make them any wetter. They were soaked through. Eventually on arriving at their destination, just after dawn, they searched for a suitable area to dry out and rest. Fortunately, the inhabitants of a nearby hamlet, after initially thinking these dishevelled soldiers were 'Jerry' paratroopers, offered help to dry them out. It was an offer gladly accepted before pushing on.

Back at Weymouth and elsewhere in the South other Commando soldiers were undertaking similar marches, equally strenuous and arduous, but in better weather. Their turn to spend freezing wet and windy nights, trying in vain to get some sleep, on the slopes of inhospitable Scottish mountains, was yet to come – all too soon.

Within a matter of weeks new standards of military marching, over all types of terrain, were being established. Marches of up to thirty miles in FSMO (where one carried all one's personal needs for prolonged action, i.e. spare clothing, socks, washing gear, some rations etc.) were an accepted part of normal training. But there was greater emphasis on the shorter distance marching/doubling as rapidly as possible and carrying just the basic operational essentials for a raid. The aim was to cover seven miles in the hour and be able to fight at the end of it.

We had problems at first with the speed marches. It took time and plenty of marches to get a Troop of fifty men of different heights and strides, and with different backgrounds of marching paces, to blend together in step as a team – and more importantly to be ready to fight at the end of it. To this latter end the marches usually finished with an obstacle or assault course, or, ideally, if one could arrange the finish near a range or open piece of ground with a firing practice.

With volunteers from so many regiments – Guardsmen used to a stylish, but leisurely 110 paces to the minute, Light Infantry and Riflemen with their faster rate of 140 and the rest of us about halfway at 120 – the first thing to do was to get a standard number of paces, so with speed the main consideration, the going rate was fixed at 140. It wasn't easy and most of us unaccustomed to this high rate found it hard on our calf muscles, in particular. The pace was set from the start of the march by the Troop Sergeant Major and after, say, ten or fifteen minutes at this speed, we'd prepare to break into double time. Out would ring the warning order, 'Prepare to double,' followed almost immediately by 'Break into double time . . . Double march . . . Left, Right, Left, Right . . .' until the new rhythm was established and had settled down. Most would agree that the speed marches were the most tortuous and stamina-testing aspects of our training.

In contrast the long marches at a more normal pace, although of longer length and duration, were less arduous, but apt to be boring affairs.

The long-distance route marches varied from twelve to twenty-four hours in duration, but with rests could continue over three or four days, as in the case when Colonel Newman had to move his No 2 Commando base from the Paignton area to Weymouth. Newman led his Commando the whole 120 miles. They bivouacked where they arrived each night, sleeping in nearby fields, farms and barns. Four days later, footsore and weary, the Commandos shouldered their arms and there was a spring in their step as they marched down the High Street.

Route marches were enlivened by a spot of singing. The songs, traditional, period 'pop' or bawdy, ranged from the old First World War favourites such as 'Pack up Your Troubles' and 'It's a Long Way to Tipperary' to the then current war hits such as 'Roll Out the Barrel', although after Dunkirk a favourite of the soldiers', 'We're going to hang out our washing on the Siegfried Line', had a hollow ring. Singing took one's mind off aching and weary limbs. Each Troop had its own song leader (and wit too) who came to the fore at such times. But it wasn't always that easy, especially in foul weather; it was difficult to chase away the blues when wet through, tired and battling against rain, hail or snow – or in the other extreme in a heatwave, and we did have those even in Scotland during the War!

If songs were not forthcoming, a Troop Leader or TSM, more in hope than in sadism, would shout out a choice, 'Sing or Double . . . ' This often did the trick. I didn't realize how often I used this ruse until many years later I was asked at a reunion by one of my ex-trainees if I knew the nickname they had for me at Achnacarry. I confessed I didn't – it was 'Double-Dunning', he told me. It was a revelation and a reminder.

Within weeks of being formed, within each Commando, and later between Commandos, there was rivalry to see how far a Troop could march in a day, without anyone falling out. One notable early achievement was attained by B Troop of No 12; they had been raised in Northern Ireland, and marched from Crumlin to Londonderry, a distance of 63 miles, in FSMO, in nineteen hours. It was an outstanding feat, but not an isolated one.

Both speed marches and the long-distance marches were usually carried out on roads, but they were not the only training marches. There were the cross-country ones too; these were quite different, needing a completely different style. More about this in a later chapter, except to mention a couple of typical examples.

Firstly, from the ME Commandos, where cross-country marches were more appropriate to their prospective operations. One Troop of No 52 covered 33 miles across the desert in 11 hours, whilst in No 51 the four sections in one Troop competed against each other on a 50-mile jaunt over rocky and hilly country. The fastest section took just 16 hours with the slowest taking almost 18 hours.

Nearer at home in North Wales, Captain Brian Hilton-Jones (he had served his 'apprenticeship' in C Troop, No 4, before taking command of X Troop, No 10 Commando) once completed a 53-mile march from Harlech to the summit of Snowdon and back in 17½ hours, which included a three-hour rest on the summit.

Nowadays when looking at these achievements it is essential to appreciate that the men on all these training marches – and on other exacting exercises – carried weapons, ammunition plus the rest of their equipment, often weighing well in excess of 60 lb.

As a result of these marching achievements standard timings etc. were established and these were the targets laid down in the curriculum for training reinforcements at Achnacarry – see Chapter VI.

Foremost among other subjects was weapon training and musketry; although this is dealt with later, it warrants mention here because of a connection with marching.

Because of the obvious dangers connected with firing ranges they were – and still are – usually located in remote places on land owned by the War Department (now the MOD), well away from built-up areas, such as the bases where the Commandos were billeted. Weymouth was no exception. This situation posed problems as we had no troop-carrying transport.

Fortunately, there were a couple of officers in most of the Commandos who still had their own cars or were able to borrow the family car. In spite of petrol rationing they somehow managed to beg, borrow or scrounge – no questions were ever asked – enough petrol to ferry their troops, stores or ammunition, particularly the latter, to the far-off ranges. The use of private cars was quite a feature of the early days of the Commandos and it added to the atmosphere of informality and unorthodoxy that was prevalent at the time. However, such luxuries were not always at hand so the problem of 'no transport' was either overcome by a route march or, not infrequently, by the simple expediency of telling the troops to muster at 'X' range at a certain time on the next day, then leaving it to them to get there under their 'own steam' . . . or else. It was a novel way to overcome the problem and at the same time test the initiative of all concerned. It subsequently became a device that was copied by other training establishments especially at the OCTUs (Officer Cadet Training Units) in a like manner to develop initiative and resourcefulness in potential leaders.

In No 4 Commando we overcame the lack of mobility in an entirely different way as will be explained later.

In spite of the advantages of living in civilian billets there had to be one or two disadvantages as a result of not being stationed in barracks. On the administrative side there was the absence of readily available buildings for headquarters, stores and such training facilities as miniature ranges and lecture halls.

Empty shops and houses, church and community halls usually solved these minor problems without much difficulty. We always found the local civilians most cooperative and helpful, which was more than can be said for our military 'lords and masters' on many occasions.

In Weymouth, the Pavilion on the sea front was requisitioned and at a stroke solved the problems of HQ, stores, lecture hall and facilities for other indoor training. It was ideal.

Incidentally, some fifty years later, in 1990, we were to place on record, in a permanent way, the cooperation, kindness and hospitality afforded to No 4 Commando by the people of Weymouth when we commemorated the 50th anniversary of the raising and founding of No 4 in their town, and a suitable marble plaque and illustrated history of No 4 was unveiled by the Mayor in a civic ceremony.

Within each Commando Troop Leaders organized their own training programmes based on the guidelines and priorities laid down by Commanding Officers. The following outline represents a typical day's training on the basic subjects by 'F' Troop at Weymouth during the period July to September 1940. Talks on a variety of subjects were fitted in as and when possible, dependent on the availability of an expert.

0700 hours	Parade on the beach, whatever the weather, for PT and early morning swim, followed by run back to billets for breakfast. A good start to the day.
0900 hours to 1230 hours	Selection from the following: Weapon training, rifle and bayonet, Bren, Tommy gun, Boys A/Tk rifle, revolver and grenades. (No heavy weapons at this stage.) Short march, 8 to 10 miles, frequently to an area where fieldcraft, map reading and compass training could be carried out. Midday meal in billets, cafes or 'haversack' meal e.g. sandwiches provided by landladies.
From 1400	Selection from boating, semaphore/signalling, cross-country running, demolitions, briefing for night schemes followed by rehearsals and practices. On really sunny days we often had more swimming followed by compulsory sun-bathing. The latter might sound bizarre, but Colonel Legard was convinced of the value of sun treatment when properly supervised and also of the value of learning to relax.

Subjects such as firing on the ranges, tactical exercises and schemes, long forced or cross-country marches, extended boating exercises and cliff-climbing were normally carried on a whole-day basis or even longer. When this type of training entailed being away from our billets for a night or more we had to fend for ourselves and get accustomed to sleeping rough either in barns, empty buildings, bivouacs or simply under the stars, albeit getting sunburnt was an offence.

Obviously one of the main aims of all the training was to get both physically and mentally fit as fast as possible. As can be seen from the outline above we daily had plenty of physical exercise, with PT, swimming, marching and cross-country running. However, it soon became appreciated that a new approach to PT, as a specific subject, was needed.

During the inter-war years, when PT was generally supervised by the Army Physical Training School (APTS)* based in Aldershot, the emphasis was on a gymnastics-cum-physical-jerks philosophy closely coupled with team sports and games. Whilst this programme had its merits and did produce fit and healthy soldiers, good games players and regimental teams, it would not fully meet the requirements of the Commandos.

Furthermore the syllabi and methods of the APTS relied heavily on the provision of specific PT facilities and equipment, usually only forthcoming in barracks or military camps. Where such facilities were not available PT was invariably limited to physical jerks and games.

Within this rather formal regime the familiar order of the APTC trained instructor, 'Right, get changed for PT...', epitomized the divorcing of physical training, as then established, from the necessity to train for the physical demands of the battlefield and especially those likely to be encountered in amphibious operations. Albeit, that particular order from the PT instructor meant strip off your battledress (BD) blouse and trousers, take off your boots and put on your white (PT) vest, blue (PT) shorts and your brown (PT) plimsoles. Instead it should have implied, 'OK, you can strip off your BD blouse or even strip right off to the waist, but keep on your BD trousers and your boots and carry your rifles for these are basically the items you will be wearing and carrying when your team goes into action – not on the games field but on the battlefield! And that's where your physical fitness is going to be put to the test.'

Notwithstanding, the value of sports and playing competitive team games was not overlooked as a recreational pursuit. Generally, each Troop had its own soccer team, whilst each Commando prided itself on its football, rugby and boxing teams, resulting in a lot of healthy rivalry between Commandos – and other units. The latter, in particular, were always ready 'to have a go' at the Commandos!

It took time for the realization that a new approach to PT was needed to be adopted throughout the Army, and the Commandos initiated this change in 1940. But it did not happen all at once. Our first sessions of PT

---

*In 1940 the title of the Army Physical Training School (APTS) was changed to the Army Physical Training Corps (APTC).

at Weymouth were in PT kit, but gradually we came to appreciate that the old-fashioned style army PT was not for us. This change of attitude came also from the almost complete lack of the traditional PT facilities already mentioned. They do say that 'necessity is the mother of invention' and here we had a good example of that old adage. Having to improvise we rapidly found that the environment, no matter where we were located, had plenty of PT challenges. There were walls to climb, fences to negotiate, streams and ditches to jump and rivers to wade through. Obstacle and assault courses followed in the wake of these changes. And so was born a new concept of PT.

Improvisation and ingenuity became key words in this new concept.

Once the seeds were sown for more purposeful and imaginative forms of PT all sorts of exercises with improvised equipment were developed. Logs appeared and were used for a whole variety of exercises – with fun. Even long-forgotten childlike games were resuscitated and brought back: 'fireman's lift', wheel-barrow races, 'piggy-back' fights and races provided plenty of variety, amusement, yet strenuous competitive exercise. None of these activities required any specialized equipment and could be enacted any place at any time. At the same time efforts were increasingly made to integrate PT activities into other areas of training so that it was no longer looked upon as a separate entity divorced from action on the battlefield.

With the obvious belief that raiding missions would be undertaken during the hours of darkness a priority was naturally given to night training. Looking at that old Troop Diary I noted that we averaged two or three full night schemes per week during those first few weeks.

All our night training was, of course, carried out against the backdrop of the wartime 'Blackout'. Added realism came from searchlights and ack-ack fire whenever a raid was in progress. Even when Jerry was not active overhead the ubiquitous presence of guards on Vulnerable Points (VPs) such as bridges, centres of communications and military installations all created the right atmosphere for such training.

There were snags. Because of the threat of a Nazi invasion the coastline and inland waters were constantly patrolled by regular troops or the Home Guard so we had to ensure that all were informed of our nocturnal activities or we might have been mistaken for enemy parachutists – with dire consequences.

Nearly all of our early exercises were based on likely raiding tasks, such as the destruction of both strategic and tactical targets, detailed reconnaissances, capture of enemy sentries and the destruction of selected enemy installations and equipment on the coastline and inland. It is pertinent to recall that we had foreseen the possible destruction of enemy aircraft and airfield installations as early as August 1940.

The F Troop diary records that for Exercise No 4, to be carried out on the night of 20 August, the declared intention was 'to attack the enemy airfield (imaginary) at Maiden Castle (near Dorchester), destroy two hangars at point 432 and also destroy as many aircraft as possible'. Surely, this is a clear indication that, from the outset, this type of raid was considered as a suitable one for Commandos. Sadly, it did not materialize until David Stirling started his own SAS for such raids in the Middle East in November 1941. So it is worth recalling that his organization and military philosophy was undoubtedly based on the original concepts of the Commandos initiated in 1940.

Attacking a target guarded by either the Regular Army or the Home Guard was always regarded as potential fun. But it also provided valuable training for both the defenders and us. Naturally rivalries built up and the defenders were always determined to put up 'a good show' when they knew the Commandos were coming.

Limited to blank ammunition and thunderflashes to simulate gunfire, grenades and explosives these exercises were however carried out with surprising realism and excitement. Scuffles and 'free-fights' invariably took place when the action was at close quarters.

Bruises and bumps were soon forgotten by the combatants afterwards, especially if there was a get-together in a canteen or mess where the pros and cons of the exercise could be discussed over a pint – or two – of beer.

Towards the end of August the Battle of Britain gathered momentum for Göring, Hitler's air chief, had launched the Luftwaffe's first major attack with 1,500 aircraft on 13 August. Thereafter, there followed daily raids on airfields and objectives in the south and east of England. We witnessed scores of air battles and 'dog' fights high above us as we trained in the Weymouth area. The blue skies of those sunny August days were patterned with tell-tale, criss-crossed white vapour trails as the young RAF pilots of Spitfires and Hurricanes took their toll of their numerically superior aerial enemy in the opening rounds of the crucial Battle of Britain.

With typical bravado, and wishing to offer moral support, we declined to seek cover in the air-raid shelters when the sirens sounded. Instead we watched the air battles overhead and loudly cheered whenever a Jerry plane, smoke pouring from its fuselage, came hurtling earthwards. But standing around had its dangers too, as I found out, for I still have a little scar on the top of my right foot where a tiny piece of 'friendly' ack-ack shrapnel pierced it as we interrupted our training on Weymouth beach to watch the outcome of a German daylight raid.

Daily the threat of the invasion increased as the Battle of Britain raged overhead. And as it did every man under arms – both full-time soldier and part-time volunteer – was called upon to stand by ready to repel and beat back the invaders. As a result of this imminent threat the Commandos in the south of the country, instead of remaining under direct War Office command and control, were placed temporarily under the command of local district commanders to assist in the defence of their area. Under the circumstances this made sound sense.

Fortunately, certain limitations were imposed on our employment; briefly, we were to be given counter-offensive roles and not deployed on static defence, staring out to sea by day and night. Such a decision suited us, for it allowed us to carry on training, although for a while the emphasis shifted from preparing for tip-and-run raids to preparing to act as a mobile reserve against an enemy landing force.

Sad to relate there didn't appear to be any definite plans for our anti-invasion role, inasmuch as we didn't carry out any practices as such either on our own, or in conjunction with other army units in the area. There is no doubt that we were ill-prepared for this situation. The speed of the German success in Europe, the retreat from Dunkirk and the sudden and unexpected prospects of facing a German invasion had caught us unprepared. Hasty defence plans were drawn up and infantry units deployed along the length of our vulnerable coastline. But being a hitherto independent and new unit we seemed to be excluded from any coordinated plan, except for being designated as a mobile reserve. How we, without any motor transport, were expected to fulfil that role is hard to fathom. Subsequently we were 'mobile', but that's a story to follow.

Consequently it seemed to many of us that our detailed operational role in the event of 'Jerry' landing would be based on a 'wait and see' policy.

Not unexpectedly when our first real test in this role came and we thought it was the real thing – there was chaos. It came on the evening of Saturday, 7 September. We were all off-duty. Not being concentrated, as we would have been in barracks, we were scattered throughout the town, in billets, cinemas, pubs and the like with only the Orderly Officer and the Main Guard on duty at Commando Headquarters in the Pavilion. The order came through for the whole Commando to muster, in fighting order, in the main car park. The only means of passing on this vital message was limited to just one way – 'word of mouth'. As a result the mustering took hours and the whole thing was an absolute fiasco. It all took place in the

Blackout with repeated shouts of 'Put out that light', etc. The situation was aggravated, at about 2300 hours, by the ringing of church bells, whereupon rumours abounded fast and furious, and for good reason. Under the wartime regulations the ringing of church bells was prohibited, they were only to be rung in the event of enemy invasion, by sea or by air. Within minutes the word soon spread that 'Jerry had landed'.

But where and what were we going to do about it?

It is hard to believe that no one had quite imagined this scenario. We had no firm information nor any orders for immediate action. It had been assumed that we would have some advance warning instructions, followed by specific orders. But we had none. Neither did we have any pre-planned course of action. We should have had a contingency plan of some sort.

Too much reliance had been placed on the 'wait and see' policy. And it hadn't worked. No one knew what to do, except to sit and wait.

It was almost midnight, some four hours after the initial order to muster had been given before all the Troops reported that they were sufficiently mustered to be considered operational and ready to proceed.

We waited and waited, but no further orders came down to us. We sat in that car park, with our rifles, Brens and other personal weapons, ammunition and grenades until dawn. Soon after we were ordered to 'Stand down'. Before being dismissed we were told, in spite of the church bells and the rumours, there had been no enemy landings. It had been a false alarm. No doubt it was just as well. We had been taught several valuable and salutary lessons.

Years later it was interesting to read in Winston Churchill's memoirs an account of what happened that night. We were not the only people unprepared. Apparently, the General Headquarters of Home Forces had received substantial information, backed up by aerial photographs, that the Nazis had been assembling barges and practising the embarkation of troops and equipment at several places along the French coast. The signs were ominous. The worst fears of the General Staff were increased when four Nazis were captured after landing on the South-East Coast and, after confessing to being spies, confirmed that the enemy were ready to invade.

Our Intelligence staff also reported that moon and tide conditions, vital factors in any amphibious operation, between 8 and 10 September were considered ideal. So with this information and the evidence at hand, GHQ concluded that the possibility of an invasion had become imminent. Accordingly, at 2000 hours on 7 September they issued the codeword 'Cromwell', which meant nothing more than 'invasion imminent'. The message was passed down the chain of command to all units speedily and without any problems. However, it was the reaction and responses to this message that had caused the chaos – and it was by no means limited to Weymouth. Church bells had been rung in many areas provoking widespread rumours of an invasion and causing confusion and alarm akin to that experienced by us.

Not even Churchill or his Chiefs of Staff were aware that the codeword 'Cromwell' had been issued, and consequently were much concerned at the resultant muddle and chaos. Churchill recalls: 'The next morning instructions were given to devise immediate stages by which vigilance could be increased on future occasions without declaring an invasion imminent.'

He added that, 'as may be imagined, this incident caused a great deal of talk and stir . . . it served as a useful tonic and rehearsal for all concerned.' He was right.

Certainly, we in No 4 Commando had exposed several shortcomings which had to be redressed. Most important was concern about our role as a 'mobile reserve'.

The obvious question that needed an answer was: 'How can one have an effective mobile force if the force earmarked for this role has no means of mobility apart from the CO's vehicle, the Admin 15 cwt truck, a few private cars and 500 pairs of feet?' The answer is simply – impossible.

It might have been possible to requisition or commandeer civilian vehicles in an emergency, but the recent disastrous call-out had convinced Colonel Legard that he must have his own integral means of mobility, available at all times for the duration of our assigned role. But how?

Any issue of War Department transport was, under the circumstances, regrettably out of the question, so he decided on a typical expedient to find an independent and unorthodox solution. Through the Troop Leaders he made an appeal to all ranks to go out and 'beg, borrow or scrounge' any form of transport on wheels, without breaking the law.

The next few days saw the arrival of a small and motley collection of wheeled transport, only the odd motor car and motor cycle, but several old bikes, including those of errand boys, one still bearing its trade plate boasting 'Lipton's Tea Is Best', or words to that effect. However, not all had been honestly obtained and under police pressure, several of these vehicles suddenly and mysteriously found their way back to their place of origin – without (too many) questions being asked.

The Colonel was almost back to square one, but the outcome of his appeal did suggest a possible simple solution – the issue of army bicycles, 500 of them.

Once the decision had been taken to equip us all with bicycles for our mobile role it was effected with typical Commando alacrity. Within a day or so we were all taken in 'charabancs' from Weymouth to the military Ordnance Depot at Tidworth, in Hampshire. The weather was ideal for a 'country spin' so we sported shirts and shorts. On arrival in Tidworth we were marched through one end of the Depot and out the other end wheeling a brand new khaki-coloured Service bicycle. It was no lightweight pleasure job, but a sturdy single-speed model complete with fittings to fasten our rifles along the frame, with the butt strapped under the saddle and the muzzle just below the handlebars. And off we set back to Weymouth, all 500 of us.

In the Diary entry recording this adventure, Captain Young restricted himself to this bare sentence: 'The Troop rode very well together and covered the 73 miles in $5^{1}/_{2}$ hours.' He didn't mention the inevitable mishaps that took place on those Hampshire/Dorset roads that day, or the bewildered looks of locals as we cycled south. Considering some chaps had not cycled before it was a creditable first time. There were some sore bums, but next day we were off on our newly acquired mounts to practice cycling in tactical groups.

First, however we had to face our landladies. It shouldn't be difficult to imagine the looks of perplexity on the faces of those good ladies as we took home our new 'charges' and carried them through the house to stable them in the back garden, shed or coal house. The looks on their faces clearly posed the question 'What ever next?' For after all they had only just got accustomed to having an arsenal of ammunition and grenades in their homes, when there we were wheeling bicycles through the kitchens. Bless those good souls, they took it all in their stride. 'For after all,' they would tell their neighbour over the garden fence, 'don't you know, there's a war on.'

Midway through September, whilst the invasion threat was still with us, we were deployed on Ridgeway Hill, a prominent feature alongside the main Weymouth to Dorchester road. There we set up a base to carry out anti-invasion exercises. We bivouacked and with our civilian-size rations of tea, sugar, milk, bread and other basic foods bought on the strength of our ration cards, we set up camp. We used a small old hut on the site as the Troop store/HQ and central cookhouse. There, a chirpy, but capable, cockney RASC corporal was installed as 'chief cook and bottle-washer'. He did a great job. His main task was to cook a decent meal for all at midday. The rest of the meals each day were the responsibility of each man, or rather each pair of men and in essence this saw the beginnings of the accepted 'Me and My Pal' system.

Photograph from Troop Diary entitled 'One Night's Bag, Ridgeway Hill.' The author, in shirt sleeves, is second from right.

We bivouacked in sub-section areas, using whatever was at hand to provide temporary shelter. The most popular being a 'lean-to', made by draping our groundsheets from the the stone boundary walls.

We also took advantage of our nocturnal forays to forage for supplementary rations in the form of chicken, rabbits and vegetables from the neighbouring farmland. This was a very important aspect of our training, not only because we might after a raid be forced to make our way through enemy-occupied country to escape, but also had the Germans occupied this country we may well have been used as a guerilla force.

As luck would have it, we had, in Stan Harris, ex-poacher and regular soldier of the Royal Tank Regiment, an excellent instructor and mentor where it came to foraging for food. He showed us how to lay traps for rabbits, how to approach chicken coops and other poaching ruses. Equally important were his tips on how to overcome obstacles, climb fences and gates, and deal with barbed wire without being heard or raise an alarm. This was put to good use on our night exercises, both for our military training and our commissariat needs.

*During the invasion scare the Commandos were often called upon to act as 'Fifth
Columnists' to test the Regular and Home Guard defence forces. Here a group of No 4
Commando dressed in 'civvies', but armed and mobile on their newly acquired bicycles,
are seen acting in that role in Dorset, September 1940.*

It was a pity that there were no opportunities for poaching on rivers in
that part of Dorset, however we were able to make good this apparent
deficiency a couple of weeks later on a cycle expedition to Clovelly in
Devon.

Stan was also an expert in imitating bird calls and tried to pass on his
expertise to us so that we could possibly use this method for signalling at
night, but we had limited success in this subject compared with poaching.

I must admit our nocturnal foraging outings were not always
appreciated by the local farmers and smallholders, but on the odd
occasions when we were found to be the culprits compensation was
offered, yet frequently, in the spirit of the times, was not always accepted.

From the 'bivvy' camp we sallied forth on our bicycles to selected
targets some miles away on the coast to repel imaginary enemy invaders or
areas inland to deal with equally imaginary 'Fifth Columnists'. These
forays were carried out by day and night, but the latter was always difficult
and hazardous. The total 'blackout' precluded the use of any cycle lights
whatever, fore and aft, and great care was needed when on the move as a

body of some 20 to 25 cyclists. Needless to say we had our fair share of mishaps – to put it mildly.

Life wasn't made any easier by the removal of all road signs as an invasion precaution and this added to problems of finding one's way round the countryside on a dark night.

Finally, on the use of bicycles, mention must be made of our 'excursion' to Clovelly in North Devon. Although the main aim of this particular exercise was to provide experience of a long ride (about 150 miles) done as quickly as possible, but compatible with arriving there as a unit, there were other training factors such as boating, weapon firing (out to sea), bivouacking and 'living off the land'.

At Clovelly we were able to do a lot of rowing in boats lent to us by the local fishermen. They passed on to us not only practical tips on seamanship, but also helpful advice on mackerel fishing which we soon put to profitable use.

Deliberately denied any proper fishing tackle other than some twine/string and a pin, we set off like Robinson Crusoes, five in a boat to fish for our suppers. We had no bait but were told that a sliver of silver paper, taken from a packet of fags, and wrapped around the makeshift hook at the end of the line would do the trick. The silver 'spinner' was trailed behind the boat as we rowed about 400 yards off-shore, and parallel to the coastline, in a likely stretch of water recommended to us by an old salt. He had based his advice on the presence of seagulls flying over this certain patch of water. He was right and we netted some twenty-odd mackerel in as many minutes. Thrilled with our success we returned to the little harbour and soon the freshly caught fish were sizzling away in our mess tins over campfires. In addition to boating and fishing at Clovelly we also had the chance to test-fire all our Troop weapons at improvised targets floating off-shore. Ammunition was still in short supply so we had only a few rounds each, but it was better than none at all and did at least allow us to fire our individual weapons, whereas in many units soldiers didn't get that opportunity.

By the time we returned to Weymouth after a very wet, almost non-stop cycle ride it was late September, and the outcome of the Battle of Britain had been decided. 'The Few' had saved these islands and, although we didn't know it at the time, Hitler had decided to postpone Operation Sea Lion indefinitely. Instead, he decided to bomb the civilian population of our cities and towns. The Blitz was about to start . . . and we were about to begin a new phase in our training. Although the narrative so far has been concentrated, for obvious reasons, on No 4, the other Commandos and

Independent Companies elsewhere in this country, with one notable exception, were following similar training programmes.

The exception, of course, was No 2 Commando, the one designated for parachuting.

If we had problems starting much of our training from scratch, we had good cause to pity – and later admire – our comrades in No 2 for there being no parachute school or recognized specialist instructors – they, themselves, had to pioneer the way, but more about their experiences later.

So much for the newly-formed Commandos in the United Kingdom, now for a word or two about those raised in the Middle East. There, the British and Commonwealth Forces were facing the Italians in North Africa – the Germans didn't arrive until late 1941 – and Nos 50, 51 and 52 were busy training in the desert, being based mainly in a tented camp at Geneifa.

Their primary role was seaborne raids along the coast of North Africa and on any enemy-held islands in the Mediterranean, plus – because the Italians were on the same land mass and shared a mutual front line – possible deep inland penetration raids behind the enemy lines.

Basic training in the ME Commandos was similar to that of their UK counterparts, except for some obvious differences attributable to terrain, climate and the additional role of deep penetration raids by land. For the later role it was initially suggested that camels would be used, an idea undoubtedly prompted by the exploits of Lawrence and his Arab raiders in the First World War.

With the priority for all the major supplies of arms, ammunition and supplies firmly needed for the defence of Britain, the ME Commandos faced the same sort of problems as their UK comrades, the main one being the complete absence of any powered landing craft of any type. They were dependent on naval cutters and whalers, requisitioned motor launches and any other local craft, plus home-made rafts for possible river crossings.

Recalling some early training, Charles Messenger wrote:

> A typical exercise carried out by No 50 involved marching to Port Said and embarking in the boat 'Saggita', a boat belonging to the manufacturers of Branston pickles, requisitioned for the purpose. After landing on the coast of the Red Sea, they marched back to Geneifa carrying out schemes and practice demolitions on the way. The whole exercise lasted three days.

In spite of the unavailability of purposeful landing craft throughout 1940 for either training or operations the ME Commandos persisted with whalers and local craft. The latter were often unseaworthy and required extensive repairs in order to make them serviceable. However, No 50 did manage to devise a drill whereby about sixty men could be landed using a diesel-engined caique towing two 'strings' of local boats.

By autumn 1940 Commandos both in this country and in the Middle East were established, had embarked on their innovative training and, indeed, had carried out some raids although none of these could be hailed as successes. Without any shadow of doubt the failures were not due to any lack of enthusiasm and spirit, on the contrary, but due to a lack of the proper landing craft and insufficient training.

As we shall see in the next chapter during the winter of 1940/41 the problems of suitable landing craft and related amphibious training were tackled with increasing urgency and resolve, due in no small measure to the drive and resolution of Admiral Sir Roger Keyes.

CHAPTER IV

On the Water –
Small Boats and Landing Craft

It is a sad reflection on our military planners during the inter-war years that little or no thought was given to the training – or even study – for amphibious warfare and operations.

Admittedly one reason for this neglect was the usual one – a lack of money to pay for such an apparent non-essential, especially when all the pundits reckoned that if there was another war it would again be fought on the mainland of Europe and our forces would get there as they did in 1914-18. It was firmly believed that combined operations involving seaborne assaults were not a priority matter in preparing for any possible future conflict.

In the twenty years spanning 1918 and 1938 the limited thoughts and preparations given to this type of operations were confined to academic Staff College discussions and papers, plus a couple of exercises with troops in Scotland and also on Slapton Sands in Devon. Ironically, although it was not foreseen at the time, those same beaches and the hinterland in Devon were to become a major and vital training area for the largest combined operation of amphibious warfare in history, the Normandy landings in June 1944. For it was there that thousands of American soldiers prepared for D-Day and it was also on Slapton Sands that one of the giant rehearsals for D-Day was held, which ended in catastrophe and the loss of precisely 749 US soldiers and sailors, when German E-boats attacked the Allied convoy transporting the force, whilst they were still at sea. The story of this disaster was for some forty years a closely guarded secret.

In 1938, however, possibly as the result of a study paper prepared by the Royal Naval Staff college at Greenwich, the Chiefs of Staff did decide to set up a team of four officers and some clerks to look into specific problems appertaining to amphibious operations.

Known as the Inter-Service Training and Development Centre (ISTDC), this team – in reality it was nothing more than a 'think-tank' to provide recommendations on the given problems – was based in Fort Cumberland near Portsmouth. Without going into details, suffice it here, in the context of Commando training and operations to record that among the specific tasks they were instructed to study and advise upon was that of suitable ships and craft required to launch seaborne assaults.

In their study of the parent ships that could be suitably adapted for the envisaged amphibious role, they looked favourably at two cargo/passenger ships then being built for the Alfred Holt Line for service in the East and duly earmarked them for possible requisitioning in war. In the event they were taken over and became well known to many Commandos en route to battle overseas, the *Glengyle* and the *Glenroy*.

The wisdom of this choice was further enhanced by the ISTDC decision to recommend the building of the assault landing craft designed by the famous shipbuilding firm of Messrs Thorneycroft. Their prototype, suitably modified, became the standard landing craft assault (LCA) for all the major amphibious landings not only in Normandy, but throughout the Middle and Far East theatres of war.

These sturdy and reliable little landing craft had a RN crew of four – skipper, coxswain, 'stoker' and deckhand – could carry up to 35 fully equipped troops, had lightly armoured sides and with two V8 engines had a range of between 50 and 80 miles at a cruising speed of about 7 knots (see illustration).

Although some LCAs were in action in the ill-fated Norwegian campaign and at Dunkirk there were only eight left in service when the Commandos were formed, and these were needed to train crews.

Bernard Fergusson, a distinguished soldier of Chindit fame and who later became the Deputy Director of Combined Operations, in the authoritative history of Combined Operations, scathingly commented in his book *The Watery Maze*, of our unreadiness at that time, summer 1940, and being woefully unable – left with just a handful of landing craft – to mount any amphibious operation, however small. He wrote: 'It was not much to show for three hundred years of vaunted supremacy in maritime arts. We had been kicked ignominiously off the continent of Europe. We had not prepared, we had not planned.'

This then was the position when Churchill ordered the Commandos to be formed for raids on the enemy coastline of Europe.

Nevertheless, being based mainly in seaside resorts around the coast the Commandos were able to train in seamanship and acquire some skills in the handling of boats plus making a start in beach landings. We did so in a motley range of boats ranging from small rowing boats and naval cutters to

'Out Troops' – an early training picture (late 1940) of disembarking, during a mock assault landing, from a LCA, which carried up to 35 troops. (Photograph by courtesy of the Imperial War Museum.)

locally owned motor launches and fishing boats. Although these boats were not really suitable for training for the operations envisaged, they represented all that was available to use at the time.

Thus it was in the early days, with no alternatives at hand we had to accept the situation as it was and press ahead with seamanship training with whatever boats and craft that were available.

Indeed, the Middle East Commandos not only had to carry out most of their amphibious training in whalers and cutters on the Great Bitter Lakes, but also use them for their operational landings on the island of Castelorizzo in the Dodecanese, in February 1941, the whalers being lowered from the parent destroyer – a scenario reminiscent of Gallipoli in 1915.

Apart from the 'hotchpotch' collection of small boats available at the seaside bases, a few Eurekas became free. Indeed they were used for the early abortive raid on Guernsey, mentioned later. These craft were the brainchild of an enterprising Mr Higgins of New Orleans, who had originally designed them for the American Coastguards, not for amphibious operations. As a result they had many limitations for our needs. With an overall length of 36 feet, they could carry some 25 troops, and although speedy they were very noisy. Furthermore, to disembark troops had to jump off the prow, which was relatively high above the water line, not an ideal way to make a landing, especially if the water was more than waist deep.

In the initial stages of training, prior to the use of LCAs, sliding over the sides of rowing boats, or jumping off the prows or gunwales of launches and their like was regarded as normal. Invariably all such landings were 'wet-shod' – and not always readily accepted. For as can be imagined it made for a very wet and cold start to an exercise especially in the winter months. Water would find its way into battledress tunics and trousers, boots or rubber-soled plimsoles, and ammunition pouches, only to cascade out as we plodded and squelched up the beaches.

Water wasn't the only problem. One serious early problem was the noise created by ourselves in various ways and for various reasons. Obviously the aim was to land as quickly and silently as possible, but this is easier said than done, especially by inexperienced novices to this aspect of warfare. As a result many of the early exercises were chaotic. We had no set or established drills, consequently verbal orders had be given, which were not always clear or even heard, and had to be repeated frequently by shouting them afresh. Then there was the inevitable swearing and cussing – often aloud – during disembarkation when the boat lurched and someone lost his footing or was thrown off balance and fell into the 'drink', not to mention the verbal tirades that ensued when a wave knocked a wader off his feet or the depth of water suddenly, without rhyme or reason, got deeper – and deeper – as we floundered ashore.

In fairness, it is true to comment that these were natural teething problems resulting from our ignorance, lack of experienced instruction and basic training in seamanship and boating.

As might be expected we also had some dangerous moments in the water, plus the occasional accident. There was a narrow escape early on at Weymouth on one of our mock raids. We had returned to the beach having successfully accomplished the exercise mission, but our boat was unable to come in to pick us up. So there wasn't any alternative but a mere 50 yards swim. Halfway one of Lieutenant Munn's chaps got cramp and went under. Fortunately, it was a daylight exercise and Munn was near at hand, saw what had happened, was able to quickly reach the hapless fellow and, in the approved Royal Life Saving Society manner, tow him safely to the waiting boat. Munn had reacted quickly and capably in deep water, but only just in time. It was a near thing.

We were not so fortunate a year or so later when stationed at Troon. We were involved on a night landing on the Isle of Arran, disembarking from a landing craft, tank (LCT). As we silently approached the beach the ramp was lowered and the order 'Out Troops' given. The two leading soldiers went straight ahead off the lowered ramp into the water which was almost five feet deep. As they did so the LCT continued to drift inshore on the incoming tide, pushing the two soldiers under. Seeing what had happened the following Commandos jumped off the sides of the ramp, assuming their mates had recovered and were now clear. At this stage, having had plenty of training and also been on a raid in Norway, our self-discipline and silence could not be faulted. There was no indication that anything was amiss as the landing continued as planned. It wasn't realized the two were missing until much later, the normal drill being that if anyone was initially missing all troops 'pressed on regardless', anticipating that any straggler would catch up as soon as possible.

Unfortunately when the two did not appear at any stage during the exercise, our worst fears materialized in the light of the morning when two bodies were found washed up on the foreshore. Both were popular members of D Troop and the tragedy was compounded by the fact that one had recently married a local Troon girl. Now she was a widow.

Afterwards it became a Standing Order that the inflatable 'Mae West' lifebelts were to be worn under equipment on all seaborne exercises and operations. But back in 1940 Mae Wests were not always available.

There was another occasion in September 1940 when, had our exercise been the real thing, six of our Troop would have ended up as POWs. This time we were on a simple little daylight scheme in the Ringstead Bay area to the east of Weymouth.

We had landed satisfactorily and the rest of the exercise had gone well; perhaps we had done too well, because when we got back to the beach to re-embark we found the Troop Leader had ordered the launch and boats to lie off about 250 yards out to sea. We had to swim to them. We were all fully clothed and armed. This was to be our big test. We waded in and although the actual swim was reduced to about 150 yards, it was too much for six men. They gave up and returned to the beach, much to the chagrin of Captain Young. He recorded his disappointment in the Troop Diary in no uncertain terms, when he wrote: 'At the end of the scheme we pretended that the boats had been lost and the Troop would have to swim out to the launch . . . We lost six men, which is not good. I intend to do much more deep sea swimming.' He kept his word and we did plenty.

It is important to appreciate how vitally important swimming was at that time bearing in mind the types of boats we had and also before the general issue of Mae Wests. This is borne out by the fact that on the very first Commando raid on Guernsey in July 1940 the only casualties suffered were three lost because they had been incapable of swimming out to the RAF Eurekas used on the operation. After the landing the boats withdrew to 'lay off'. Unfortunately when the time came to re-embark the raiders the RAF boats were unable to get close inshore because of rocks and a swell that had developed with the tide. So the Commandos had no option, swim or... All made it except three. They spent the next four years as guests of Adolf Hitler. It was a salutary lesson for all weak swimmers.

Colonel Legard was very aware of the high priority that swimming should have in our training and he even introduced it to the nightly Staff (Defaulters) Parades whilst we were at Weymouth. The men on this punishment parade for minor misdemeanours paraded at 2200 hours at the end of the Pier. Following the inspection by the Orderly Officer, the 'janker wallahs' – an old army term (India inspired) for those on minor punishments – had to strip off, put on swimming trunks or PT shorts and then go down the steps and into the water to swim the 70 or 100 yards, dependent on the state of the tide, to the shore. Once ashore each man quickly shook himself and ran as fast as he could back to the sea end of the pier to redress. If the Orderly Officer thought that the time taken was too long, the defaulter was called an 'idle man' and had to repeat the performance. Maybe the punishment didn't always fit the crime, but no one could deny that it did fit the needs of our training. Furthermore it was novel and in keeping with the innovative philosophy of the Commandos was readily accepted – even by the janker wallahs.

By the beginning of October 1940 the situation regarding landing ships with their own LCAs was improving and No 4 Commando became one of the first to graduate on LCAs operating from a parent ship.

We left Weymouth and travelled north, overnight on the inevitable steam troop train, to the Clydeside docks where we embarked on one of those converted cargo/passenger ships of Alfred Holt, now HMS *Glengyle* of the Royal Navy.

For practically all of us it was the introduction to life on board. It was vastly different to life in army barracks and, regrettably, civilian billets. What's more there was a different language too.

The *Glengyle* had been converted, more or less, as recommended by the ISTDC, and was now complete with its ten LCAs slung on davits.

Below deck the passengers' accommodation had been adapted as officers' cabins.

No such comforts for the troops, who were consigned to the original cargo decks, although, admittedly, they had been converted sufficiently to be called 'Troops' Mess Decks'. Here all NCOs and other ranks, with the exception of the RSM, were quartered. To say that these mess decks were cramped and uncomfortable would be a gross understatement.

Each sub-unit in the Commando was allotted areas on the mess deck and split up into groups of eight NCOs and men to form a 'mess'. The living space for each mess centred on its wooden table and the two wooden forms each side of the table, plus the immediate surrounding floor space; in addition, the sleeping arrangements were hinged (quite literally) on hooks in the bulkheads. On these we nightly slung our hammocks, which were collected last thing just before 'Lights Out', then immediately taken down at reveille to be packed and stowed before anything could be done on the mess deck.

Now this is where the new language of the Navy should be mentioned. There were, of course, no bugle calls on board to punctuate and regulate the day's routine. Instead the boatswain (bo'sun) acting rather like an army orderly sergeant would make various announcements over the ship's tannoy. Each announcement was preceded by the shrill call of the bo'sun's pipe to be followed by 'Do-yer-hear-there, do-yer-hear-there', and then the relevant order or announcements for either the ship's company or the Commando troops on board.

At six o'clock each morning, or at four bells in the ship's time, the bo'sun's pipe prefaced, 'Wakey, Wakey; Rise and Shine; You've had your time!' Some minutes later, just time enough for the previous order to take effect, came the more demanding one from the same source, 'Lash up and stow.' In the time-honoured tradition of the Royal Navy we then had to take down our hammocks, although under the restricted conditions it was impossible to do this together, fold up the single blanket, take out from the canvas hammock any personal items kept there overnight and with the cords tie up the hammock before returning it to one of the nearby stores. One might add that we were so packed on the *Glengyle* at that time that there were not enough hammocks or hammock spaces for everyone, so some had to sleep on the forms, in odd corners or the vacated hammock storage spaces. It was all rather chaotic, like so many conditions in those early and formative days of Combined Operations.

Surprisingly it didn't take long to get used to sleeping in hammocks; the fact that we were usually dead tired after a hard day's training no doubt contributed to this rapid familiarization; most of us found the hammock extremely comfortable and the single woollen blanket ideal. Of course, on the first night or two there was a fair amount of hilarity – and a certain amount of horse-play – in getting into and out of the swinging hammocks, especially as they were so close together. They were a novelty and source of amusement that helped to offset some of the exasperation and frustration induced by the crowded conditions. It was understandable that we all, with typical 'Tommy' resigned humour, christened the *Glengyle* the 'Altmark', after the infamous German prison ship that had been captured earlier that year off the coast of Norway. It was a name that stuck even when the Commandos of Layforce travelled in her to the Middle East.

The announcement 'Cooks to the Galley' was most misleading. An orderly was appointed daily from each mess, and in the eyes of the Navy he was our 'cook', but only in name. So when that announcement was heard, it was the mess orderly that went off to the galley, not to cook, but to collect the grub for his mess. He returned with large tins of food and a bucket of tea. Back at the mess table this was distributed under the strict supervision of the NCO i/c of the mess. As there was no separate Sergeants' Mess on board, it was one of the senior NCOs.

Most days were spent away from the parent ship, on practise landings and/or training ashore, so there were dry rations for the midday meal to be collected in bulk by the mess orderly. Some idea of how we fared for food on board the *Glengyle* can be gauged from the following entry in the Troop Diary: 'food on board was not good and in fact some of the best appreciated meals were just plain bully beef and navy biscuits ("hard tack") with a mug of tea round a fire on the edge of the loch'.

Let me break here and explain the significance of the 'loch'. Shortly after having boarded the *Glengyle* we set sail from Port Glasgow, past Greenock and Gourock, then, rounding the Isle of Bute, we headed north and into Loch Fyne for our destination and training area around the picturesque highland village of Inveraray. On arrival there, however, the scene was anything but picturesque, for a typical Scotch mist had all but blotted out the landscape.

We wasted no time in starting our training on the LCAs. However, at first it was almost a case of the blind leading the blind, inasmuch as the ship's company had little or no experience of working with the Army and by the same token we with the Navy. There was much to be learnt by both sides. The first priority was to work out routes and timings for speedy, silent and simultaneous movement of all the troops from their different mess decks to the embarkation stations, then embark in the suspended

LCAs. This took several practises and quite a bit of coordination to ensure that we took the quickest routes on board without crossing the paths of others engaged on the same task but from different mess decks. However, once that problem had been solved and practised to the mutual satisfaction of both sides, we were ready – and more than anxious – to move on to the next stage: positions in the LCAs, the sea passage, disembarkation and clearing the beach.

The tactical loading and positioning of the thirty troops to travel in each LCA was most important, as we were soon to find out. Initially we didn't bother with this aspect. 'Get in and get out' was the immediate object of the exercise.

Then came the moment we had all been waiting for: the run-in and and the landing. After all our boating in cutters, rowing boats and on launches, to be packed in the LCA without any view of the outside was very claustrophobic and one felt very much committed to the care of the crew – who at this stage were an unknown quantity.

'Lower away LCAs' was ordered over the tannoy and down we went to meet the water with an undignified flop, then a roar of the twin V8 engines and away we went. The journey from the *Glengyle* to the lochside didn't take long and as we approached the beach we were ordered, 'Prepare to disembark'.

After all those wet landings down in the South it was wonderful to hear the flat bottom of the LCA harmlessly crunching its way on the pebbled shore as the ramp was lowered and, when the order 'Out troops' was given, to disembark dryshod.

We had trained to clear the beach as quickly as possible but that had not been easy wading ashore from the motley craft we had used down at Weymouth, but now we were being delivered to the beach in style. Hopefully, less wading, just a little jump off the ramp and we would be ashore, not even wet feet! That was the theory, but it didn't always work out that way and we were in for a lot more unpleasant wading . . .

From the beginning we had been trained to dash up the beach as quickly as possible to a forming-up place (FUP), a preselected spot where we could muster on disembarkation. It was again drilled into us that we must not succumb to the natural self-preservation instinct of wanting to go to ground if the beach was being swept by fire. The hope of avoiding being hit was a false one. So at Inveraray from the very first landing we always cleared the narrow lochside beach and up to the road before stopping. This basic disembarkation drill became automatic and sacrosanct.

The practice landings were repeated time and time again, always against the clock to see which Troop could be the fastest. The aim became to empty the LCA and all clear a 30-yard beach in under half a minute.

When we returned to the parent ship we had the task of boarding via scrambling nets which hung over the sides, a challenging way to end the day's training. LCAs were never hauled back on board with troops still in them – just in case.

Once we had mastered the drills for embarking and disembarking, we spent more time on training schemes, exercises and weapon training including the field firing of all our Troop weapons.

On one of the day's training our Troop was given permission to go deer stalking. Unfortunately, but for obvious reasons, the numbers were limited to just one party. Consequently only the best shots were chosen, ten in all. They were successful and they bagged three deer, including a 12-pointer. Somehow the hunters managed to 'dress' the animals and get the carcasses aboard. However, word got around to higher Headquarters who didn't approve. The Troop Diary takes up the story: 'The shooting was not accorded a popular reception from Scottish Command and the CO got a good rocket. Nevertheless in the meanwhile the venison was eaten and much appreciated.'

We spent a fortnight on board the *Glengyle* at Inveraray and during that time became quite proficient on the LCAs, whilst the intensive training ashore, which included four of five night exercises, enhanced our previous training and was far more realistic than the boating exercises carried out in the Weymouth area. Furthermore, it was the beginning of integrated army/navy cooperation, but I hasten to add that this early joint training was not always harmonious or smooth. Although it would have been natural to expect problems because of the inexperience in amphibious training on both sides, we were, unfortunately, subjected to some gross inefficiency in administration on board, particularly appropos feeding which, added to the very unpleasant and cramped living conditions on the mess decks, was too much for some. Meals invariably were late and, on the whole, unsatisfactory and inadequate. It was quite common to be called for a meal, only to find it wasn't ready and waits of half an hour were quite normal. This affected our training schedules, making it necessary to alter them at short notice. So frequent were these changes that we coined a new – and appropriate – cliché, 'Order, Counter-order, Disorder...', prefaced by typical army adjectival expletives. The outcome was often a shambles with a lot of us, as senior NCOs, not knowing what was going on and consequently having little or no information to pass on to our subordinates, so adding to the problems of life on board. This, coupled with training mishaps and frustrations inflicted on us through the inexperience of the crews of the LCAs caused much moaning and groaning.

However, the collective impact of all this showed up the whingers who couldn't take it when things didn't go smoothly and were not prepared 'to grin and bear it'. Such teething problems of Combined Operations revealed the 'Moaning Minnies', the types who upset everyone else and as potential Commando soldiers were unsuitable and undesirable. They were earmarked for RTU as soon as possible – we didn't want them at any price.

We left the *Glengyle* by LCAs in full battle order and, carrying all our Troop weapons, landed on the shore of the loch to march the 12 miles to the nearest rail station at Dalmally. In itself this was no problem, but the gods were not smiling on us that day. It rained, or rather 'bucketed down' for every inch of the way, as it can in the Scottish highlands, and we arrived at the small, lonely station soaked to the skin, only to hang around for the special steam troop train that was to take us to a new coastal base at Ayr. Of all the most unpleasant physical predicaments none is so demoralizing as being cold AND thoroughly wet through. One can endure cold, snow, hail, mud and wind if the body is kept dry, but worse even than the severest cold is when all clothing, boots and the body are soaking wet. And we were that day as we waited for the train and the rain continued to teem down.

However, once aboard, the hot water pipes in all carriages – a feature of the old steam trains – were on full blast and were quickly festooned with wet clothing. As we sat in the steaming atmosphere in near nudity, the scene presented a cross between a Chinese laundry and a Swedish sauna.

We eventually arrived at Ayr late at night to be met by the Advance Party who had left the *Glengyle* two days earlier to sound out the possibility of finding billets in Oban. They drew a blank there and so pressed on to Ayr where they were more successful. Most of us were lucky and got billets that night, but a number of the unlucky ones spent a chilly November night in the grandstand of Ayr Race Course.

It was whilst we were stationed on the Ayrshire coast that we were introduced to the collapsible Goatley boat that was to play quite a part in future training. This extremely useful little boat had a flat wooden bottom and green collapsible sides.

Originally planned for use on rivers the Commandos used the Goatleys extensively in training on the sea and other waterways. Thousands of Commando trainees had their baptism of fire in amphibious warfare in

Goatleys at Achnacarry. But probably the most daring use of Goatleys in training during the Second World War was Exercise 'Brandyball', a cliff assault on the formidable Cornish sea cliffs near Land's End. But more about the Goatleys at Achnacarry and Exercise 'Brandyball' later.

There were several other types of boats, dinghies and canoes which the Commandos were trained to use.

Arguably the most useful small boat used exclusively by the Commandos was the sturdy 18-foot dory. Robust and reliable it was very popular and much used for clandestine raids by SSRF, Forfar Force and detachments from Nos 4 and 10 Commandos.

One of the training centres to use dories extensively and, indeed, to pioneer the techniques for rocky landings from dories was the Commando Mountain Warfare Training Centre (CMWTC).

The dories were extremely seaworthy and many Commandos were very grateful for this characteristic both on training exercises and in action, none more than those returning from a reconnaissance raid on Walcheren prior to the landings there in 1944. The raiders were all from the CMWTC and attached to the Commando Brigade for special duties, but they hadn't bargained for a ten-hour battle through gale force winds and seas to return to their base at Ostend.

The basic technique of going inshore for a rocky landing from dories hinged on sound judgement of tide and swell, plus close coordination between the coxswain and the kedgeman. The latter was responsible for throwing out and controlling the kedge anchor, which had grapnel-like prongs to make it hold fast on the seabed and so not only control the approach to the rocks, but also helped to pull away after the landings and subsequent re-embarkations.

These two key men in the dory worked as a team; invariably the coxswain, a senior NCO and usually a climbing instructor as well, chose his own kedgeman and was largely responsible for his training.

Of the landing party one was nominated as the bowman. His job on approaching the rocks, the kedge having been thrown out, was to be ready, rope in hand in the bows, to be first ashore and help to steady the dory for the remainder of the landing party to land. This type of landing needed, as can be imagined, plenty of practice, first by day, before attempting it in the dark.

Dories were used with considerable success for operations in Holland and then on the river crossings in Germany by the Commandos in their advance from the Rhine to the Baltic.

One simple and humble little craft used by the Commandos was the inflatable rubber dinghy, so popular and familiar after the War both in its own right for 'messing about' in the water and as a tender for yachtsmen.

The first recorded operational use of dinghies was from the Middle East in 1941. Geoffrey Keyes and the Layforce Commandos used them to get ashore from their parent submarine for their raid on Rommel's Headquarters in North Africa.

Although dinghies were subsequently used by the smaller Commando raiding groups, they were not generally included in normal Commando training, which was a pity as they were fun to handle and being light, easily transported and inflated would have been ideal for individual training in seamanship skills. However, they were frequently pressed into use by the Heavy Weapons Troops of the Commandos to ferry their mortars, MMGs and ammunition in wet landings and river crossings.

In the later stages of the War, more sophisticated amphibians, Landing Vehicles Tracked (LVTs) mostly Buffaloes, and their smaller relations, the Weasels, were used by Commandos in operations in Holland and on the river crossings in Germany.

The use of Buffaloes by 45 RM Cdo on the Rhine gave rise to a typical Mills-Roberts quip: 'Hannibal crossed the Alps using elephants, but my Commandos crossed the Rhine using buffaloes.'

Generally the LVTs were manned and maintained by Assault Squadrons, Royal Engineers, but for a short spell No 48 RM Cdo did have its own fleet of Weasels with drivers trained by Captain Bonner of that Commando. He had his 'school' on Walcheren and not only trained drivers for his own Commando, but also for the other Commandos.

Meanwhile in Italy No 2 Commando Brigade used a mixed armada of LVTs, Goatleys and storm boats for their bloody action on Lake Comacchio in April 1945, an action in which two Victoria Crosses were won by Commandos, Major Anders Lassen and Corporal Tom Hunter. Sadly both were posthumous awards.

Briefly these were the main boats and craft on which most Commandos were trained. In addition, there were some others, such as those used by special small units, e.g. SBS and SSRF. However perhaps the most unusual and unorthodox boat used was the Brixham trawler, 'Maid of Honour', acquired by Captain 'Gus' March Phillips of SSRF.

He had persuaded Combined Operations that a wooden hull sailing boat with an auxiliary engine, not affected by mines and primarily a sailing ship, could be used for night raiding without drawing enemy attention. Having got agreement in principle, but no written authority, to obtain a trawler, Gus proceeded to Brixham and requisitioned one of the typical fishing trawlers, with the winsome name. Not only did Gus get the boat but he also managed to 'hire' the skipper, and together they sailed back to Poole Harbour in Dorset.

The account of their secret training on the 'Maid' on the coastal waters from Poole contained in the book, *Geoffrey (Being the Story of 'Apple' of the Commandos and Special Air Service)*, makes fascinating reading and captures the development of the Commando spirit.

The Admiralty did not take kindly to the idea of a sailing ship operating against the enemy coastline, however there did arise a clandestine job for March-Phillips and the 'Maid of Honour' operating off the west coast of Africa, which they fulfilled with great success, plus the award of the DSO for Gus. On return to England he was instructed to expand his force, with hand-picked Commandos, with the express aim of raiding the coast of France, not from the 'Maid', but from small boats including dories.

During 1941 many Commandos spent a lot of time at sea involved in the training for one or other of Sir Roger Keyes' grandiose raids that never materialized. I remember when No 4 Commando was part of Force 110, formed to take part in Operation Pilgrim. The aim of this operation was to seize the Canary Islands in an attempt to thwart the Spaniards, thought, at the time, about to enter the War on the side of Germany and Italy.

The training for this operation necessitated a series of landings. We sailed from Gourock, down the Forth of the Clyde, past the Isle of Arran, rounded the Mull of Kintyre, before making for the Western Isles to carry out a series of landing exercises on South and North Uist. There we used, not for the first time, bamboo ladders to climb up from our LCAs onto the decrepit old jetties before pressing on across the bogs to our exercise objectives guarded by the local Home Guard. It was here we saw for the first – and only – time some of the men armed with pitchforks and other crude home-made weapons resembling old pikes. One shudders to think what might have happened if our raid had been for real . . .

Thereafter we sailed on, sighting the isles of Muck, Eigg and Rhum, names that raised a laugh, in spite of some atrocious weather and the tail-end of an Atlantic storm, to the Orkneys.

There we carried out a series of 'crash-landings' by night, onto the quayside of the port of Kirkwall. As the name suggests, instead of landing in the usual manner from LCAs on a beach, the idea was for the ship itself to go right alongside and disembark its troops direct on the quay under the cover of darkness. Quite a tricky operation as the exercise proved . . .

Each time as we came alongside there was a shuddering crunch as the ship lurched into the quay. That was our signal, we didn't need any other, to get off as speedily as possible by various routes and means. Officers, naval and army, recorded the time taken for the disembarkation.

It wasn't a success, and we were quite relieved when after several attempts we left Kirkwall and sailed back to Gourock not knowing whether this was just another exercise or whether it was for real. We were not told, but it all seemed to fizzle out. Our return to Gourock was quite pleasant, mainly because we enjoyed glorious weather and were able to spend a fair amount of time on deck. It was on this trip back that Charlie Vaughan introduced 'milling', one-minute all-action boxing, that became a feature of Commando training, especially at Achnacarry.

One of the most spectacular successes of the Second World War was the build-up of the mighty amphibious force that invaded the Normandy beaches on 6 June 1944. Many of the assault ships, support craft and amphibians were not even on the drawing board when the Commandos were first formed four years earlier.

Commando veterans, who stormed ashore on that momentous day, could not have foreseen, as they started their amphibious training in the motley collection of seaside rowing boats, naval cutters and whalers, and requisitioned motor launches, the subsequent wide-ranging fleet of assault ships, support craft and amphibians that would be developed and which they would use in training and operations during those four years.

The success of Operation Overlord and the other major assault landings elsewhere was directly attributable to the initial joint Royal Navy/Commando training, experiments, trials and exercises carried out on Loch Fyne and the stoney beaches near Inveraray in the autumn of 1940. There the Commandos and their naval comrades pioneered methods, drills and techniques that set patterns for all the many worldwide Combined Operations that followed. It is a fact worth remembering – and acknowledging.

CHAPTER V

Weapon Training –
Shoot to Kill

During 1940, especially after the fall of France and in the face of a threatened invasion, the availability of all weapons and ammunition throughout the British Army was woefully short and inadequate. This was most apparent when we began our special training and prepared for raids at Weymouth in July 1940.

Initially, in No 4 Commando – as in all of the other Commandos – we had just the basic pre-war infantry weapons. These consisted of the short magazine Lee Enfield rifle (SMLE), with its formidable long 18-inch bayonet, Bren light machine gun (LMG), Boys anti-tank rifle, .38 Smith and Wesson hand pistol and the veteran grenade of the First World War, the Mills (36). Ammunition was scarce.

We had to wait for several weeks before receiving the first consignments of the US Thompson sub-machine carbine (the 'Tommy gun', TSMC) and the US .45 colt automatic pistol, plus a few boxes of .45 ammo.

Following the decision in late 1940 to add large-scale combined operations to the original small raids other weapons were added. The first new one was the useful little 2-inch mortar.

From late 1941 the supply of Tommy guns improved considerably and these carbines were supplemented, from 1942, by the arrival of the cheap British-made Sten Machine Carbine (SMC), albeit it would be fair to add that the more sophisticated US Tommy gun was generally preferred to its rough and ready British counterpart.

By 1943 the ungainly and unpopular Boys anti-tank rifle had been replaced by PIATs (an acronym of Projectile, Infantry, Anti-Tank).

The Commandos placed special emphasis on close-quarter fighting, indeed they usually carried their famous fighting knives into action, and were taught to improvise and use other hand weapons, including sticks, coshes and even the enemy's steel helmet. They all made lethal weapons if one knew how – and the Commandos did. 'Mad' Jack Churchill had his claymore and bow and arrow but this was the odd exception because in action the Commandos, although trained to use a wide range of weapons and devices, fought mainly with the standard infantry weapons outlined above. Notwithstanding, it was how they started to use new techniques and skills in the use and firing of these weapons that initially raised the eyebrows of the pundits in other training establishments, but ironically as the aggressive philosophy of Commando Training became accepted and integrated into 'Battle Training', these same training units prided themselves on their own standards of 'Commando Training'. There is no greater form of flattery than copying . . . now for the weapons themselves.

The Lee Enfield (SMLE) had been the standard rifle throughout the First World War. It was proven as sturdy, reliable and accurate. Although a bolt-operated, single-shot weapon, with a magazine holding just 10 rounds of .303, in the hands of a well-trained soldier a rate of rapid fire of 15 rounds per minute was possible. It was reported from Flanders in 1914 that the Germans often thought they were up against British machine-gun fire when, in fact, it was well-aimed rapid rifle fire. To achieve similar standards became the norm to aim for in all Commandos. Fortunately, a rifle expert became available to exert a great influence on the training, namely, Captain 'Wally' Wallbridge. As an instructor at the Special Training Centre, Lochailort (STC) and later at the Commando Basic Training Centre, Achnacarry, (CBTC) he aimed to get all those on his special courses up to a speed of 25 well-aimed shots in a minute and he also reckoned he could get most squads up to 20 shots per minute with a programme of just one hour's tuition per day over six days. Those on his special courses left for their respective Commandos with this latter aim in mind.

The Commandos owe a great debt to the inspirational tuition of Wally Wallbridge, one of the great Commando instructors whose influence was considerable. Together with that formidable couple, Captains Fairbairn and Sykes, at Lochailort he brought a new dimension – an aggressive one – to weapon training and musketry. He created and nurtured a new breed of weapon training instructors who passed on, in turn, his philosophy and methods to their charges with great success. But back to the weapons . . .

From 1941 onwards the SMLE, with its long sword bayonet, was gradually replaced by the No 4 rifle, although in some Commandos the SMLE was retained, as a firm favourite.

The No 4 rifle shared many characteristics of the SMLE, including calibre – .303 – and magazine capacity – 10 rounds – but the main differences were the types of backsight and accompanying bayonet.

The SMLE was the favourite with all Commando snipers. Fitted with a

The Bren gun was the standard light machine gun of every Commando sub-section, here No 1 is seen with his loaded weapon and a spare magazine (holding 30 rounds) tucked into his leather jacket and available for immediate reloading. Other spare magazines are in the pouch; his personal weapon, 45 Colt automatic, is tucked into his belt. Around his neck is his personal face camouflage net.

Numbers 1 and 2 on the Bren gun apply the 'Me and My Pal' principle to tackle and cross this barbed-wire obstacle.

telescopic sight it was used – quite literally – with deadly effect on raids and campaigns wherever Commandos went into action.

Finally the SMLE, fitted with a cup discharger, could eject the lethal 36 grenade and so be used in the role of a simple mortar. Although essentially still the SMLE, when used in this way it was referred to as an 'EY rifle'. A cup was fitted to the muzzle end of the rifle and into it, when ready for action, was placed an attached base plate and the grenade, primed with a seven-second fuse. Using a ballistite cartridge, instead of ball ammunition, the grenade could be ejected up to a distance of 200 yards.

The employment within Commandos of the EY rifle varied. In No 4 we took ours on the Dieppe raid, whilst those Commandos who fought in Burma found it a most effective weapon for jungle warfare.

Ever since its introduction to the British Army in the seventeenth century, the bayonet, the last of the purpose-made hand weapons – following in the wake of clubs, fighting picks, axes, daggers, swords and pikes – has long been associated with heroic charges, fierce hand-to-hand fighting and last-ditch defensive stands.

Traditionally, training with the bayonet was always accompanied by blood-curdling screams, oaths, curses and fearsome lunges at all types of dummies. Notwithstanding, almost as much time was spent on ceremonial drill with the fixed bayonet as was spent on weapon training!

Next to the rifle in the Commando armoury was the popular Bren light machine gun (LMG). It had been introduced to the British Army in 1935 when it replaced the old Lewis gun, although some of the latter were still in use during the Second World War. The LMG was relatively light weighing only 23 lb (10.4 kg); gas operated it could fire single rounds or automatic bursts. The magazine which fitted on to the top of the gun held 30 rounds, although to save wear and tear on the magazine spring it was normal to load with just 28 rounds of .303. The barrels were air cooled, so after sustained firing the heated barrel had to be changed, but this was a simple operation and only took a couple of seconds.

The spare barrel and other spares were carried by the No 2 on the gun. In every Commando the Nos 1 and 2 were inseparables, a splendid example of the Commando 'Me and My Pal' system at work. The two shared all the chores of maintaining and cleaning their cherished weapon. In training and on active service they worked and moved together, with No 2 ever ready to support his No 1 with a helping hand.

There was one unique innovation by the Commandos concerning the firing of Brens. It all started in the autumn of 1940, occasioned by the return of NCOs to their Commandos from weapon training courses at

Lochailort – taken by Captain Wallbridge – and the arrival of the US Tommy guns. The main characteristic of the latter was that it was a quickfiring, short-range weapon with great stopping power, fired mainly from the hip in a hosepipe fashion. This last feature posed the question why not, when within short range of the enemy, try and also fire the Bren from the hip too? We were at Weymouth when we tried out this new theory. It was quite exciting and to our delight we found it was a practical possibility, very much in line with our 'aggressive' policy, and it worked successfully.

Firing the rifle also from the hip followed, and one little ruse when firing in this way was to keep the thumb and first finger around the bolthead and use the second finger on the trigger. This speeded up the bolt action – and rate of fire.

Success in these techniques, as for all firing, depended on regular practice in building confidence in handling and aiming. The Commandos paid great attention to 'Pokey Drill', as the daily exercises with the rifle were known. A lot of improvised ones were added to the standard range of rifle exercises.

Early on it was appreciated that it was essential to integrate weapon handling into other areas of training, such as PT, fieldcraft, and on the assault courses, and not to regard such training as a separate independent subject unrelated to the others. In fieldcraft it was not sufficient to move unseen and unheard but to move in such a way that one's weapon was readily available for immediate use, taking great care to ensure the working parts of the weapons were not fouled with dirt, mud or sand.

Commandos spent a lot of time on board ship either on training, en route to operations or, all too frequently, preparing for operations that were cancelled. The latter were far too commonplace during 1941. Facilities for training on board were severely limited, but it was always possible to carry out some forms of weapon training. The limited facilities encouraged fresh ideas. One particular strengthening exercise that owed its origin to the cramped conditions on board was a form of wrestling. The men were paired off with one holding his rifle, standing toe-to-toe, as in Cumberland wrestling; the unarmed man had to try and disarm the rifleman, who had to retain his grip on the rifle, or throw him in any way. The armed man, for safety sake, was restricted to defensive action only. It was very strenuous – as it was intended to be.

When at sea we always managed to fire a few rounds from our Brens and rifles in particular. Boxes and crates would be thrown astern and, floating in the wake of the ship, provided 'opportunity' targets – not ideal, but always better than nothing. Such shoots were invariably the subject for a little friendly betting. And so to other weapons...

The TSMC, firing a snub-nosed .45 bullet at a rate of nearly 700 rounds per minute at short range, had great stopping power. It was a popular and formidable weapon, sturdy and reliable, rarely guilty of any stoppages or malfunctions.

Originally it was supplied with a choice of two types of magazines: a drum holding 50 rounds or a box mag holding just 20 rounds. The smaller box magazine was less liable to jam and for a variety of handling and operational reasons was preferred and adopted for general use throughout the Commandos.

One of the major weaknesses in the early days of training with the Tommy gun was the tendency to fire long bursts, which was natural because of its high rate of fire and the unaccustomed use of firing from the hip. However, this could become a bad habit for two reasons. Firstly, it was wasteful of ammunition, especially with only 20 rounds in the magazine, and secondly, just as important, long bursts tended to make for inaccuracy on account of the accumulative effect of the the recoil forcing the muzzle upwards and the shots to go high. As a result strict fire control with just short bursts of 3 or 4 well-aimed shots became the rule.

Although essentially a short-range weapon, the Tommy gun did have both a foresight and a backsight, enabling it to be fired from the shoulder, but like all short-barrel weapons it had a limited range and on the whole was seldom fired other than from the hip in close-quarter fighting.

When we were issued with the Tommy gun in 1940 we had to devise our own training instruction and develop our own firing practices. The latter meant improvising the type of ranges and targets that resembled likely battle situations – snap targets, 'pop-up' targets and suchlike. There was no end to the improvisation shown to create worthwhile and realistic range practices. Often 'battle ranges' were created in the blitzed areas of some of our bombed cities and towns.

Provided we had the 'ammo' and the location was not fraught with safety problems, we never missed an opportunity to fire our weapons. Typically, in No 4, en route from Scapa Flow to raid the Lofoten Islands, we even managed to land on one of the remote Faroe Islands and fire all our weapons at makeshift and specified natural targets, i.e. bushes, trees and rocky outcrops, although the latter invited the risk of some ricochets. The plus side of this 'shoot' was that we didn't have the irksome chore of having to apply to a higher authority for permission.

Much consideration and practice was devoted to the reloading and magazine changing of the automatic weapons, under all sorts of conditions, and especially in the dark. Blindfolding the weapon handlers provided one simple and useful way of simulating darkness during daylight hours.

Much of what has been written here on the training with the TSMC applied, of course, to the British Sten gun. These machine carbines fired a 9mm round, but their magazines held 32 rounds – more than the Tommy gun – but again it was customary to load with just 30 rounds to avoid excessive strain on the magazine spring.

Undoubtedly the most unpopular weapon in the Commando armoury in the early days was the unwieldy Boys .55 anti-tank rifle. Introduced to the British Army in 1936, it was a bolt-operated rifle with a high muzzle velocity and considerable recoil. It fired a solid armour-piercing bullet which, in effect, was only capable of penetrating the lightest armour. The magazine held 5 rounds. When fired it had a pronounced muzzle flash, which was reduced by a flash eliminator, but unfortunately this refinement did not reduce the kick to the shoulder of the firer, almost as bad as a nasty kick from a mule.

Heavy and very cumbersome, it was normally fired from the lying position, although, supported, it could be fired from a standing position. It did not prove very effective against tanks, but on the other hand it was very useful in the house-breaking role and against bunkers and emplacements.

As an unpopular weapon – murder to carry on speed marches and a menace on field training – it was always difficult to get volunteers for the job of the Boys anti-tank rifleman and consequently there were no regrets when its replacement, the PIAT, made its appearance in early 1943.

The Commandos received their PIATs in the beginning of 1943. This fired a much lighter and smaller bomb projector. Simple in design and easy to fire, it was an effective anti-tank-weapon, its only snag being the size and weight (2^1/$_2$ lb) of the bombs. As a result only a limited number could be carried between the Nos 1 and 2 on the weapon. The maximum range of the PIAT was about 100 yards; the bomb was so designed that, on impact, the concentrated force of the hollow charge ensured penetration and maximum interior damage to the tank – and crew. Although primarily an anti-tank weapon, it, too, was a useful weapon to have at hand in street fighting or when held up by an enemy strongpoint.

Finally, in each fighting Troop there was the effective 2-inch mortar, capable of firing HE, smoke and illuminating flares. It had a maximum range of 500 yards, but was more accurate up to 300 yards as the bombs were apt to be affected by the wind in flight.

Basically this crude weapon consisted of nothing more than a tube, simple firing mechanism and a base plate. It was reasonably light and with the hinged baseplate at 90 degrees to the barrel could easily be carried over the shoulders. The No 2 carried the bulk of the bombs which came packed in convenient containers, with handles, and held six bombs. More bombs could be carried in the side pouches of the webbing equipment. In 1944 a lighter version of the 2-inch mortar appeared. Instead of the long hinged base plate, it had a little fixed 'spade' base plate.

Training to handle this little mortar was simple enough, but it required a fair amount of practice with live ammunition to attain accuracy.

Now to recall how these weapons were used in the battle training developed by Commandos.

One of the flaws of the splendid instruction and coaching on the use and firing of small arms as taught at the Army's Small Arms School, Hythe, was that it seemed to be conditioned by peacetime conditions with slow, deliberate, albeit accurate shooting at long distances as exemplified by the prestigious annual Bisley rifle meetings. Accordingly the years between the Wars had seen a tendency to limit the role of the rifle, the major weapon of the infantry on the battlefield, to classification practices and competitive shooting. This was fine in its way, but the Commandos sought to bring the rifle and the supporting small arms, back to their proper place and real purpose – to kill the enemy on the field of battle, not to win cups and medals.

This emphasis meant moving away from the traditional four-foot targets, with their bull's-eyes and concentric scoring rings, to more realistic targets such as silhouettes and head and shoulders targets. Nevertheless, the Commandos still recognized the need for using the four-foot targets for the basic practices of zeroing and elementary shoots.

No one would disagree that the best position for accurate fire with the rifle is the basic lying position – rifle well forward, elbows relatively close to each other to act as a pivot to bring the rifle cleanly and comfortably into the shoulder for the aim, with the legs spread out firmly and flatly on the ground at a slight angle to the axis of the body. Such a text book position is fine on the ranges, but in action it is seldom possible to take up this ideal firing position. So whilst accepting that it was fundamentally essential to acquire the basic skills of musketry and learning how to fire accurately and quickly in the time-honoured traditions on the open ranges, the Commandos began to move on from these customary practices to new ones, more in keeping with the 'real thing'.

This meant leaving the formal and established open ranges, with their graduated firing points at neat 100 yards intervals, protected butts and sliding targets, to find open areas where live firing at a variety of improvised static and moving targets, positioned in likely operational settings, could safely take place.

Nevertheless, this did not mean forsaking the old open ranges altogether, because for many reasons it wasn't always possible to find or requisition suitable areas of open land for this new requirement of firing under simulated battle conditions. So with typical resourcefulness and ingenuity the Commandos thought up new 'action' practices for the formal ranges incorporating 'fire and movement' using 'falling plates' as targets. For anyone not familiar with the latter, let me explain. These were squares of cast iron, about 10 inches by 10 inches with a flanged bottom strip about 4 inches wide which acted as a platform stand, but when the plates were hit, like a coconut at the fair, they fell down with a most satisfying metallic-sounding 'ping'.

In the early days of the Commandos, Commanding Officers frequently incurred the wrath of higher headquarters when their troops 'loosened off' their weapons at makeshift targets on isolated and remote areas in the otherwise quiet countryside in their well-intended and zealous efforts to create realistic battle situations. Not a few COs received 'rockets' over this score, but not before they had made their point and in so doing accelerated the process of requisitioning land suitable for field firing.

Gradually from 1941 onwards whole areas of remote countryside throughout Britain were made available for extensive field firing with live ammunition from the full range of artillery, tank and infantry weapons. For the Commandos these included areas in the highlands of Scotland around Lochailort and Achnacarry where they took every opportunity to exploit these ideal facilities for realistic training.

The first step in field firing was the organization of simple individual and section firing practices at opportunity targets. The next stage from, what one might call these 'one-sided' field firing exercises was to create a battle scenario with controlled firing and explosive charges representing enemy fire. This was far removed from the practices that prevailed before the War and even up to late 1940 when 'enemy fire' was limited to firing blank ammunition, thunderflashes and the use of rattles, the last named representing machine-gun fire.

Using the newly acquired field firing ranges, the 'enemy' fire initially came from LMGs firing on pre-set 'fixed lines'. This safety measure ensured that the 'enemy fire' was overhead, but only just, or to the flanks

*Disembarking from Goatley folding boats in a rehearsal for the
Opposed Landing at Achnacarry.*

of the advancing troops. Such firing enabled the trainees to experience
the crack, whine and thump, characteristic of hostile small arms fire,
whilst controlled buried explosives – detonated by remote control –
simulated mortar and artillery fire and enemy mines. Smoke canisters were
ignited to add to the realism and 'fog of battle'.

Collectively these innovative practices gave rise to a new military
training term: 'Battle Inoculation'. And it came in all shapes and sizes.

However for the Commando trainees, the undisputed showpiece of
their Battle Inoculation was the 'Opposed Landing' at Achnacarry. This
was a set-piece mock raid with live ammunition, pyrotechnics and
explosives initially based on No 4 Commando's action at Dieppe.

To set the scene and provide an insight to the style and nature of this
particular battle inoculation I can do no better than to refer to the book
Castle Commando, written by my old Commando friend, Donald Gilchrist.
He devotes a whole chapter in this book to the Opposed Landing carried
out by the US Rangers in the final exercise on their course at Achnacarry.
For them, like all other trainees at Achnacarry, it was the climax – an
experience none ever forgot. Indeed, Peter Young, the much-decorated
Commando leader, in his book *Commando*, recalls that as they left the

French beach after the Dieppe Raid, one of his men turned to him and said, 'Jesus Christ, sir, this is nearly as bad as Achnacarry...' But back to Donald Gilchrist's graphic and detailed description of the exercise.

Donald begins with 'it was by far the most spectacular of all the Achnacarry training exercises. And like the superb showman that he was, Vaughan [the Commandant of CBTC] kept it up his sleeve until the end of the training programme... a performance to top any bill... a dazzling cross between Blackpool illuminations and Guy Fawkes night... (it) was as close to battle conditions as Vaughan could get to without slaughtering half the trainees...'

The Opposed Landings – there were both day and night ones – were terrifyingly realistic; they were meant to be for they represented an enactment of a seaborne raid; from preparation to the action itself. With this in mind the preparations were carried out as they would have been operationally.

Not until all these preliminaries were satisfactorily completed did the exercise go ahead, and only after the final last-minute checks had been made – issues of ammunition and explosives, faces blackened, equipment tested for unwanted rattles and noises, pockets turned out to ensure that no incriminating items were being carried that could aid enemy intelligence if captured, field dressings (handy little first-aid packs carried in purpose-designed pockets on the front left thigh of the BD trousers) checked, and passwords issued – was the ultimate operational order, 'Let's go', given.

Everything was as grimly realistic as possible.

Silently, in the pre-arranged tactical order of march, the trainees left camp for the boat station at Bunarkaig, a short distance away on the shores of Loch Lochy. There they quietly embarked in the Goatleys (folding assault boats) to paddle line ahead towards the centre of the loch before forming up to assault the selected beach.

All was eerily quiet. Orders, where necessary, were whispered and passed on. Nothing could be heard except the dull plop of the paddles. Then just as the raiders began to make out the outline of their landing points and were smugly beginning to congratulate themselves for getting this far apparently unseen and unheard 'all hell was let loose'. Machine guns and mortars spat out a lethal welcome. Tracers and flares vied with controlled explosives and thunderflashes to create the baptism of fire that all had been promised.

All the firing, pyrotechnics and battle effects were controlled by the WTO and each in turn stamped his mark on this exercise as Captain Ken

Allen did during his spell at Achnacarry. He introduced recordings of the awesome Stuka dive-bombers relayed on loudspeakers and the ingenious 'Allen EY Rifle Thunderflash Projector' whereby he could produce some sixteen airburst thunderflashes almost simultaneously with, as he recalls, 'very spectacular effect, especially at night'.

The instructors with each section of trainees shouted and howled, 'ON, ON, ON . . . ' Out of the boats and across the beach. There was but one immediate aim, to clear the beach as fast as legs could carry them.

This was a fundamental lesson taught to all trainees at Achnacarry.

Once the beaches had been cleared, the mock attack, proper, got underway. Assault groups began to work their way uphill towards the main objective under the covering fire of their own Bren support groups. For safety reasons this was pre-arranged and under the control of instructors. Meanwhile the 'enemy' fire continued unabated as flares silhouetted the raiders as they struggled and stumbled their way through the bracken and heather towards the enemy gun positions.

By now stealth and silent movement had long been abandoned in favour of speed, on and upwards. Once the perimeter wire had been reached it was time to let the support groups know that the final assault was about to be launched, Very light flares, 'White over Green', being the pre-arranged signal to lift the covering fire off the objective.

Then a momentary pause, no more, a prelude to the bayonet charge, plus Tommy gun fire, on the enemy position. 'Charge—', shouting, cursing, firing, bayoneting dummies, on, on, and beyond the enemy gun position; just far enough to protect the demolitionists. Explosives were placed and fuses lit. That agonizing wait and suspense, until an almighty blast echoed around the Lochaber hills to announce success and mission accomplished.

But the exercise didn't end there, any more than it would in real action. Still to come was the withdrawal, re-embarkation and return to base. These drills too had been rehearsed, leaving nothing to chance. There was no letting up either in the firing, foe or friend. Explosions and grenades in the beach area simulated enemy mortar fire intended to harass the re-embarkation. Even as the trainees managed to clamber aboard their waiting boats large and noisy explosions in the waters of the loch threw up debris and spray to beset the crews.

Nevertheless, as the little convoy of raiders drew away the firing gradually ceased until all was silent again except for the sound of the paddles entering and pulling through the water.

It wasn't until all were back at the boat station, sections and weapons checked, that the exercise was declared over and the trainees marched back to camp for the inevitable post-mortem and discussion on the conduct of the exercise. And no punches were pulled for mistakes made.

The training experience of those two hours or so was significant. Men who hitherto had not been in action were subjected to the frightening sounds of battle, having encountered the fearsome noises of gunfire dangerously near – some too near for healthy comfort. They had sniffed the unmistakable acrid smell of explosives and smoke. It was their Battle Inoculation, and it could not be more vivid.

High-ranking military visitors to Achnacarry, and there were many from both the British and Allied forces, were always much impressed by the spectacle of the Opposed Landing, even if they missed the main aim and real purpose of the exercise, namely, that of being placed 'under fire'. Invariably all were astounded by the intensity and volume of the live firing and explosives. One, jokingly, compared Vaughan's expenditure of ammunition with that of Montgomery's at Alamein.

On a sadder note it is pertinent to record that to achieve this high degree of operational realism risks had to be taken and it was so dangerous that it was not achieved without accidents, even though all reasonable steps were taken to ensure safety for all the participants. Some of the accidents were, regrettably, fatal. Such was the high price the Commandos paid in their training to ensure success in their subsequent desperate and demanding battles.

Obviously not all the Commandos' field firing exercises – and there were many – were as elaborate as the showpiece Opposed Landing, however, grand or not, they were invariably based on setpiece attacks in which newly devised Battle Drills were involved.

In No 4 Commando we originated our own Battle Drills based on 'fire and movement'.

It all started with Captain Dawson's appreciation that the Germans in their Blitzkrieg methods, from 1940 onwards, must have used pre-arranged 'drills' for immediate action on meeting opposition. We discussed this possibility and Dawson reckoned that something akin to the set-piece drills used in American football was most likely and comparable. How else, we queried could they deploy with such speed and attack with supporting fire?

With this in mind Dawson started to think of applying this theory to the smallest sub-unit in the Troop, the sub-section, which was led by a sergeant and contained a Bren gun, Tommy guns and rifles. This small sub-unit could be broken down into two groups, namely a Bren group and a rifle group. These, he contended, could ideally be used as the two basic elements of 'fire' (the Bren group) and 'movement' (an assault group of the Tommy gunner(s) and the riflemen).

We then set about devising simple drills which could provide patterns for immediate action on meeting enemy opposition at this level, i.e. the sub-section level, and this was likely to be a small enemy outpost or a determined sniper.

The essence of this innovation was immediate response and to react speedily with everyone aware of what was expected of him, plus – equally imperative – knowing what his mates would be doing too. The sub-unit in this type of operation became a self-contained team of two groups which were interdependent, yet ready and rehearsed to employ 'fire and movement' to close with the enemy and destroy him.

Our proposed drill was simple enough and based on the following tactical picture. When the section came under fire all took cover and every man tried to locate the exact position of the enemy fire. Having pin-pointed the enemy position the Bren group engaged it with well-aimed, controlled fire. Meanwhile the sergeant in charge, having assessed the lie of the land, covered approaches etc., told his subordinates of his planned route and any other necessary details such as the signals to control the covering fire.

Then under the support of covering fire from the Bren, the section sergeant led his assault group by the best covered approach and as rapidly as possible to within, say, grenade range where they would make the final assault with bayonets fixed and firing from the hip on to the enemy position.

At first all movements were done at walking speed with no regard for any other considerations except to inculcate the basic principles of 'fire and movement' and the need for deployment with the minimum of orders.

Once these fundamentals were thoroughly understood and well practised, almost as 'barrack square' movements, we moved on to carry out the drill on pieces of ground that resembled possible battlefield scenarios, and moving tactically, first without any actual firing and then finally with 'all guns blazing'.

The Troop, as a whole, recognized the value of the new idea, and trained enthusiastically to make it a success. Then came the crucial test of selling our ideas to the CO, Lord Lovat, and the rest of the Commando, who were bound to be sceptical of another Troop's ideas.

We put on a demonstration with blank ammunition and other pyrotechnics on a suitable piece of training ground at Troon. Thankfully it all went well, and much to Dawson's credit – and satisfaction – our basic Battle Drill was immediately adopted throughout No 4.

We might not have been the first in the field with such a Battle Drill, but we must surely have been among the pioneers. Within a year similar drills were being taught in all the Infantry Battle Schools plus other training centres. It was part of the general adoption by all training establishments to a more aggressive, vigorous and offensive style of training.

Next in the Commando armoury was the standard 36 (Mills) grenade, named after Sir William Mills who invented it in 1915. It was invaluable to flush out an enemy behind cover, i.e. in a machine-gun emplacement, pillbox or a room in a house.

The range depended upon the ability of the thrower, but was generally reckoned to be about 25 yards.

Because of its shape and segment casing it was nicknamed the 'pineapple'. Filled with amatol it had a 7-second fuse, which was activated by releasing the safety lever just prior to throwing.

It was a very handy little grenade and practice in throwing was standard training, using dummies. These were ex-live ones, but the explosive and detonator/fuse had been removed.

As mentioned earlier the 36 Grenade was used in a 'mortar' role by discharging it from a cup on the EY rifle.

During 1942 two more useful grenades were introduced: the '69' and the '77' grenades. Both had different roles to the Mills grenade.

The '69' grenade, with its black bakelite casing, was distinctly lighter than the Mills grenade; it relied solely on the blast effect of its HE filling to inflict shock and limited damage. It was, therefore, not lethal like the Mills grenade, but had a different purpose, being invaluable when there was a need to immediately follow up an explosion, as in house-clearing and on any other assault when in close contact with the enemy.

The '77' grenade was a handy little smoke grenade in a tin casing, but its phosphorous filling could – and did – inflict nasty burns if thrown at the enemy.

One other so-called grenade was the 'sticky tank grenade'. This was a misnomer as it was more a hand-positioned explosive charge. It was developed from the 'Molotov' cocktail concept, which was introduced in the Spanish Civil War.

We found that the sticky exterior was subject to deterioration and although the 'bombs' were stored in cases, they always presented problems. As far as I know they were never used by Commandos in action, although we did use them extensively for a while in 1941/42 for training in demolition tasks, street fighting and house-clearing.

Following the decision to extend the role of the Commandos beyond the limits of the 'butcher and bolt raids' to more sustained combined operations, involving the holding of ground after an initial landing (first experienced by Nos 1 and 6 Commandos in North Africa), it became painfully apparent that the limited Commando armoury was woefully inadequate. This shortcoming was exacerbated when Commandos were employed as normal infantry battalions to hold positions 'in the line'. In such roles they lacked the vital heavier infantry support weapons of 3-inch mortars and .303 Vickers machine guns (MMGs), plus the logistic and communications back-up of infantry battalions.

Although 3-inch mortars, manhandled ashore from assault landing craft, had been used on the Vaagso (December 1941) and Dieppe (1942) raids with some success, these formidable infantry weapons were not in general use at those times with all Commandos.

However by late 1942 to early 1943 battle experience and envisaged future roles for the Commandos made it imperative for the issue of these heavier weapons. Accordingly, a Heavy Weapons Troop became an inherent, albeit separate, Troop in every Commando.

It was commanded by a captain, and consisted of a little HQ, one Mortar Section and one MMG Section.

The Mortar Section was commanded by a subaltern and his little HQ comprised a section sergeant, signaller, batman and two jeeps with drivers. There were two 3-inch mortar detachments, each with a crew of four men (including an 'ammunition handler'), plus two jeeps with drivers.

The MMG Section was also commanded by a subaltern and his HQ was similar to the mortar's, but in addition he had a rangefinder, a necessary addition for this long-range weapon. There were two detachments in the section, each of one machine gun with a crew of four, all were lifted in jeeps.

With all these jeeps (total of 14) this Troop had a high degree of mobility – in striking contrast to the lack of transport and mobility of the original Commandos in 1940. However, it must be emphasized that on the landings, in training and in action, the heavy weapons and ammunition, if needed for immediate and close support, had to be manhandled and carried ashore as the jeeps could only arrive later in the follow-up waves of landing craft. As a result all the heavy weapons detachments endured plenty of strenuous and exacting manhandling and marching as part of their routine training.

The Vickers machine gun and the 3-inch mortars were well established infantry weapons. The machine guns, having been first introduced to the British Army in 1912, had been widely used in the First World War. So formidable were they in the static nature of trench warfare that a whole corps, the Machine Gun Corps, was formed. It was a rather complicated, but nevertheless reliable weapon. Recoil action enabled it to fire, automatic, at a rate in the order of 500 rounds per minute. Using .303 ball ammunition, there were no complications over supply.

A heavy weapon with its bits and pieces, including a condenser can as part of the cooling system, it weighed, complete, some $88^1/2$ lb (40.2 kg). The gun was belt-fed and, with the aid of a dial sight, it could fire at long ranges (up to, say, 3,000 yds) on compass bearings.

The 3-inch mortar – one of the last of the muzzle-loaded weapons – was crude, but able to fire high-trajectory bombs most effectively. It too was very heavy, but could be broken down into 3-man portable loads, basically consisting of base plate, barrel, bipod and sights. One of the main snags of this weapon for the Commandos in the assault role, when it had to be manhandled, was the carrying of the bombs (HE and Smoke). They each weighed 10 lb, HE and smoke alike. This was a snag, especially when every round had, in the seaborne assault, to be carried ashore. However, it was mitigated as Captain Knyvet Carr (OC Heavy Weapons Troop, No 4 Commando, 1943-5) records: 'Every man in the Troop carried at least two 10 lbs mortar bombs, including myself . . . ' In addition extra bombs were often carried by men in the other Troops as resupply.

Now for the training. Fortunately in 1943 there was, generally, in the Commandos a fair sprinkling of officers, NCOs and men with experience in these heavy weapons, but in addition selected officers and NCOs were also sent on specialist courses. So, initially all training of the crews was carried out within the Commando; but later specialist courses were run at HOC (Holding Operational Commando, Wrexham), for selected volunteers on their return to Wrexham after successfully completing their basic training at Achnacarry. In this way, a steady stream of qualified mortarmen and machine gunners enabled the Commandos to be reinforced with trained men for their Heavy Weapons Troops.

Knyvet Carr MC, whom I mentioned above, recalls that when he was chosen to command this new Troop in No 4 it was partly because he was a Gunner (Royal Artillery) and therefore had experience of rangefinding etc., but also partly because he had been MTO (Motor Transport Officer), and with all those jeeps to look after this background was more than useful.

He records that the initial training of his mortar detachments took two months, but that of the MMG, 'which was a precision and longer range weapon', took up to three months. In both cases this period of initial training included plenty of live firing.

When plans for Overlord were made and it was clear that Knyvet's Heavy Weapons Troop would have to manhandle their weapons and ammunition ashore and be without their jeeps until D+1, their main continuity training reflected this decision. Knyvet writes: 'My special memories of the training for D-Day were the strength and stamina that was displayed by all the men in carrying the mortars, MMGs and our heavy Bergen rucksacks on speed marches and over hilly and rocky country, plus in and out of the landing craft.'

Rehearsals included getting out of the craft and up the beach quickly to proposed mortar and MMG positions. It doesn't need much imagination to visualize the implications of this training with Commandos laden down with over a hundredweight of weaponry, ammunition and personal survival kit wading, stumbling ashore through the surf and up sandy and rocky beaches under (in training) simulated 'enemy fire' in readiness for the real thing on 6 June.

Lord Lovat, then commanding the Commando Brigade of four Commandos for Overlord, with his customary thoroughness for training, delighted in pitting the military skills and sporting prowess of his individual Commandos against each other, The Heavy Weapons Troops were not allowed to escape such competitions and became involved in inter-Commando shoots using 3-inch mortars and MMGs. These competitions and the 'Brigaded' heavy weapons live firing battle inoculation exercises, states Knyvet, 'were truly memorable'. Incidentally, he took great pleasure when his mortar detachment won the Brigade 'shoot' prior to D-Day.

CHAPTER VI

Training Centres –
Lochailort and Achnacarry

Without any reservations the Commando Basic Training Centre (CBTC) at Achnacarry was regarded as one of, if not the finest, of all the Allied special training centres established in the Second World War. Its reputation was widespread and held in the highest regard by all the Allies, for not only were soldiers and marines of the British forces trained there, but also those from the USA, France, Holland, Belgium, Poland, Norway and, surprisingly, some Germans. These were 'Free' Germans and included Jews who had escaped from the clutches of the Gestapo. In addition, volunteers from the Royal Navy and the Royal Air Force were trained there too, after it had been decided by Headquarters Combined Operations to raise RN and RAF 'Commando' units for special operational roles peculiar to the two services.

The training centre was originally set up in early 1942 as the Commando Depot, but was more appropriately renamed as the Commando Basic Training Centre soon afterwards and continued to train Commando soldiers for the rest of the War until it was closed down at the end of 1945.

One reason why the area around Achnacarry was ideal for Commando training has already been mentioned in the context of field firing, but that was only one of several good reasons.

However, the actual origins of the choice of location in this remote part of the Highlands goes back to 1940, before the issue of Churchill's directive to form the Commandos, when the Special Training Centre (STC) had been set up at Lochailort, some 27 miles to the west of Fort William on the road to Mallaig – and the 'Isles'.

Because of the links that grew up between the STC and the CBTC it is worthwhile tracing the birth of the former and its influence on the latter. It all started in February 1940, when following the invasion of Finland by the Russians the War Office decided to raise a British ski battalion, to be known as 5th Bn the Scot Guards. About 1,000 skiers answered the call, but the big snag was that well over half of the volunteers were officers, so all except the regular officers had to resign their commissions and revert to the ranks. Spencer Chapman, a Polar explorer of pre-war fame, became an advisor to the Battalion and in his book, *The Jungle is Neutral*, describes the problems faced in raising the Battalion. Somehow, the unit managed to get to the French Alps for ski training with the French Chasseurs Alpin before being recalled to this country and earmarked for Scandinavia, but then the Finns signed a peace treaty with the Soviets so the idea of a ski Battalion was dropped and the unit disbanded. However, in the unit were some outstanding officers keen to 'do battle' in the Arctic and they managed to persuade the 'powers-that-be' to send them, as a small force, to Norway and link up with some partisans there.

They duly set off, with stores and explosives, in a submarine from Scotland but after only a few hours had the misfortune to hit a mine and just managed to limp back to port. As no other submarine could be spared for the mission it was cancelled and the party sent on leave. One of them, Captain 'Bill' Stirling, a wealthy landowner in Scotland invited the rest to spend their leave at his country seat. It was during these few days' leave they hatched up the idea to start a special training centre in the Highlands for raiding and guerilla operations. Stirling managed to persuade his cousin, Lord Lovat, also to join in on the scheme. It says much for the power of the 'old boy' net and knowing the right people in the corridors of power that within a few weeks an area around Lochailort was acquired for their project.

A main camp, of Nissen huts and tents, was created at the head of Loch Ailort, with the headquarters installed in Inverailort Castle. A powerful team of instructors was gathered. Many became well-known leaders of irregular forces including Commandos, Chindits and the Special Air Service (SAS), to wit, Lord Lovat, Brigadier 'Mad Mike' Calvert, Colonel Spencer Chapman, Major Peter Kemp (a veteran of the Spanish War and later an operator in SOE) and the Stirling Brothers (Bill and David) plus other officers and NCOs who between them had a wide range of experiences from Arctic exploring to rugged campaigning on the North-West Frontier of India plus those well versed in signalling, demolitions and shooting.

In addition there was a most extraordinary couple of seemingly elderly gentlemen, Messrs Fairbairn and Sykes of Shanghai Police fame, and they, more than anyone else in the British Army, were responsible for the introduction of unarmed combat and close-quarter fighting.

In and around the camp were held the main courses of fieldcraft, (directed by Lord Lovat), demolitions (Mike Calvert), close-quarter combat (Fairbairn and Sykes), weapon training (Wally Wallbridge) and a signals wing organized by Peter Fleming, famous author, explorer and brother of Ian Fleming, the post-war author/creator of '007 Bond'.

Further properties were requisitioned in the neighbourhood where activities included boating at Dorlin House, Achcaracle, under the control of a colourful bearded RN character, Sir Geoffrey Congreve – his brother won a VC – and he himself was later also decorated, only to be subsequently killed on a raid.

At that time Achnacarry Castle was used as a holding wing for STC, a role it continued to have until 1942 when STC was closed as such to become a naval training centre, and by which time most of the original instructors had long since left for active service.

From July 1940 onwards officers and NCOs from the newly formed Commandos attended STC courses and returned to blend the techniques and skills acquired with the other new ideas being developed in their own Commandos.

I attended a course on demolitions during the summer of 1941 after our raid on Lofoten. At that time 'Mad Mike' Calvert had left for the Far East. Notwithstanding, another 'madman', Captain Bobby Holmes, had taken his place and he, with similar enthusiasm, began to teach us to blow up everything from 'battleships to brigadiers'.

For three packed weeks we were introduced to the mysteries – and satisfying delights – of explosives and demolitions. We learnt the basic principles governing demolitions, how to tackle the destruction of bridges, railway lines, boats and factory plant, how to make Bangalore torpedoes and pole-charges, crater roads and airfield runways, the different types of explosives, primers, detonators and means of detonating, including time, pull and pressure switches plus, of course, the intriguing use of 'booby' traps. We all had some knowledge of explosives and demolitions through demonstrations by our own experts in our respective Commandos, but now with an intensive course in an area where big bangs were acceptable as the norm it provided an ideal chance for all Commandos to increase their numbers of demolitionists so that each Troop had its own quota.

Holmes made us all, regardless of our backgrounds or knowledge of the subject, start at the beginning, combining lectures, demonstrations and practical sessions in a well-organized progressive programme. In spite of his tremendous enthusiasm and infectious zeal for the job – qualities he had also instilled in his NCO instructors – he made sure that we didn't 'run before we could walk', a policy he applied quite literally for he made us all walk away after having prepared and set off our first little charges of timed safety fuses, detonators and primers. Through this insistence he inculcated in his trainees coolness and thoroughness, two essential qualities for success in demolitions.

We were taken through the various types of explosives and their main uses for demolitions. At that time there were three main types: guncotton, amatol and plastic '808'.

Guncotton, ideal for cutting purposes, be it for metal (railway lines and iron girders) or masonry (bridges or for use in a pole-charge against a strongpoint or houses) was supplied in handy sized slabs, measuring (in inches) 6x3x$\frac{1}{2}$ and weighed about 19 oz. In the middle of the slab was a tapered hole to take the 'booster' primer which was made of a composite explosive and set off, in turn, by a small detonator.

The standard detonator was a little metal tube, just under 2 inches long and containing a sealed explosive; one end was open, into which was inserted either the safety fuse – for timed detonation – or cortex, an 'instantaneous' fuse. Once either fuse was placed into the detonator it had to be crimped to make the chosen fuse secure. There was a simple little tool for this, a crimper, but the 'old hands' preferred to use their teeth!

Amatol was the favoured explosive for cratering, but gradually its use gave way to more efficient methods, including the prepared 'Beehive' charge. The use of amatol, a dark-grey powder, for cratering involved boring a small detonator hole, about 6 feet deep, and blowing a small underground cavity to take the main charge of amatol, which could be poured down then sealed by tamping before detonation.

Introduced during the War, 808 plastic explosive was a great success on several counts. A stable explosive, it was powerful, ideal for cutting and supplied in a very convenient form, inasmuch as it came in wrapped cartridges, each one weighing only 4 oz. But above all it was malleable and so could be moulded and fashioned around a target. It looked like marzipan and had a sweet, unmistakable smell; unfortunately it tended to induce a nasty headache if handled for a prolonged period out of its wrapping. That apart, it was ideal for many of the jobs envisaged by Commandos, including underwater explosions. Charges using 808 plastic could be made up before an operation, indeed such ready-to-use charges were prepared well beforehand for both the St Nazaire raid, the Dieppe raid and, of course, on the many small raids by the SBS. The latter were able to fix ready-made limpet charges, held by magnets to a ship's side, to be detonated by a time switch. These charges with just 2 lb of 808 were able to cut a hole of about 6 feet in diameter in the plates of the average merchant ship.

Indoor sessions included lectures on the the various types of targets and the best ways of demolishing or causing maximum damage to them. With the Highland railway only a few yards from the camp we were able to practice the laying of dummy charges on the lines and on the nearby bridges. With only one train per day in either direction we had plenty of scope for both day and night training and exercises.

We made up Bangalore torpedoes (used for blowing gaps in barbed-wire fences) and pole-charges, and were instructed in the making of improvised bombs and the use of incendiary devices.

True to form our course had to end with an exercise involving a long tactical cross-country march into the mountains to destroy an imaginary enemy target. We marched by night and lay up by day, as was customary for raids that involved a long advance through enemy-held territory. It wasn't much fun after a night's march in the rain, spending the daylight hours in wet clothing to await the next night's march.

I enjoyed the course, found it interesting and a challenge, and it provided all with a sound practical background knowledge of explosives and demolitions. Ironically I wasn't called upon to put this training to use in action, except for the supervision of preparing Bangalore torpedoes for the Dieppe Raid. These metal tubes, 8 feet long and about 2 inches in diameter were packed with 10 lb of explosives, sealed at one end with the detonator inserted at the other end.

The explosion disintegrated the iron casing into countless fragments which dispersed and in so doing cut through the barbed wire, thus clearing a gap. There was an added bonus because the explosion could also set off some types of mines that might have been placed under the wire obstacle. It was a handy device, especially as the the overall length could be increased by adding and linking extra Bangalores.

However, back in 'C' Troop I was frequently called upon to make up charges for field exercises, I recall one such exercise in North Wales where we were called upon to test the Home Guard in the Conway-Bangor area. We carried out a wide flanking movement from the direction of Bethesda, over the mountains, moving only in darkness, to a vantage position above the quarries at Penmaen-mawr. We detonated just small token amounts of guncotton slabs, but even so, shifted sufficient rocks to demonstrate to the Home Guard etc. how easily the defile coastal road could be blocked by creating a landslide with just a small amount of explosives.

Later on the demolition course at Lochailort stood me in good stead in Palestine in 1947. After the demise of Army Commandos I returned to my county regiment, the Royal Hampshire Regiment, and we were stationed in Jerusalem during 'the troubles' there. It was 1 August, the anniversary of our battle honour, 'Minden Day', and the terrorists decided to mount an attack on our billet area. There were several explosions and an outburst of small arms fire. I take up the story from the official Regimental History:

> Two sentries held the terrorists at bay whilst a party led by Lieut Arden raced round behind them ... the Terrorists realising their error tried to withdraw. One was shot dead as he was running away and the others were driven into houses and captured. With great presence of mind, Capt J.E. Dunning removed the fuses from two 50 lbs bombs which had been left on the wire. The Battalion then continued its Minden Day celebrations.

So you see, the instruction on explosives I had received at Lochailort in 1941 was put to good use even after the standing-down of the Army Commandos.

One of the outstanding then-novel features of the instruction at Lochailort was that of close-quarter fighting and unarmed combat, which had been introduced by the redoubtable duo, Fairbairn and Sykes, who had seen plenty of action long before arriving at Lochailort, for both had served for many years in the Shanghai Police. They had undertaken first-hand studies of every known method of personal attack and defence in that notorious city where gangsters, robbers, kidnappers and smugglers abounded and thrived. Fairbairn founded the Shanghai Riot Squad and both he and Sykes had organized the training of its members. Fairbairn's techniques were based on a wide experience of self-defence and ju-jitsu; as regards the latter he was the first foreigner outside of Japan to be awarded the Black Belt degree by the Kodokan Ju-Jitsu University of Tokyo.

Both became legends in the annals of the Commandos and Special Forces, not because they achieved great deeds in action, but for their joint influence on military philosophy and their personal instruction on close-quarter combat.

They were responsible for introducing a new personal aggressive dimension in our fighting forces that had been lacking in peacetime and during the 'phoney war' of 1939-40. Throughout both these periods the development of any spirited, aggressive and ruthless attitude to close-quarter fighting was limited solely to bayonet training. Our traditional and national love of 'fair play' and adherence to the Queensbury rules had precluded our resorting to 'dirty tricks' when it came to fighting for one's life.

Fairbairn, in the introduction to his wartime book, *All-in Fighting*, first published in 1942, puts forward the basis of his philosophy in the following words:

It must be realised that, when dealing with an utterly ruthless enemy who has clearly expressed his intention of wiping this nation out of existence, there is no room for any scruple or compunction about the methods to be employed in preventing him.. There are very few men who would not fire back if they were attacked by a man with a gun, and they would have no regrets if their bullet found its mark. But suggest that they retaliate with a knife, or any other methods explained in this book, and the majority would shrink from using such uncivilised or un-British methods. A gun is an impersonal weapon and kills cleanly and decently at a distance. Killing with bare hands at close quarters savours too much of pure savagery for most people. They would hesitate to attempt it. But never was the catchword, 'He who hesitates is lost', more applicable. When it is a matter of life and death, not only of the individual but indeed of the nation, squeamish scruples are out of place. The sooner we realise that fact, the sooner we shall be fitted to face the grim and ruthless realities of total warfare.

Without going into the details the following headings outline the six main sections of Fairbairn's and Sykes's courses.

1. **BLOWS** (Delivering blows without a weapon)
   a. Using the edge of the hand
   b. The chin jab
   c. Using the boot, side kick
   d. Defence blows using the boot
   e. Using the boot, bronco kick

2. **RELEASES** (Getting free from grasps, holds etc.)
   a. From wrist holds (two methods)
   b. From strangle holds (two methods)
   c. From bear hugs (six methods)
   d. From hair hold

3. **HOLDS** (To use against an enemy)
   a. Thumb hold
   b. Sentry hold
   c. Japanese strangle hold (two methods)
   d. Handcuff hold
   e. Bent arm hold
   f. Head hold

4. **THROWS** (To use against an enemy)
   a. Hip throw
   b. Wrist throw
   c. The back break

5. **MISCELLANEOUS ITEMS AND ADVICE**
   These included fighting with a knife, machete, cane, stick etc.
   Vulnerable points of the body. Defence against knife attack.
   Securing prisoners, etc. In all some fifteen different sub-subjects.
6. **DISARMING** (When held up by an enemy with a pistol)
   a. From the front (two methods)
   b. From behind (two methods)

As the reader might imagine some of these concepts were regarded as alien to our traditional ideas of waging war and the involvement of such 'un-British' weapons and methods attracted and provoked controversy.

Antagonists of the concepts of the Commandos began to seize on this type of warfare, weapons and training and suggest that the Commandos were no better than thugs, cut-throats and gangsters. These views were expressed publicly and had to be countered. This was done, and one such counter-action will be recalled later.

However, those in authority were won over and within a short time this aspect of Commando Training, as with others, became a standard subject in the training of all soldiers, mostly under the syllabus heading of 'Unarmed Combat'.

Fairbairn and Sykes continued to instruct at Lochailort until the STC was closed. Their pupils were many and varied for not only did they teach the Commandos, but also many others ranging from those engaged in clandestine operations organized by the Special Operations Executive (SOE) to potential instructors of the Field Forces Divisional Battle Schools. None ever forgot this intrepid couple and their teachings. Among their unlikely protégés was the famous film star David Niven, who as a pre-war regular army officer responded for the call to arms in 1939 and returned from the glamour of peaceful Hollywood. He initially volunteered for the Commandos in July 1940 and went on the course at Lochailort. In his entertaining book, *The Moon's a Balloon*, he recalls the ex-Shanghai Police duo – 'they concentrated on teaching us a dozen different ways of killing people'. David Niven did not join the Commandos, but he did become OC of 'A' Squadron of 'Phantom', the specialized signals organization.

Fairbairn's and Sykes's training of the agents of SOE is recognized in the new permanent exhibition 'The Secret War' at the Imperial War Museum in London. Among the related artefacts there is the US Legion of Merit awarded to Captain W.E. Fairbairn for his services in instructing agents and operators in the US clandestine organization, 'OSS', a role he carried out in the USA after the closure of the STC.

Unarmed Combat. Above, a member of No 3 uses the hip throw;
below, Commandos were taught to use any potentially lethal object
as a weapon, here a steel helmet is used for the 'coup de grace'

Perhaps, the most lasting memorial to Fairbairn and Sykes is the Commando fighting knife, which they jointly designed and was manufactured in very large numbers by the Wilkinson Sword Company.

Furthermore, their fighting knife was also adapted as the shoulder emblem of the wartime Commandos and the post-war Commando Association, whilst it still is in fashion as the shoulder flash of today's Royal Marine Commandos.

And so on this interesting historic note we leave the STC Lochailort, and some of their instructors and teachings, to look at its more famous successor, the Commando Basic Training Centre at Achnacarry.

Achnacarry Castle, the hereditary seat of the Clan Cameron, was a victim of punitive ravaging by the Duke of Cumberland's troops after the Jacobite Rising of 1745. But, like the legendary phoenix it rose out of the ashes to recontinue its traditional role, with the head of the clan, Sir Donald Cameron of Lochiel, in residence there when the STC requisitioned it as the Holding Unit. He and his family, taking with them many of the clan's historic artefacts, moved into voluntary exile for the duration of the War in a nearby estate house at Clunes.

But it wasn't until the camp was taken over as the CBTC under the command of Lieutenant Colonel C.E. Vaughan, in early 1942, that it was fully developed. Like its predecessor at Lochailort, perhaps even better, it was in the centre of an ideal area for the rugged and demanding training.

Located on the banks of the river Arkaig, which connects the deep water lochs of Arkaig and Lochy, the Castle is flanked by daunting and desolate mountain terrain. Britain's highest mountain, Ben Nevis, at 4,406 feet high, is but 18 miles away and so was there – and waiting – as a final challenge at the end of most of the courses.

On the windswept waters of Loch Lochy the trainees were able to master the basic skills of seamanship in a variety of small boats, whilst there was no shortage of different assault landing places and points for 'dryshod', wet and rocky landings. Any exercise over 24 hours in duration, at practically any time of the year, also put the trainees to the test with trials of endurance, 'living off the land' and personal survival in a hostile environment – especially so in the middle of winter.

In the immediate vicinity of the Castle, hutted accommodation was erected, amongst which a large multi-purpose hut, aptly sited in the shadows of a couple of giant Douglas firs, was dominant. Around the drill square, hard asphalt on what had been, in peacetime, a luscious green lawn, were the austere Nissen huts with their rounded corrugated-iron

There was no need to construct obstacle courses where the terrain used for Commando Training was as rugged and varied as the highlands of Scotland – seen here above and below. (Photographs by courtesy of the Imperial War Museum.)

98

The stately grounds of Achnacarry were transformed into a stark Nissen-hutted camp. The pre-war lawns were converted to a parade ground surrounded by accommodation, cooking, dining, ablutions and NAAFI huts.

sides and roofs providing spartan accommodation, dining 'halls', ablutions and the NAAFI canteen.

Periodically on the periphery of the huts, tents were pitched to accommodate extra intakes of trainees beyond the normal quota. These were the famous old 'Bell' tents that had been a feature of the old colonial campaigns from Queen Victoria's time and countless military camps and manoeuvres dating from the nineteenth century.

The Nissen huts could, at a pinch and by using double bunks, house about forty men but about twenty-five was normal, including a Lance Corporal junior instructor as NCO i/c hut. Beds consisted of scrubbed wooden planks supported on red bricks onto which three square brown 'biscuits' (covered coir), when laid end to end, formed a mattress for a covering of three rough army blankets – no pillow, but the back pack acted as a substitute. The only other facilities in each hut were a pot-belly cast-iron stove for solid fuel fires, electric light and a bucket for use as a night urinal. As it was nearly always raining in this part of the Highlands the ground and tracks from the huts to the parade ground and dining hut were invariably ankle-deep in mud so duckboards were placed around the huts and under the wooden benches on which metal bowls and running

Colonel Charles Vaughan, Commandant of the Commando Basic Training Centre, Achnacarry, with Lord Lovat during a visit by the latter to CBTC in November 1943.

cold water provided the means for daily washing and shaving. Hot showers were a weekly luxury reserved for the 'Make Do and Mend Day' – the so-called free-from-training day.

So much then for the location and the general layout and conditions at Achnacarry. If these were seemingly as near-perfect for the demanding training then the choice of the man to organize and control this task could not have been bettered – Lieutenant Colonel Charles Vaughan, who was briefly introduced in Chapter 1. A veteran of the First World War, he was one of those in the Retreat from Mons in 1914. In the inter-war years he had graduated from Drill Sergeant in the Coldstream Guards to RSM, but he was much more than just a bawling barrack square man, although he could do that if needed.

His obvious military potential as an officer was recognized and he was duly commissioned.

A Londoner by birth, and proud of it, Charlie's standards for soldiers and soldiering were set by his long service, in war and peace. He accepted nothing but the best, whether it be in fitness, weapon training and musketry, fieldcraft and tactics, drill and turnout, or even in the more apparently mundane matters of administration which included feeding and hygiene. Together all these factors made the 'whole' – and the self-disciplined and reliant Commando soldier, 'fit to fight and fighting fit', with high morale, willing and capable of tackling any military task, under any circumstances and against any odds.

In appearance Charles Vaughan was striking, upright but rather portly, and although he had a florid complexion he also had the rugged countenance of a seasoned campaigner, which indeed he was.

At a time during the War when a popular misconception was rife that the Commandos were a gang of reckless desperadoes and cut-throats, he invited a group of war correspondents to visit Achnacarry to see the trainees and and watch their training, then to report on what they saw.

Setting out to dispel the somewhat ill-gotten reputation of Commandos, Charlie told the reporters, 'I would like you to tell your public that we are not a band of "cut-throats" ... Go anywhere you like about the camp and form your own impressions. You will soon realize we are not the undisciplined mob of toughs some people think we are.'

They did just that and according to the reports saw all aspects of the training, including the spectacular showpiece, Opposed Landing. They were impressed and duly reported, 'Yes, the Commandos are tough, but they are not "toughs".' Charlie Vaughan had made his point, but then he usually did.

In early 1943 I was recommended by my Troop Leader, Robert Dawson, for a commission. It was a time when many warrant officers and NCOs throughout the Army, with battle experience, were also being recommended. It was a sound and wise policy for it provided an immediate supply of junior officers with experience who had already demonstrated their ability to lead men in action.

Many Commando WOs and NCOs were commissioned in this way and went on to serve in the Commandos both in action or as instructors.

Arguably one of the most outstanding of the officers commissioned from the ranks was Lieutenant George Herbert DCM MM of No 3. After surviving raids in Norway and France, and further operations in Italy, he was killed in Normandy leading his section against a German strongpoint.

Unfortunately, space precludes mention here of others whose contributions to the many and varied operations of the Commandos were considerable, which is a pity...

With a single bright new 'pip' shining on each of the epaulettes of my battledress I arrived at Achnacarry in May 1943. No introductions between Colonel Vaughan and myself were necessary. We knew each other from our No 4 days, indeed he was Second-in-Command when Lord Lovat promoted me TSM of 'C' Troop.

I started as a Section Training Officer, but after a couple of intakes Charlie promoted me to captain and I took over the responsibility for fieldcraft training, before ultimately being put in charge of Haydon Commando, one of the three training Commandos. But now for a closer look at the syllabus and programme for the basic six weeks courses.

When I started to gather material for this book I naturally sought aid from my old comrades and one of them, Captain Jack Clovis BEM, contacted me and offered some papers and photographs relating to Achnacarry. This was too good to be missed, and among them was Jack's old battered copy of 'The Commando Basic Training Centre – Instructions & Key to the Programme of Work for New Intakes to Commandos', some thirty pages of authentic details.

This particular set of instructions was issued after I left Achnacarry, at the time when the War in Europe was nearing final victory and consequently, in many minor details, the emphasis was on fighting in the Far East against the Japs. Nevertheless over 90 per cent of the programme and syllabus was the same as I had followed in the previous months with, literally, hundreds of Commando trainees.

As a result of this excellent authentic record I am able to recall exactly what we taught in those exacting – but also exciting – days.

Some time after the receipt of the syllabus I was asked to talk on 'Commando Training' at a seminar at the National Army Museum in London, so used it, but I also did a breakdown of the time allotted to the various subjects. It was so interesting that I have no hesitation in repeating it here as a prelude to detailed descriptions of the contents of the course:

Weapon Training, incl Foreign Arms	19%
Fieldcraft, Movement and Tactics	13%
Firing of Weapons/Grenades/Field Firing	11%
PT incl Ropework and Unarmed Combat	10%
Boating	9%
Map Reading	8%
Speed Marches	6%
Night Training	5%
Mines and Demolitions	4%
Drill	4%

Climbing	3%
Set-Piece Exercises (incl Opposed Landing)	3%
Training Films	3%
Medical Lectures and First Aid	2%
Plus Final 36 hours scheme and Final Day Activities	

Of course, I must add that there was quite a lot of overlapping of subjects within the above breakdown, for example in fieldcraft a lot of practices in movement was part of night training, likewise some field firing and even boating came under the same heading. One might be surprised to see no specific mention of assault courses above – they were included in various other subjects and at the end of speed marches.

Now for the standard course, bearing in mind there were others that were different and tailor-made for special intakes. However, all courses did, in fact, start before the trainees' arrival at Achnacarry. This may sound odd, but all arrivals came by one way only – steam train from Glasgow. For most of them it was their first sighting of mountains and lochs as they journeyed alongside Loch and Ben Lomond, passing lonely Crianlarich, Tyndrum and across the bleak and forbidding Rannoch Moor to Spean Bridge station, their immediate destination, to be met by a kilted piper... and some of their future Commando instructors. The latter in their camouflage Dennison smocks ('jumping jackets') and all wearing the coveted green beret complete with their own parent regimental badge and the colourful backing of the Cameron of Lochiel tartan – the only distinguishing emblem of the Achnacarry staff.

No matter what the weather, rain or shine, as the new arrivals tumbled out of the train, in marching order and carrying their rifles and kitbags, the orders ran out like a burst of machine-gun fire: 'Kit bags on the truck and get fell in on the road.' No 'cushy' ride in trucks for the 7 miles to Achnacarry, their training was to start right there and then.

It was a stark introduction and left none in any doubt of what was in store for the next six weeks. However, as Charlie Vaughan used to say, 'We always like to welcome them in style, so I send out the pipe band to greet them and lead them in for the last half mile to camp.'

But things looked even worse on arrival at the camp, for there just past the Guard Room, on the grass verge alongside the drive to the Castle, was a row of well-kept graves with wooden crosses and on each was written the cause of death: 'This man failed to keep his rifle clean', 'This man looked over cover and not round it', 'This man stood on the skyline', and so on. This unexpected cemetery prompted a dramatic and salutary reaction. Initially it also posed the question, 'Real or phoney...?'

The 'graves' at Achnacarry; on the cross of each 'grave' was written the military fault which resulted in the soldier being killed in action – salutory silent lessons for trainees!

There was the story concerning the arrival of Darby's US Rangers at Achnacarry for their training, when one of them, on spotting the graves commented with some feeling, 'Jesus, the sons of a bitch, they kill us on the march from the railroad, and when we get here they bury us . . . '

The first day of every course started with the Commandant's Opening Address, in the big multi-purpose 'Iris' hut.

Charlie Vaughan set the scene and the tone with typical forcefulness and clarity, there was 'no messing'. It is sad that none of his talks were recorded for posterity. They were gems of direct, honest-to-goodness, no-nonsense talking from an old experienced warrior to his young braves. Charlie knew exactly what he wanted to achieve and how to do it.

He pulled no punches – not all those present would pass. Those who couldn't keep up would be RTU'd; generally speaking they would be given one chance and one chance only – as in action. Perhaps there might be exceptional circumstances, say, in the case of an injury which might mean, after recovery, joining a later course. Nevertheless, he asserted, and assured them, they were all capable of passing, or they would not have been selected for the course. It wasn't a question of being physically strong and tough, physical strength was just one factor, not even the major one; far more important was mental strength. On this he was always unyielding. 'It's all in the mind', he never stopped insisting.

Then followed his customary tirade on the so-called 'toughs', the bully boys, those who fought in brawls and on the streets after the pubs had turned out. 'Give them two pints of beer and the smell of the barmaid's apron and they'll fight anyone. We don't want them, we don't need them, we won't have them,' he told all and sundry.

An outline of the course then followed and amidst all the exacting and demanding aspects of the training in the surrounding mountains and on the lochs, it came as a surprise – and a shock to many – that there would be drill on the square and a high standard of 'spit and polish'. 'I know, and you will find out too, that a soldier who keeps his weapons and equipment clean, no matter the conditions under which he is living, will also keep his body and his mind tidy and alert too,' he maintained.

'I've got the best Commando instructors 'ere,' he asserted. 'Learn all you can from them and remember they will never ask you to do anything that they cannot do themselves, likewise your officers too; furthermore they will lead you from the front. By the time you leave here, you will have had the best training there is – make no mistake about that! And having passed the course and I have given you your green beret, you will belong to the finest troops in this war – the Commandos.'

Then came Charlie's concluding salvo, delivered in his unapologetic Cockney accent with convincing force: 'Then when the time comes for you to face the 'Un [Hun] and 'e sees the determined glint in your eyes and the cold steel of your bayonet, 'e'll drop his rifle and run like 'ell!'

Such rhetoric sounds far-fetched and almost absurd to readers today, but it is impossible to convey the psychological impact of Charlie's opening address and how much it contributed to the success of the courses.

Normal intakes of trainees were allocated to one of the three training Commandos: 'Keyes', 'Haydon' or 'Sturges', named after pioneers of Combined Operations and the Commandos – Admiral Sir Roger Keyes, our first beloved boss, and his son, Geoffrey, who won the first Commando VC; General Haydon, the original commander of the Special Service Brigade and leader of the Lofoten Islands Raid; and General Sturges, a Royal Marine, who after the Madagascar operation became the first overall commander of the Commando Group of four Commando Brigades.

Each Training Commando was commanded by a Captain, with a minimal headquarters of a CSM, a clerk and a storeman. The Commando was organized into four training Troops, each under an instructor-officer, assisted by a Troop Sergeant.

Many trainees then – and years after – reckoned the speed marches were, possibly, the most gruelling of all the training, requiring both the mental and physical stamina that Charlie Vaughan alluded to in his opening address.

The trainees' dress for all these marches and for most of the other training consisted of denims (blouse and trousers), boots and anklets, whilst head-dress throughout the course was the woollen cap comforter. As for arms and equipment, unless there was a specific exercise requiring the use of the 'Troop' weapons, i.e. Brens, TSMCs etc., every trainee carried a rifle and wore FSMO.

Trainees were introduced to their first speed march on the first or second day of the course; they didn't have to wait long. It was a relatively gentle five miles around the 'Dark Mile' in under the hour, the aim being to get down to 50 minutes. This scenic route which circumnavigated the camp had a special history of it own – although few of the trainees were interested in that at the time. The wooded hillside rises steeply from the road whilst on one side alongside the little stone bridge, is the spectacular wee waterfall of Chia-aig, above which somewhere in the glen is where Bonnie Prince Charlie is reputed to have hidden in a cave after his defeat at Culloden. What is not in doubt is that this picturesque spot was used for background shots in the film, 'Rob Roy', in 1994. However, going back to the 1940s and speed marching . . .

This first march was followed by other weekly jaunts progressing in stages from 5 to 15 miles and after each one was an added task as follows:

7 miles under 70 minutes, followed by digging a defensive position
9 miles under 90 minutes, followed by a firing practice, usually at falling plates
12 miles under 130 minutes, followed by a drill parade on the square
15 miles under 170 minutes, followed by assault course and firing.

These times were basic guidelines inasmuch as Troop Leaders were expected to aim for faster times 'according to the fitness of the trainees on arrival'.

On all speed marches everyone was expected to help flagging comrades to keep up; support on either side was often sufficient or carrying a second rifle helped too.

Trainee officers, as well as their men, were sometimes glad to take advantage of this 'sharing the load' philosophy as they, too, often struggled to keep up on the speed marches. Even a colonel was expected to help carry a rifle if need be, as Charles Vaughan used to tell all senior officers on the courses. Indeed Colonel Moulton, whose No 48 (RM) Commando underwent their basic training at Achnacarry in 1944 makes a point of describing his experiences in 'load-sharing' in his book, *Hasten to the Battle*.

It is relevant to emphasize that the officer and NCO instructors, on the speed marches and all the other training led by example: they encouraged, they helped stragglers and 'Oh, Yes,' they shouted and chivvied, but never, never, did they result to bullying. This was a fundamental and significant feature of all Commando training.

No matter how hard the training nor how frustrated and exasperated instructors were, they never 'lost their bottle' or became sadistic. At Achnacarry Charles Vaughan would never have allowed or tolerated it.

When I had it in mind to write this book I wrote to Lord Lovat with an outline of my intentions and asked for his views and advice. I was pleased to receive his reply because he favoured a book devoted entirely to our training and made the point that I should emphasize emphatically and in no mean terms, this aspect of Commando philosophy: that throughout training, as in action, Commando officers and NCOs relied on leadership to achieve results. Certainly this basic principle was well applied at Achnacarry, where it led to a healthy respect and genuine regard between instructors and trainees.

Perhaps this relationship is best summed up by a quotation from Robin Neillands' book, The Raiders. It was made by one of those who did his initial training at Achnacarry and had this to say of his old instructors: 'They were as hard as nails, but totally lacking in brutality or malice . . . we were their lads for the duration of the course and we were not expected to fail.'

The instructors were devoted and as keen as the trainees themselves for a 100 per cent pass rate, but this was never possible. Failures and RTUs were inevitable on such a demanding course.

Quite different to speed marching on the roads was the other type of marching – cross-country, better known today in modern Commando parlance as 'yomping'.

To start with the formation was different – instead of column of three's, it was single (Indian) file, led by an officer or NCO marching on a compass bearing or picking his route from the map. The leader also set the pace. Over the heather and swampy moors, through the glens, across shallow burns and deep, fast-flowing rivers, and up and down the mountains the trainees trailed in file. For practically all of them it was the first time they had been in such wild and rugged mountain terrain. The weather invariably added a further challenge, rain was never far away and in winter snow, sleet, icy winds and mist were added hazards; and remember at Achnacarry we had no special clothing or equipment for mountain trekking, just the standard army issues.

Dressed in FSMO and carrying rifles the trainees found marching over the challenging terrain hard going; they struggled to keep up especially on the steeper slopes and when reliable footholds had to be searched for on the treacherous boggy moors.

I can still hear the curses and swearing as they sweated uphill, and one Royal Marine trainee, Lishman, who, incidentally played football for Arsenal after the War, muttering quite audibly, 'Bloody hell, they think we're bloody machines not bloody marines . . . '

Gradually they got the knack of hillwalking, then came the task of making everyone realize they must be observant. Instead, keeping eyes glued to the ground, they had to look up as well and maintain a watchful eye; as one would if operating in enemy-held territory. It was essential that they all understood the need for this type of vigilance even though 'they were 'shagged' and finding it difficult enough to cope with the physical demands of moving over such unfamiliar and exacting terrain.

To drive home the necessity for all-round observation on the move, ambushes and 'enemy' snipers were introduced to the cross-country marches, thus providing realism and also reminding the trainees that the object was not just an introduction to mountaineering, hill or fell walking but preparing to fight in the mountains under hostile conditions. True to form the 'enemy' fired live ammunition.

The cross-country marches were developed into 36-hour schemes so that the trainees slept out and learnt to make the best of any shelter or use natural materials to construct simple bivouacs. They also had to cook their own meals in mess tins over little individually prepared fires. It was on these particular exercises that the 'Me and My Pal' system came to the fore. One man prepared the 'bivvy' while the other got 'cracking on the grub'.

These schemes made the trainees put into practice the instruction they had received from CSM 'Ossie' Moon on 'Survival'. Alongside the river Arkaig Ossie had erected a collection of different types of improvised bivouacs, made from materials one could expect to find in all types of countryside. He demonstrated the basic principles of building to provide shelter from the rain, wind and cold. But his great joy and expertise was demonstrating how to live off the land, how to procure all kinds of food, animal and vegetable, and prepare and cook the same on a wide range of makeshift and improvised fires. He showed how to skin deer and other wild animals, also how to cook birds in clay with their feathers on, but his pièce-de-resistance was an apparently mouth-watering stew bubbling away in a mess tin on one of his little trench fires. It smelt delicious and he always had plenty of volunteers to take up his offer of tasting it. When all had supped he posed the question, 'What's the meat?'

It was cut in slithers, dark in colour and tasted fine. Answers fired in, 'Venison, mutton, hare, ptarmigan, beef...'

'No, you are all wrong,' drawled Ossie, with a sardonic and evil smile on his lips. 'It's Achnacarry rat...' Unbelievable thought some, others just thought and wondered, but all survived. Before they left Ossie made them promise not to tell others of this particular menu of his, for it would spoil the fun!

When the trainees were preparing to go off on an overnight exercise they drew, from the cookhouse, individual rations of raw foods – some meat, potatoes, carrots or another root vegetable – plus a couple of slices of bread; sufficient tea, sugar and some tinned milk was collected in bulk by the instructors to be shared out later. No tinned rations, 24-hour ration packs, self-warming soups, blocks of dehydrated meats, oatmeal or the likes for Vaughan's boys. Neither were they allowed Tommy cookers or blocks of solid fuels. 'You go out into the mountains 'ere with what we've got 'ere...You 'ave to light your own fires and get on with it...or you go without,' warned Charlie. 'After all it's only for thirty-six hours... remember Colonel Laycock and Sergeant Terry lived in the desert for forty-one days after the raid on Rommel's Headquarters, and all they had were the berries they could pick and the rain water they could gather as they trudged along or rested overnight.' As he never tired of telling all and sundry, 'It's all in the mind, so get on with it.'

Dependent on the time of the year the instructors were able to show what wild fruits and vegetation could be picked and eaten. I always found boiled stinging nettles a ready favourite with those who like spinach.

At Achnacarry were members of the staff with first-hand experience of surviving and existing on raw vegetables or wayside plants, some on their escapes or treks back to Allied lines.

One such Commando was J. Byrne, who was an original volunteer in 1940 and went to the Middle East with Layforce, then afterwards was in Stirling's SAS until he was captured. Imprisoned, he twice escaped and eventually made his way back to Britain via Sweden; he was so weak and underweight when he eventually got back that, still wanting to stay in the Commandos, he was sent to Achnacarry to be built up and retrain! He recalls his days there: 'The food was plain, well balanced and plentiful. In addition to the normal rations I frequented the canteen for slabs of cold bread pudding and rock cakes. But it rained every day without exception,

IT HAD TO BE TOUGH

and at night when we returned to our huts wet, tired and ravenously hungry we knew it would be the same next day.'

In spite of his track record in action with both the Commandos and the SAS in the Middle East, plus his experiences as a successful escapee, Byrne, in his book, *The General Salutes A Soldier*, pays a glowing tribute to the instructors and the contents of the course at Achnacarry. This is particularly pertinent when one records that although he was already permitted and entitled to wear his green beret, he had been told by General Haydon that he had to pass the course and prove himself fit enough to join an operational Commando. Consequently he had no cushy ride – no one got that at Achnacarry and Byrne wrote:

> There was a lot to learn, so we had no spare time or days off, although we were allowed half a day each week in which to repair our equipment, sew on buttons, darn socks, wash our clothing etc. Every one took it in good part. No one ever complained, for it was the only way to obtain the coveted green beret and become a Commando soldier. Among the instructors were specialists in everything imaginable, and we learned something new every day.

Gradually Byrne returned to full fitness: 'my body filled out, and I gained in confidence, until, full of surplus energy, I got up to the same daft tricks as the others, such as leaping off the top of a hut, eating a raw cabbage at a sitting and firing the anti-tank rifle from the hip'. Charles Vaughan wanted Byrne to stay at CBTC as an instructor, but he declined and was posted to No 6 Commando to be one of those who landed on D-Day.

More time was devoted to weapon training and firing practices than any other single subject – and for good and obvious reasons. All this training, the organization and supervision of all firing – field and target shooting – was the main responsibility of the Weapon Training Officer (WTO). The original WTO has already been introduced, namely, Captain Wally Wallbridge; he was succeeded by a young regular officer, Captain Ken Allen of the Sherwood Foresters, and when he left to help run a Commando training centre in Bari in Italy, Captain 'Spud' Murphy took over.

The basic instruction consisted of a thorough revision of rifle, Bren, TSMC, Boys A/Tk rifle, PIAT, revolver and grenades, followed by plenty of handling practices and lots of firing. Some introductory instruction was given on the heavy weapons (Vickers MMG and 3-in mortar) but it was very elementary and limited because more thorough and specialized instruction was given at HOC, Wrexham or on posting to an operational Commando for those going to serve in the Heavy Weapons Troop.

Popular with the trainees was the chance to handle and fire some of the enemy infantry weapons and those of our major ally, the USA. Among such weapons were the German Schmeisser, Spandau and Luger, and the US Garand automatic rifle, the M1 and M3 carbines.

A total of some seven hours instruction was given to Mines and Demolitions. Obviously in this time one could provide no more than a basic introduction to the subject, keeping it simple without too many technical details.

About 10 per cent of the instruction was, as might be expected, spent on physical training. This was wide ranging, including unarmed combat and climbing and swinging – like monkeys – on ropes. In the latter the Commandos became unrivalled innovators, and the various forms of training on ropes gave rise to such Commando labels as 'Tarzan Swing', 'Death Slide', 'Toggle Bridge', 'Cat Crawl' and 'Postman's Bridge', plus, of course, in the context of climbing, 'Roping down/abseiling'. Not only were these activities adopted throughout the Army during the War, but afterwards they were readily incorporated into Outward Bound and Youth Adventure Training schemes and activities.

By the time I arrived at Achnacarry in 1943 all these challenges were in position as part of the PT syllabus and were under the control of the Chief Instructor and his excellent PT staff, headed by a splendid warrant officer, CSMI Frickleton. His right-hand man was the legendary 'Sonny' Bissell. This popular NCO had quite a background in the 'Met' Police and it is interesting to recall how he and hundreds of other policemen arrived as volunteers for the Commandos – straight from 'civvy street' – in 1942.

Early in that year Brigadier Haydon, who was then the overall commander of all the Commandos, met the Metropolitan Police Commissioner, Sir Philip Game, and asked if fit and active policemen might be allowed to volunteer direct for the Commandos. It was a novel request which was put to the test and nearly 500 came forward.

In successive intakes during the summer and early autumn they arrived at Achnacarry in plain clothes to be trained and moulded into Commando soldiers. In the vanguard of these volunteers was 'Sonny' Bissell, seven times national wrestling champion and black belt (1st Dan), physical training and self-defence instructor at the Metropolitan Training School.

Writing in the *Police Review* after the War, Charlie Vaughan had this to say about Sonny: 'Well do I remember this chap. He reported to me at Achnacarry in a blue suit, complete with his bowler hat and small case . . . ' He made a great impression and his instructional ability and

One of the uses of the handy little toggle rope, standard issue to all Commandos, was the making of a simple bridge; as such, however, it was mainly used in training as part of an obstacle or assault course. (Photograph by courtesy of the Imperial War Museum.)

experience was soon put to use in training his colleagues in those subjects in which he excelled.

Of the others Vaughan had this to add: 'Their enthusiasm and keenness made my task easy... There were only a few huts and tents in which to accommodate them and equip them with uniforms and the accoutrements of a soldier, and the conditions at Achnacarry, I can assure you, would have horrified the War Office recruiting agents or any Commandant of any ordinary infantry training centre. But, believe me, nothing deterred those chaps. They entered into the spirit of the situation and within two months I had the pleasure of presenting to those who had passed their green berets, the hall-mark of a trained Commando... they were the finest material that I ever had to deal with in all my soldiering,' concluded the respected old warrior.

A few of the ex-policemen, such as 'Sonny' Bissell and 'Jock' Holland, who had special qualifications and attributes as instructors, stayed on at Achnacarry to pass on these skills, but all the rest were posted to the various operational Commandos and fought worldwide. Without exception they all acquitted themselves gallantly and proudly; every CO spoke highly of their influence and achievements. Colonel Durnford-Slater (No 3) wrote: 'The intake of police was perfect Commando material. The men were big, strong and intelligent and had all their police discipline and training behind them. They were real volunteers, keen for the contest . . . the best intake we ever received, and every man was a potential leader; many of course were later commissioned and others exerted a fine influence as senior NCOs.' So much then for the police who learned their fighting skills and were imbued with the indomitable Commando spirit at Achnacarry.

The small staff of PT instructors, Frickleton, Bissell and a couple of others, had a formidable workload, but they thrived on it and seemingly enjoyed every moment of it. Their enthusiasm was infectious.

For most of the instruction on PT, the Tarzan Course and Unarmed Combat the trainees wore 'clean fatigues' - denims, boots and gaiters, but no headdress. For most of the year, even in wintry weather, it was 'strip to the waist' for the active PT sessions.

Much of the PT consisted of agility and strengthening exercises and teaching the drills and skills of tackling obstacles. All the equipment and obstacles were home-made at Achnacarry by a small staff who utilized local materials for not only these aids, but the obstacles on the assault courses and some of the unusual snap targets etc. on the ranges. Fortunately they had plenty of the main material - wood - close at hand.

The rustic walls, fences and climbing frames for PT were sited alongside the 'Square'; also kept there were a dozen or so hefty tree trunks of varying diameters - and weights - but all about 15 to 20 feet long. On most the rough bark still remained. These 'logs' were heaved, lifted, hurled into the air and caught in a variety of different improvised strengthening exercises demanding, in addition, plenty of team work and cooperation.

There alongside the square, amongst the trees, was another strengthening aid, also home-made, a large disused oil drum filled with cement and with rope, block and tackle anchored to a tree. 'Heave ho, my hearties,' was the clarion call for using this device.

The undoubted showpiece of the PT staff was their 'Tarzan's Course'. This was erected in the beech trees that formed an avenue from the Castle along the bank of the river Arkaig. There, a series of rope crawls, bridges, swings and scrambling nets culminated with the 'Death Slide' across the river and nearby was the means of returning – the 'Toggle Bridge'.

The average height above the ground was about 25 feet. The various rope 'walks' and 'crawls' had their own individual names. They all looked very frightening, and the instructors knew that, so they weaned their 'lads' first on simple upright ropes, teaching them the fundamentals of gripping the ropes with hands, knees and the use of the boots, then on to the techniques of climbing inclined and horizontal single ropes, such as the 'Cat Crawl'. The technique was to lie on the rope with arms outstretched in front to pull, one leg dangling below the rope to act as a balancing 'keel', the other leg and foot on the rope to grip and assist the movement along it. The hardest part, as one can imagine, was to regain the cat-crawl position once it was lost, it was tricky, but like most seemingly difficult tricks quite easy once you mastered the knack. Confidence was the name of the game and Frickleton's NCOs certainly knew how to instil that with calm, patient but firm instructing that followed their demonstrations. One of their favourite jibes was, 'You can do it, 'course you can – even the officers can do it! 'That was usually enough to get them going.

Each section on the ropeway was introduced and tackled separately at first – even the Death Slide and the Toggle Bridge. Once these were mastered then the trainees were ready for the whole course as a continuous series – done in FSMO with the added excitement of a few detonations in the river as they crossed the Death Slide and the Toggle Bridge.

No one who did their training at Achnacarry ever forgot the Tarzan's Course with its Death Slide and Toggle Bridge. The Death Slide originated at Achnacarry and like many other features of Commando training was soon copied by others both during the War and afterwards.

I never knew whose brainwave the Death Slide was – I rather fancy it was one of those seemingly boisterous ideas that used to develop at places like Lochailort and Achnacarry, such as jumping off Nissen huts and landing by going into a parachute roll.

The Achnacarry Death Slide started with a climb up a riverside tree on which, admittedly, man-made footholds had been inserted on the trunk, to a little platform about 35 feet above the ground, a pause to take off the toggle rope worn around the waist, then threading the toggle through the eye at the other end make a hanging strap for sliding down . . . and away. Great fun, but a bit awkward in FSMO and encumbered with a rifle slung over one's back.

Once on the far side of the river the way back was, over the Toggle

*The crossing of obstacles using just ropes was practised
in all types of locations, here over water.*

bridge, made as the name suggests from the ubiquitous toggle rope. This handy little piece of equipment, unique to Commandos, consisted of a 6-foot length of thickish rope, with a spliced eye at one end and the approximately 5-inch wooden toggle at the other end. Trainees were taught to use these ropes for a variety of jobs, including, of course, a rope bridge. Crossing over a toggle bridge was plain sailing provided one kept the two top ropes well under the armpits and used the bottom toggle joints for footholds.

The third feature of the PT staff's instruction was the much publicised Unarmed Combat. It was based wholly on the Fairburn/Sykes programme and routine. The Achnacarry course started with a demonstration in an erected boxing ring in the Iris Hut. The usual trio providing the spectacle consisted of Frickleton, Bissell and Sgt Bellringer. The latter was an ex-member of the 'grunt and groan brigade' (all-in wrestler) and one of the few survivors who got away from the St Nazaire Raid. He also had a most unfortunate stutter, but in spite of this defect was a good and convincing instructor, who, understandably, was nicknamed 'Ding-Dong'.

RSM 'Jimmy' James provided a well-scripted commentary. It was a star performance, well rehearsed and with a cast could have been nominated for the 'Oscars'.

It started with a summary of the vulnerable points including, quite naturally, the 'goollies'. How to deliver disabling blows followed, then attacks on sentries, breaking free from holds, how to break falls, throws, the use of the knife and other makeshift weapons plus defence against such attacks and so on . . . It was a very 'professional' and stimulating demonstration that had the trainees raring to 'have a go'.

Each sub-section of trainees had seven sessions of instruction under one of the three experts. These were done in the camp area area where realistic settings were readily available and not under gym conditions, with a 'mat' to fall on. Unarmed Combat was always a popular subject.

Maybe in action few ever had to use it 'in anger', but it was there in the back of one's mind, stored away ready to be brought into use at a second's notice. Furthermore, it was another section of special training, the mastering of which gave added confidence to the fighting soldier.

The location of Achnacarry was ideal for training in fieldcraft especially as one had the opportunity to create realistic battle conditions with live firing. It did, of course, lack facilities for street fighting, although attempts to compensate for this apparent deficiency were addressed with the mock-up front of a house.

Although I had no specific qualifications for the job of Officer-in-charge of Fieldcraft, apart from having been in action, I had been on an extended course on camouflage, and been heavily involved in the early development of No 4 Commando's Battle Drill tactics and patrols – I was greatly pleased when Charlie appointed me to that post, and not just because it meant promotion to Captain.

I was given quite a lot of scope with the way I organized the subjects to be covered within the programme and timetable. This was quite a challenge. Fortunately I had two expert instructors to assist me. Both were highlanders, one was a ghillie in civilian life and the other, although not actually employed as a ghillie, was brought up from a lad with a shot gun or a rod in his hand.

Staff Sergeant Davidson, of the Lovat Scouts, was a ghillie. Of medium height, lean and wiry, his weather-beaten features and his taciturn character exemplified his hard mountain background. On the other hand Sergeant Archie McClelland of the Seaforths was quite different. Nearly 6 feet tall, stocky, good looking with a flowing moustache and a twinkle in his dark eyes, he was ever ready to share a joke.

They seldom spoke to each other; maybe the fact that one was a Catholic and the other a Protestant accounted for their obvious social disregard for each other. But at work it was a different matter.

116

Both were deadly shots with the rifle, they moved over the most gruelling, mountain terrain with ease and the lithesome movements of a cat stalking a bird. Born and bred in the Highlands they had a thorough knowledge of – and respect for – the vagaries of the mountain climate. As a team, in spite of their obvious differences away from the job in hand, they were excellent. To see them in action together one would never have believed they were other than close comrades.

As a role model Davidson was ideal. His movement in the hills was that of a hunter as he eyed the skies and smelt the wind. Then when he spotted his quarry, be it a beastie or a group of trainees, his rifle seemed to be an integral part of him as he slithered effortlessly to the ground to take cover and take up a firing or observing position, his eyes never leaving his quarry. I often used him as an example of how it should be done. All I needed to say was: 'Just watch him and see how to do it...'

All-in-all the three of us had a very harmonious working relationship, and off duty, or when we were in 'the hills' living rough, I seemed to be able to bridge the gap between them without any problems.

Our contribution to the overall course was considerable, if less spectacular than some of the others, although that's debatable. Our work load invariably involved us where subjects overlapped. For example we provided the setting and opportunities to put into practice many aspects of weapon training, unarmed combat (i.e. stalking a sentry) and we frequently acted as 'enemy' with live firing on exercises.

However our primary brief was to provide expert instruction on movement over all types of terrain by day and night, the use of ground and cover to avoid detection by the enemy, camouflage and concealment, and methods of locating the enemy with both 'eye and ear'.

A lot of our instruction hinged on demonstrations by both my two NCOs and the Achnacarry Demonstration Troop. The latter had a busy time for it not only gave demonstrations, but also doubled as the Pipe Band. This was another example of Charlie 'MacVaughan's' ingenuity and its activities are recalled by Bill Millin (who was in the Demonstration Troop/Pipe Band when I organized the Demonstrations, but later left Achnacarry to become Lord Lovat's piper on D-Day in Normandy and to lead the Commandos over Pegasus Bridge) in his book, *Invasion*.

An important demonstration was the 'Crack and Thump' one. The main object was to show how an enemy position could possibly be located by listening for the origin of the firing, and a secondary object was to familiarize the intake with distinctive sounds of our own weapons and also those of the enemy.

117

The trainees were brought at a steady double – normal practice when moving from one place of 'work' to another – to a piece of ground just outside the camp. There, once in a viewing position, I said they were all in the weapon sights of the 'enemy' and most of them were only 150 to 250 yards to the front.

'Try and spot them,' I challenged.

I didn't get many takers, and those I did get were mistaken. It was surprising how a clump of heather could be mistaken for the head and shoulders of a man lying in a firing position. While they were still looking I passed on some tips on 'searching the ground': how to search systematically, bit by bit, and to look hard at features that don't seem to blend or fit into the background or surroundings. We also passed around some binoculars to help them, but to no avail.

After a while I got the individual 'enemy' to fire over the heads of the watching trainees.

But before they started to fire I explained the importance and sequence of 'crack and thump'. When a shot is fired at one, the first thing one notices, given that it hasn't 'got your number on it', is the distinctive crack, like that of a whip, as the bullet flies overhead or to a flank. Then, as the bullet moves quicker than the speed of sound, it is followed by the 'thump' (sound) of the actual discharge of the round in the weapon and it is this 'thump' they had to try and locate. Forget the crack, it's missed you and gone forever...

One by one the weapons were fired, a whole miscellany of small arms, single shot and automatic, plus some overhead fire from the mortars. A large number of rounds were fired, so that the trainees had a good chance of locating the firers by sound alone. Gradually as they gained experience of the different weapons they began to pinpoint the area of the firing, if not the exact position, and equally important what type of weapon was being fired.

Again the Demonstration Troop was used to illustrate some of the 'do's and don'ts' of camouflage. Without going into great detail I used to emphasize the major factors and provided a simple four-worded memo on the basics: 'Shape, Shine, Shadows and Skylines'.

In addition to the practical demonstrations we also showed training films on various aspects of fieldcraft, such as preparing for patrols and the application of fieldcraft to terrain totally different to that at Achnacarry, for example, in the jungle.

One of the 'perks' as Fieldcraft Officer was to spend some off-duty hours going into the mountains with either Davidson or McClelland for

On the loch at Achnacarry a little fleet of various craft was assembled for training in basic seamanship and landing drills. Seen here on the far bank are eight dories and a rigged cutter, mid-stream trainees row past the landing craft (LCA) partly visible. The Goatley collapsibles were stored in the boathouse.

stalking. Sometimes we were able to take a party to bring back 'a beastie' or two to supplement rations, but generally we went just for the fun of pitting our skills against the deer. This made ideal military training, and it was a shame we couldn't extend it for more trainees.

One of the 'fixtures' on the Staff at Achnacarry during the period 1943-45 was a Royal Marine officer, boating-officer, Jim Keigwin. He was most competent, a first-class instructor and an excellent organiser, with his fleet ever-ready and in good condition. Furthermore, his cheerful countenance, ready wit and sense of fun always dispelled the agonies of even the coldest and wettest landings through icy waters.

His was a mixed armada of whalers, cutters, landing craft, dories, canoes, rubber dinghies, kapok bridge rafts and the ever-faithful Goatley folding canvas boats, all moored alongside, or housed in, the little stone boathouse at Bunarkaig on Loch Lochy. It was a fleet built up over the years from the original collection of a whaler, a cutter and some twelve folding boats in 1942.

The instruction started with a film on the role and functions of Combined Operations, and the various craft used for training and operations. Elementary watermanship in the folding boats, canoes and rubber dinghies followed with the correct handling and use of paddles and oars for steering and propulsion.

Once these fundamentals had been mastered it was on to the normal craft for operational landings, the assault landing craft, concluding with the Opposed Landing.

Captain Bill Nash, an ex-ranker in the Parachute Regiment, assisted by CSMI 'Spider' Leech and one other NCO (during my time at Achnacarry he was Sgt 'Spike' Pike, who had been with us in 'C' Troop, No 4, when we started climbing in Snowdonia) were the climbing instructors. 'Spider' was an old hand from No 5 and had been with them in Madagascar. A droll Cornishman, he had been a steeplejack on the tin mines before joining up and was a natural climber and instructor, furthermore he was in Geoffrey Rees-Jones's original 'climbing' troop back in 1940.

All three readily admitted that in the short time they had allotted to this subject, just under seven hours, split into forty-minute sessions, they could do no more than to provide 'a taste'. Fortunately there was an excellent outcrop of suitable solid rock only a few hundred yards outside the camp for learning the basic skills and techniques, so very little time was wasted in getting to the site for this training. On the rock face the trainees were able to carry out individual scrambling and bouldering, go through the drill for climbing roped in a team of three, watch a demonstration of hauling heavy equipment up a rock face and the use of the Neil Robertson stretcher for lowering casualties, and practise abseiling, although the initial abseiling was done on the 35-feet-high walls of the Castle. This descent from the parapets of the Castle was yet another spectacular highlight of Achnacarry, and arguably provided the inspiration for house assaults, such as that carried out by the SAS many years later on the Iranian Embassy in London.

One of the secrets of a good descent was to lean well out and away from the wall before pushing off. However with self-preservation urging one to stay close to the wall, it needed a bit of courage and plenty of confidence. For those with a fear of heights it posed a challenge, which some failed to meet.

Without the modern aids of web harnesses and carabiners, we had to depend on the rope alone and incurred the risks of nasty rope burns on the back of the thighs.

The basic knots used in climbing were also demonstrated including the 'figure of eight', 'bowline', 'bowline-on-the-bite', 'timber hitch' and lashings, plus maybe others I have long since forgotten. These knots, plus those taught in the boating instruction, trainees were expected to practice in their free time or at odd moments of 'stand easy'.

In fact, quite a lot of useful, and often informal, instruction took place outside the laid-down sessions of the timetable. This was possible because each evening, when not on night schemes etc., the trainees had cleaning and polishing sessions in their huts, or during the summer, when it wasn't raining or the midgies not biting, on the grass outside. There being no other distraction such as the wireless, the NCOs i/c huts had a specific list of subjects to talk over, or they would take any backward trainee on extra weapon training, map-reading etc.

It came as a surprise to most of the trainees to find that even at Achnacarry they still had 'square-bashing' and 'bull', but Charlie Vaughan – ever the Guardsman that he was – was uncompromising on its value and place in the programme. He maintained that it provided a solid and proven background for developing self-discipline.

But Vaughan knew full well that he had to procure the very best of drill instructors, NCOs who could extract results from the likes of the men volunteering for the Commandos. Accordingly he got them mostly from the Brigade of Guards and the Royal Marines, and these NCOs appreciated the challenge they faced with the type of intakes they had to drill.

Presumably the style and mannerisms of drill sergeants never alter, their jargon and wit is timeless; certainly their 'patter' at Achnacarry, although adapted to refer to Commandos and not the Guards or the 'Royals' would have sounded equally at home at Pirbright or at Chatham. Assuredly, the final passing-out parade provided evidence of the successful instruction of that rare breed whose trademark is the pace-stick firmly tucked under the right armpit – and punctiliously parallel to the ground – the Drill Sergeant.

The final week of the course provided a fitting climax. By then most of the rejects had departed – RTU'd. For the survivors it was 'shit or bust' week and included the final 15-mile speed march, the 36-hour scheme, firing tests on the ranges, the Tarzan Course and the Opposed Landing. But that wasn't all. Charlie Vaughan reckoned no course was complete without 'some 'ealthy competitions'. So for good measure the last day of training before the final parade and the presentation of the green berets saw a hectic day of an Inter-Troop Competition and an Individual Commando Pentathlon. It was quite a week.

The format of the final 36-hour scheme was left to the three individual Commando Leaders. In Haydon Commando I always aimed to incorporate

This basic mock-up was erected at Achnacarry for teaching battle skills in street fighting and house-clearing using, of course, live ammunition and explosives.

the ascent of Ben Nevis in our exercise with a couple of tactical situations en route and an ambush on the way back to a bivouac area where the expected night's rest would be rudely broken by a preplanned night attack by some 'enemy'.

I always enjoyed the 'yomp' to the 'Ben'. The actual route to Britain's highest mountain varied, dependent on whether we were able to get Keigwin's boats to take us initially across Loch Lochy to Glenfintaig, or alternatively we had to 'hoof' it towards Spean Bridge and then march westwards to Glen Nevis and the Ben itself.

This climb was always regarded by the intakes as something special, and once on the actual track to the summit I tended to treat it as a 'one-off' recreational jaunt. As a result nearly everyone enjoyed the experience, but once we were back down at the foot of the mountain it was business as usual and we reverted to tactical marching to the bivouac area, invariably around Gairlochy, by the Caledonian Canal.

The last day was 'Competition Day' and rather special. It had a great atmosphere that was a cross between Cup Final Day and Derby Day. It was meant to be a fun day, but with hard-fought rivalry between the Troops, usually as many as twelve and involving some 350 to 500-odd trainees.

All trainees had to partake, although for the Troop competition only one event was for the whole Troop, including the officer and NCOs of the staff, and this was the first one, a 5-mile Speed March. For the other four events, the Boat Race (in folding boats, one boat per Troop), Tug-o-War (team of ten from each Troop), Shooting (at falling plates, ten men from each Troop) and the 'Milling Contest' (team of ten from each Troop), the Troop Leader had to select his teams, but no man could be in more than two events.

Points were awarded for each event, timekeepers, judges, and other officials came from the specialized instructors and members of the staff other than the Training Commandos, to ensure fairness and impartiality. All the events took place during the day with the exception of the 'Milling' which was held in the evening in the Iris Hut. Often the final outcome depended on it too, producing a very exciting finale to the day's activities.

One of the fun factors was the inclusion of a tote, opened before the first event and closed before the return of the first Troop from its Speed March. For several intakes the tote was organized and run by Captain 'Tim' Balchin, a lanky, bespectacled officer with a sharp mind, quick wit and a head for figures. He always appeared in some sort of fancy dress as becoming the most outrageous bookie to be seen on any race course.

All the Troop events were self-explanatory barring the Milling. This was one of Vaughan's innovations which first appeared on the scene when he was in No 4 Commando.

It was a form of boxing, but with a difference – a big difference. It was a team contest, usually ten per team and competitors were paired off roughly by weight, and then numbered off '1 to 10'. The two teams – Red and Blue – lined up outside the ring opposite each other.

There were three officials, the MC (announcer), the judge (with two flags, red and blue) and the timekeeper with stopwatch and whistle. The MC made the appropriate opening announcements, then it was 'Number ones into the ring' – there was no time for any handshakes because when both were in the ring, the timekeeper blew his whistle, the signal for 'let battle commence'. And it did. It was all-action stuff, no quarter given and none asked, nevertheless all blows had to be legal and proper punches, none below the belt and no rabbit or kidney punches etc. It was fast and furious, as the two millers usually stood toe-to-toe swapping blow for blow, urged on by the tumultuous roars of their respective supporters. For unlike all orthodox army boxing where no shouting or other noise was permitted during the fighting, milling thrived on the cheering. For sixty seconds the gladiators battled until halted by the shrill blast of the timekeeper's

Although it was difficult to obtain much strenuous physical training on board, boxing, milling and unarmed combat was possible, as is seen here when No 4 Commando held a boxing contest during an amphibious exercise based on Scapa Flow in 1942.

whistle, when they had to stand still until the judge held up the respective flag of the fighter he considered had delivered most proper punches on the target area of head, shoulders, chest and solar plexus; no marks or consideration for clever defence or fancy footwork. The idea and aim of this game was forthright and simple enough, just one word – 'attack'.

In spite of the apparent risks and possible injuries, the rapid flurries of blows seldom produced any damage apart from a bloody nose, a split lip and the odd black eye.

The varied nature of the competitions in the Individual Commando Pentathlon accounted for surprise results, none more than the Free French trainee I had in Haydon Commando in late 1944. He was one of many Frenchmen who had made their way to Britain over the months that followed France's capitulation in 1940 and subsequently volunteered for the Commandos.

After the excitement of the Competition Day and the sweat and toil of the previous six weeks, the final day, with the presentation of green berets, the Commandant's Parade and Farewell Talk, brought not so much an anti-climax but a sigh of relief. It was all over, but was it? Not in Charlie

Vaughan's book for there was a bit more spit and polish to cope with, not to mention the rehearsal, for the final parade for the demanding wartime 'Laird of Achnacarry'.

Inevitably there was an end-of-term atmosphere as the hour to leave Achnacarry approached, kitbags and packs onto the trucks, then carrying personal weapons and proudly wearing their newly won berets, it was the march to Spean Bridge to catch the special train that would take them to the Holding Operational Commando at Wrexham for specialist training before eventual posting to an operational Commando.

As they swung out past the graves and Guard Room, onto the road, where today the Cameron Museum stands, Charlie Vaughan took the salute and, headed by the Pipe Band, the newly fledged Commandos, rain or shine, happily marched through the Glen, over the bridge at Gairlochy and up the long hill, where the Commando Memorial now stands, and down to the station where a hissing steam train awaited. Their days at Achnacarry were over, but for some not quite, for even now – fifty-odd years later – veterans return annually to pay their respects to fallen comrades, many of whom did their initial Commando training at Achnacarry.

Before leaving the story of Achnacarry one must take the opportunity to record, and even emphasize, the important integration of the Royal Marines into the Commando organization. It started in 1942 with the formation of 'A' RM Commando, later retitled No 40, and by 1944 a further eight RM Commandos had been raised. Most of all the officers and ratings in these Commandos underwent their conversion training at Achnacarry. Furthermore, from late 1942 onwards, RM officers and NCOs began to play their part as instructors there.

Finally, it is relevant to add that today's RM Commandos have their own 'Achnacarry' at Lympstone in Devon.

Achnacarry Castle Today

A couple of years ago I was asked by the Fort William and Lochaber Tourist Board to help them produce a tourist leaflet, 'The Commando Trail', to enable visitors in the area to gain an insight on the historical background to the Commando training carried out during the Second World War. Included in this leaflet was a map I drew, entitled, 'The Commando Dark Mile, as existed in war years', and it has subsequently enabled many visitors to walk the trail we blazed all those years ago.

CHAPTER VII

Special Operational Training – The St Nazaire and Dieppe Raids

So far all the emphasis has been on general training for a wide range of operations, now it is proposed to dwell on the specific and detailed training for two of the more famous Commando raids, St Nazaire and Dieppe. The preparations for these two raids undertaken in 1942 provide excellent examples of thorough and detailed training designed to ensure the success of the impending operations.

Here one must emphasize that in both cases the commanders involved were given just about sufficient time to plan and prepare for the raids. Accepting in most cases you can never have enough time, the Commanding Officers of the respective Commandos involved in these two raids did have just about enough time for training and rehearsals, although often Commandos were committed to operations with insufficient time to prepare.

Many military historians consider the combined RN and Commando assault on St Nazaire, in March 1942, was the greatest and boldest raid of the Second World War, a view that is perhaps confirmed by the award of five Victoria Crosses to participants – the highest number awarded for any single operation in that war.

The raid was a daring action of high strategy and, as such, played an important, if not vital, part in the Battle of the Atlantic, a battle that Winston Churchill called 'the dominating factor all through the War' and 'the only thing that ever really frightened me'.

The battle's true beginning was in June 1940, when the fall of France and the Germans' capture of the Bay of Biscay ports of Brest, Lorient, St Nazaire, La Pallice and Bordeaux gave their navy, with its formidable fleet of U-boats, advantageous starting points to attack our vulnerable sea supply routes in the Atlantic.

Throughout 1941 and into 1942 enemy U-boats inflicted appalling losses on Allied merchant shipping. These losses in ships, men and supplies were inflicted, in the main, by Donitz's U-boats, but there was a real fear – a growing one – that Germany's capital ships would join in this crucial battle on the seas with dire and disastrous consequences.

St Nazaire, with its drydock, the largest in the world and the focal point of the port, would play a key role in any such extension of Germany's naval plans. It was, therefore, considered imperative that immediate steps be taken to deny the use of the port to the enemy.

At that stage of the War aircraft were not available or capable for this type of mission, so it was decided to delegate it to forces of Combined Operations, whose chief, Lord Mountbatten, was keen to take it on.

Without going into the details of the plan it was broadly based on the Royal Navy delivering the Commandos to the port, and then for the raiding force, having overcome the immediate defences, to destroy and/or put out of action vital dock installations and equipment.

Because of the shallowness of the Loire river estuary on which St Nazaire is situated, it was planned that the bulk of the Commandos would travel aboard some sixteen Motor Launches (MLs); the rest of the Commandos, about 100 in all, would go on board HMS *Campbeltown*. The latter was an old US destroyer which, together with some other similar warships, had been transferred to the Royal Navy in exchange for rights whereby the Americans could use bases in Bermuda. The *Campbeltown* was to be used as a blockship to ram the massive seaward caisson gates of the drydock and subsequently destroy these gates with a time-delayed detonation of explosives packed within.

No 2 Commando, commanded by Lieutenant Colonel A.C. Newman, was selected for this redoubtable challenge.

Newman was given the outline plan for the operation and then introduced to his opposite number on the naval side, Commander R.E.D. Ryder, who because of his initials – and for no other reason – was nicknamed 'Red'. Only thirty-four years old, he already had a distinguished naval career.

From the outset he and Newman established a warm and harmonious working relationship. With just a month to prepare for the operation they immediately set about the planning and training.

The Commandos were to land at three different places in the dock area of St Nazaire: (1) on the drydock caisson gate itself from the decks of HMS *Campbeltown*, (2) on the Old Mole quayside from MLs and (3) on the Old Entrance quayside also from the MLs. From these three main landing points assault parties would attack and destroy the dockside defences, whilst the demolition parties would demolish and/or damage selected dock installations and items of equipment including the pump and winding houses and the caisson gates of the drydock.

Within this overall plan there were three distinctly different training priorities: (1) those for the assault groups; (2) the specialized tasks for the demolitionists; and (3) liaison with RN and familiarization with the craft and ship to be used for the operation.

There were no great problems over (1) and (3) although it has to be borne in mind that the planned disembarkation onto the quayside was greatly different to the accepted method from LCAs onto a beach.

However, for the demolitionists the training was not so straightforward. To start with, because the number of demolition experts required for the numerous and wide-ranging targets exceeded those normally available in a single Commando, and the time for training more from within No 2 was so short, it was decided to draft into this Commando for the specific raid extra demolition experts from the other Commandos.

Officers and NCOs were dispatched from Nos 1, 3, 4, 5, 9 and 12 Commandos. From No 4, I remember 2/Lieut H. Pennington, a rugged ex-varsity rugby blue, and several NCOs, mostly all sappers (REs), being seconded. In the event not all these reinforcements went on the raid, although Pennington did and unfortunately he was one of those who did not return. He was killed aboard his ML in the run-in to land.

Each demolition expert was destined to carry very heavy loads so it was wisely decided they would need others to protect them. Accordingly most demolition teams consisted of four heavily laden experts and four 'minders', who, incidentally, also carried additional explosives etc.

Initially all the officers and men chosen for the demolition tasks, some eighty in all, gathered at the small port of Burntisland on the Firth of Forth under the overall command of Captain William Pritchard RE. As a cover plan he told the Commandos that they had been chosen, and he would train them, for the possible demolition of our own port facilities in the event of an enemy invasion.

There was a very high proportion of officers to ORs in the party, with many of the small, mostly four-man teams, being led by an officer, so important was the rating of each potential task. Among the NCOs was Sgt Tom Durrant from No 1 Commando, who was to win the Victoria Cross, posthumously, on the raid, although it was for his heroic part in the run-in to the port – and thus in reality the only VC ever awarded to a soldier in a naval engagement.

It is significant to mention Pritchard's background and how he became involved in this operation because he was not a Commando officer, but a specialist called in for the job. Before the War he had been a dockyard engineer, having served his time as an apprentice and worked in Cardiff docks. He had joined the Territorial Army and was commissioned into the Royal Engineers with whom he had served in France 1939-40. A keen and capable demolitionist he had won the Military Cross for blowing up a vital bridge during the Dunkirk evacuation – and this under enemy fire. Back in England he subsequently became involved in the study of blowing up home dockyards to prevent their use by the enemy in the event of an invasion. But that wasn't all: he had also made a study, at some considerable length, of the feasibility of similarly destroying enemy-held dockyards by our raiding forces.

One such enemy-held port he had studied, together with another RE officer, Captain Robert Montgomery, was none other than St Nazaire. With this in mind, when the initial joint planning started, Pritchard and Montgomery already had a detailed outline plan covering the targets, the types of explosives required and other such details. This then was the background to the two men who were to direct the thorough training of the Commando demolition teams and subsequently go on the raid with them.

As trained demolitionists, many having 'graduated' from Lochailort, they were familiar with all the general methods and techniques, but now they began to acquire the specialized 'know-how' and training for destroying port facilities and equipment.

At Burntisland they were shown how to destroy anything and everything that contributed to the smooth and efficient running of a small port. In the short time available the enthusiastic Commandos theoretically destroyed all there was to be destroyed including the ships.

It was time to move on to the next stage, at two larger ports more like the one chosen for the raid. So the eighty-strong party was split into two for continuation training at Cardiff, under Pritchard, and at Southampton under the supervision of Montgomery.

Prior to their actual training of the demolition teams Pritchard and Montgomery had done their homework in some detail on the actual targets, working out the best explosives for individual tasks and sizes of charges as well as methods of detonation etc., leaving nothing to chance. Full details about this aspect of the preparations can be found in Lucas Phillips' book, *The Greatest Raid of All*.

By now all were beginning, as one Commando pertinently recalled, 'to almost dream explosives and demolitions', and they got no respite from Pritchard and Montgomery for whom nothing short of perfection was acceptable.

Sergeant Bill Portman, one of those seconded from No 4 who went to Cardiff first, remembers how they learnt, at these larger ports, such details as the differences between caissons and double lock gates, looked at steel bridges to see whether they folded or swung back, studied port and dockside machinery and equipment – all with the purpose of deciding and working out the best means and methods of destruction.

When it came to demolition by explosives the aim was to complete each demolition task within ten minutes in the dark – no mean task. It took plenty of practice and teamwork, working to a drill with each man having his own part. They learnt the drill by day, practiced it blindfolded then finally at night 'on the job' in the docks.

From Cardiff Bill Portman went to Southampton, which had been purposely chosen for training because it had many similarities to St Nazaire. At this time none of the Commandos had any idea of the real purpose of this detailed training – Pritchard's cover plan still held good.

Although the city of Southampton had suffered considerably during the Blitz, surprisingly the docks were relatively unscathed. This was most fortunate for the Commandos, especially as the giant King George V Dock was not only undamaged but lying idle and accessible for their training. This drydock, the second largest in the world, was almost identical to that in St Nazaire, and was reputed to have been modelled on the French one. Furthermore one of the engineers who had been employed on its construction was able to give the planners at HQ Combined Operations much valuable detailed information which was passed on to Montgomery.

In spite of all these apparent advantages the destruction of such a huge and formidable target by small raiding parties seemed, at first, to be a nigh impossible task. However, as one of the participants wrote after the raid, they were being trained by experts who did their job so thoroughly that they inspired confidence.

Those earmarked to land from the *Campbeltown* onto the caisson gates of the drydock practised movement on the Southampton caisson, blindfolded by day so that they could move on it with confidence at night without fear of falling or harming themselves.

Although the *Campbeltown* with its concealed cargo of twenty-four depth charges, equal to $4^1/2$ tons of high explosive, was planned to severely damage the actual caisson gates, it was the role of the Commando demolitionists to destroy all the other associated installations of the drydock, such as the Pump House, and the two Winding Stations, plus swing bridges, power station, cranes and fuel tanks elsewhere in the docks.

Pritchard made all teams aware of each other's tasks. This not only ensured that the raiders knew what their mates were doing, it added variety to the training and also introduced a degree of flexibility to the overall plan.

Not all the eighty demolitionists trained by Pritchard and Montgomery were used for the raid, indeed Bill Portman and five others out of the twelve seconded from No 4 didn't go. After all that intensive training at Burntisland, Cardiff and Southampton they were disappointed.

However, no sooner had they been taken off the job for St Nazaire than they were dispatched to another Commando which was preparing for a raid on Bayonne on the coast of France. In the event they did set sail for Bayonne, but like so many of its predecessors this became another Commando raid that was cancelled at the last minute, this time just a few miles from the objective. But that's another story, so back to to the preparations for St Nazaire, which by now had been given the codename Operation Chariot.

Following the dispatch of the demolition teams to Burntisland, the rest of No 2 Commando, who were stationed at Ayr in Scotland at the time, continued their normal training which was relevant and appropriate for their roles as assault and 'protection' parties. With this in mind their main priorities were physical fitness, firing of weapons and night fighting in a docks/built-up area as opposed to open country. All these subjects were, of course, inherent in the normal training programme, but now they needed to 'peak' at them.

Referring to the problem of the Commandos landing from the *Campbeltown* onto the caisson of the drydock, Captain John Roderick, who was OC No 3 Troop, and in charge of one of the assault groups operating from the 'old' destroyer recalls:

> We were prepared with bamboo ladders and ropes to help us off the ship, but didn't know how high – or low – we would be on arrival with the collapse of the ship's bows following the impact of the ramming the dry-docks. As it happened several of the ladders were badly damaged by gun fire and we had to improvise – very smartly.

The assault and protection parties under the supervision of Major Bill Copland also furthered their training in street fighting, specifically when they took part in a mock raid on Plymouth docks. John writes,

> This gave us a refresher in street fighting and its complications, this time in the realistic setting of the bombed part of the Plymouth dockyard and the war-damaged civilian surrounds. The Commando had previously practised in the Lockerbie area where some over-enthusiasm with explosives had caused mayhem in Ecclefechan.

131

To provide those troops earmarked to make the long sea journey on the MLs with some experience of such a sea crossing aboard these small craft, Newman arranged a trip to the Scilly Isles for them, but it was anything but a pleasure cruise. The weather was foul and the sea conditions vile, with the result that practically all who went were very seasick. Certainly at the end of their round trip to the Scillies they were painfully aware of what the sea journey to St Nazaire might be like: not very nice.

Six days before the operation was to be mounted a dress rehearsal was staged with that mock raid on Plymouth docks. The defenders, consisting of regular troops and the Home Guard, were told that it was to test their anti-invasion plans and that British Commandos would be acting as German invaders. No suggestion or hint was given that it was a dress rehearsal for Operation Chariot. For a variety of reasons it was not wholly successful, but several useful lessons were learnt, especially on the problems of navigating the small craft in the full glare of coastal searchlights.

Prominent among the final preparations on board the *Princess Josephine Charlotte* was the detailed study of the model of the docks and aerial photographs used for working out the routes to be taken after landing.

Cpl Woodiwiss, who was one of John Roderick's NCOs, elaborates on the briefing: 'Everybody was given a general briefing on the whole operation and then each man was briefed on his own particular task ... We had plans of the dock area which we had to draw and redraw, and a wonderful scale model, which we could study in different lights to help identify our own targets.'

Included in the final preparations were lectures on evading capture and escape, always a feature of the last-minute preparations for a raid. Details were given on routes to be taken and in some cases where one could find 'safe houses'. Often silk maps that could be sewn into and concealed within the collar of the battledress blouse were issued, as were little compasses that consisted of what appeared to be two trouser 'fly-buttons'. These were sewn onto one's trousers before going into action and then removed, if need be, and used in an emergency. Once the exact location of the raid was made known more information was given on the hinterland and surrounding countryside, the likely attitude of the locals to 'fugitive' Commandos, the dispositions (in general terms) of the enemy and the suggested routes to take to escape and make one's way back to Britain. In the case of those on Operation Chariot the advice was to head south. Among those who did just that to avoid capture after the raid was George Wheeler, then an NCO, who was, subsequently on return to Britain, commissioned and went on to serve in the Commandos in Italy.

The demolition teams prepared their 'tailor-made' and other charges during this stage and also packed various additional items including incendiary bombs – to set fire to buildings containing machinery and equipment, and also to ignite any oil storage tanks. In some cases the individual loads weighed as much as 90 lb.

All those travelling on the MLs had to transfer everything needed for the journey and the operation from the base ship, starting two days before the planned date for departure. They were hectic days.

On the morning of 26 March Newman, who had, the previous day, briefed all the group leaders, one by one, in his cabin, assembled the whole Commando to give them his final pep-talk, although even at this stage he hadn't got the absolute command that the operation was on.

There seems no doubt from accounts by those who were present that he described the raid as the 'sauciest job since Drake'. Newman's final talk was inspirational – 'a rousing speech... put up morale by 100 per cent... he really is a fine chap... we all realise how much he has done to make the job a success... patient, helpful and charming all the time...' Such remarks help to confirm the image one has of this clear-headed, determined, but quiet and cheerful soldier, often referred to as 'Uncle'. The heroic action of his men at St Nazaire demonstrated how thorough and encouraging his preparations had been – and what is more he demonstrated further leadership on the raid.

Prior to the raid, at the end of his speech in which he had emphasized that it was going to be an extremely hazardous operation, Newman repeated the offer, previously proferred by Lord Mountbatten, namely, that any man who considered he had family responsibilities or any other reason for not going should stand down. They were completely free to do so... and nobody would think any the worse for so doing.

Not a single man asked to stand down. All went but many did not return. In spite of the severe losses the raid was a notable success. The dock remained out of action for the rest of the War, and the *Tirpitz* was denied the waters of the Atlantic. But, perhaps, just as important was the effect on the French and the others of Occupied Europe. As the French Prime Minister told survivors of the raid in 1947 when they returned to St Nazaire: 'You were the first to give us hope.'

This spiritual factor as opposed to the material aspects of the raid has often been overlooked. I was given an equally impressive reminder of this aspect of the effects of Commando raids by a Frenchman when I attended the 50th Anniversary of the Dieppe Raid of 1942.

That expressed sentiment provides an apt introduction to a study of the training undertaken by the Commandos for the controversial raid on Dieppe.

This particular operation has, relatively, provoked more discussion and arguments than any other fought in the Second World War. In a matter of a few hours on that sunny August day in 1942 over 4,000 Allied servicemen were killed, wounded or taken prisoner at Dieppe. Some 3,000 of these belonged to the Canadian Forces. However, it is not intended here to enter into the pro's and con's of the raid – the reader must seek elsewhere to follow the arguments.

The raid on Dieppe was officially described as a 'reconnaissance in force', the aim being to land in occupied France, capture and hold for some hours a major sea port and during this short occupation to carry out various other supplementary military missions. The bulk of the land forces chosen for the operation were from the Canadian Division, which had been stationed in Britain since 1940. They were selected for the formidable task of landing on the beaches of Dieppe and capturing the town.

Plans for the operation, under the codename 'Rutter', had been drawn up in the early spring of 1942 and preparations and training for the raid carried out. In this plan the task of destroying two gun batteries that dominated the landing beaches at Dieppe had been allocated to British parachutists. But this plan, like so many Combined Operations before it, was cancelled on 7 July.

Suddenly, probably because of political pressure from both the American and Russian allies, 'Rutter' was remounted but under a new codename; this time it was Operation Jubilee and it had one major alteration: the use of the parachutists, for dealing with the enemy coastal batteries, had been written out entirely from the plan. Instead their place was to be taken by Nos 3 and 4 Commandos. (The Royal Marine Commando, which had been formed in April 1942, stayed in the plan, their major role was to land in Dieppe and bring back some German 'invasion' craft/barges.) Briefly, the raid was a military disaster.

The Canadian forces, although they fought with great heroism and suffered the horrendous casualties outlined above failed to take their objectives. The Royal Marine Commando never got further than the beach and also suffered severe casualties.

Unfortunately, No 3 Commando whose task was the destruction of the battery ('Goebbels') to the east of the town were intercepted – one of those accidents of war – by German naval forces, on the run-in to the beaches. Consequently only a small party managed to land and although they did their best to harass the battery, by sniping and with other small arms fire, they did not silence it.

No 4 Commando, whose objective was the other six-gun coastal battery ('Hess') located to the west at Varengeville, about 1,000 yards inland from the beach, in striking contrast to their comrades in No 3 Commando, were able to land their two separate parties with complete surprise on the right beaches at the right time. With great dash under the leadership of their Commanding Officer, Lord Lovat, they succeeded in their mission. They silenced and then destroyed the battery – on time and according to plan. It was the only success of all the forces that landed on that fateful morning. Subsequently, this single action captured all the publicity at the time, and accordingly, the whole operation was referred to as 'Commando Raid'. It was not explained that the action of No 4 was but an episode in a major action in which the main brunt of the fighting was borne by the Canadian forces – and at such losses.

The success of No 4 Commando captured not only the imagination of the public, but also the War Office for they saw it, and labelled it, as 'a classic example of the use of well trained infantry... and thoroughness in training, planning and execution'. In February 1943 they issued a special training publication for study by infantry officers and NCOs 'in order that all may benefit from the story of a stimulating achievement'. High praise and recognition, indeed, for the action of any single unit. Looking back at this official booklet some fifty years later provides an accurate summary of all that was involved to make this 'episode' such an outstanding feat of arms.

And how was that success achieved? Lord Lovat, in his book *March Past* comments: 'if Waterloo was won on the playing fields of Eton it is truer to say that Operation 'Cauldron' [that was the codename, within Jubilee, for No 4 Commando's mission to destroy Hess battery] owed its success to Lulworth Cove'. It was at this famous beauty spot on the Dorset coast, near Weymouth, that we in No 4 trained tirelessly and purposefully for our specific role in the operation.

It was in mid-July, about four weeks before the proposed date for Jubilee, when Lord Lovat was summoned to Headquarters of Combined Operations in London and told that his Commando was to replace the parachutists. The Commando was stationed in Troon, Ayrshire at the time, although my particular Troop was detached in the area of the village of Barrhead, some 30 miles away, carrying out general Commando training, but throughout we were 'living off the land', in little sub-section

Physical training in the Commandos relied upon the use of the facilities and resources available and at hand. Here C Troop (No 4) are using logs, and although this training session took place in Scotland, 1942, the troops were wearing 'KD' (Khaki Drill) because they had been earmarked for operations in the Middle East and so were familiarizing themselves with this type of clothing – when the weather permitted.

and section groups, bivouacking in and around the various farms and barns. Ironically enough, we were expecting to be sent to the Middle East, or even further afield, because we had been issued with khaki drill shorts and shirts plus puttees. It was lovely summer weather so we naturally discarded our battledress blouses etc. for the lighter and more comfortable tropical kit, little realizing that within a month or so we would have partaken in one of the bloodiest actions of the War – landing on the coast of France and not the Mediterranean.

We returned to Troon and with the rest of the Commando travelled south to Weymouth which was to become our base once more. We hadn't much time for preparation so we started intensive training immediately.

Lord Lovat, with his second-in-command, Major Mills-Roberts, had worked out a plan for Cauldron based on dividing the Commando into two groups. Group 1, consisting of 88 all ranks, under the command of Mills-Roberts, would land on a beach overlooked by cliffs, but in direct line with Hess Battery. Once ashore a section of this group would form a bridgehead on the cliff top to secure the re-embarkation beach and cover the withdrawal. The rest of this group would proceed as quickly as possible to woods in front of the battery and from there engage the latter with small arms fire. Group 2, consisting of some 164 all ranks, under the personal command of Lord Lovat, would land at a beach to the west of Group 1 and after landing in two waves would carry out – at speed – a wide outflanking movement of about 2,000 yards to form up at the rear of the battery, and then at a given signal assault the battery and destroy the guns and the enemy manning them.

It was a simple plan. In effect it was basically a 'fire and movement' exercise at unit level, with Group 1 overwhelming the battery with 'fire', not only to prevent them from firing their guns, but also to command their attention, whilst the 'movement' element, i.e. Lord Lovat and the rest of the Commando, carried out their wide flanking advance to assault the gun position from the rear.

Success depended on how efficiently and capably both groups carried out their separate, but interdependent, assignments. The prime factor to ensure success, accepting the fact that the plan was sound and feasible, was, of course, thorough training. And this we started on arrival in Weymouth.

Our Troop, 'C', provided the main element of Group 1, and for good reason. The beach on which we were to land was overlooked by steep precarious cliffs which had to be climbed before pressing on to engage the battery. As will be explained later, we had, under the enthusiastic leadership of Captain Robert Dawson, specialized in rock climbing and consequently became regarded as the Commando Climbing Troop. Most of our training had been on solid rock faces such as existed in Snowdonia, and apart from some climbing on the granite sea cliffs in the area of Tenby in South Wales we hadn't tackled coastal chalk cliffs like those on the Dieppe coast. Now was our chance to do just that in the Lulworth Cove area – and we subsequently took advantage of those facilities.

Much valuable information for the planning of the raid was obtained from up-to-date aerial photographs and also from some pre-war picture postcards of the area, which was – and still is – a popular seaside spot. In the cliffs that we were to tackle were two distinctive gullies, which was most convenient because the cliff faces were not only awesome but reckoned to be practically unscalable because of pronounced overhangs at the top. From a careful study of the shadows cast within the gullies it was possible for the experts to estimate the steepness of the sides. As a result we reckoned we could cope, using our established climbing leaders and techniques. However, there was an added snag in the form of barbed wire, and possibly mines, which the Germans had deposited in the gullies to make them – supposedly – unclimbable. To overcome the problem of the barbed wire we planned to use Bangalore torpedoes. The successful and speedy ascent of these gullies, or at least one of them, was a prerequisite to the success of Group 1's mission as a whole.

When describing the actual training one can do no better than to take the official report and elaborate on it.

There were two general aspects of the training. First, the collective training common to all going on the raid, then secondly, specialized training pertinent to each group, remembering they had different roles.

The first priority in collective training was battle fitness and this included every single officer and man, whether he be a signaller, Bren gunner, demolitionist, mortarman, section leader or a rifleman in the beachhead party. They all had to be capable of wading/swimming ashore, dash up the pebbled beach, cross over any obstacles whilst fully armed and heavily laden with weapons, ammunition and explosives and move off the beach at top speed. To meet these demands the training covered – and I quote – 'Hardening exercises, PT with weapons, swimming [fortunately the sea was warm and inviting, especially after a hard day's training], one mile runs every morning before breakfast. Doubling, fully loaded, over specified distances in wet clothing. Crossing beach wire with rabbit netting.'

There was also the collective boat-drill training on *Prince Albert*, a pre-war Belgian ferry which had been converted in 1941 to carry eight assault landing craft which we would use for our two groups' landings. Although during the previous two years we had been involved in plenty of practices in embarking and disembarking from LCAs we still had to rehearse embarkation/loading for this specific operation. This meant that in each landing craft the loading and seating on board had to be related to the 'onshore' tasks of each soldier.

But these arrangements could not be drawn up until the detailed plans for the operation were made known and, in this case, the allocation of landing craft to Groups 1 and 2 had been decided.

Once these details were finalized we were able to start practising the landings. Initially these did not go well, we suffered from being put ashore on the wrong beaches. But things did improve, so that after no fewer than eight night rehearsal landings, we did on 19 August land on the boulder-strewn beaches of Vasterival and Quiberville at the right places and at the right times. It was a just reward for much irksome – and patient – training.

In spite of criticisms and comments made by either service during the training, working relations between the RN and ourselves were cordial, whilst cooperation between soldiers and sailors at all levels was first class. Some of our enthusiasm and skills rubbed off onto the sailors, noticeably after we were asked to instruct them in the handling and firing of the Bren following the decision to equip each LCA with two Brens apiece. The sailors fired the Brens during some of the practice landings and also as they were lying offshore when they potted away at some expended floating smoke canisters, using them as makeshift targets.

Returning to the collective training of the Commandos, next to battle fitness came 'skill-at-arms', in other words, weapon training and marksmanship. It so happened that just prior to this 'exercise' every Troop in the Commando had spent a whole week on the ranges in Ayrshire qualifying on the rifle and Bren, with remedial sessions for those who had not made the grade; as a result a very high standard was attained, with several chaps in every Troop qualifying as marksmen on the rifle and Bren gun. Over and above we had in our Troop managed to provide some extra training for four of our best marksmen as snipers. One, L/Cpl Dickie Mann, a Reading butcher in peacetime, became very proficient. He was later awarded the Military Medal for his devastating marksmanship on his sniper rifle, with its telescopic sight, firing at individual Germans from short range in front of the battery at Varengeville.

So with that recent intensive spell of qualifying shoots standing us in good stead we were able to press on further and concentrate on field firing, under more realistic settings than those existing on the ranges. Included in this category was the firing of the rifle and Bren gun from the hip at short range during an actual assault and bayonet charge.

The priorities for specific training in the two groups were different because of the operational roles and this, of course, dictated the types of individual and section training.

In Group 1, although our major task was to provide the 'fire' element in the plan, the first job on reaching the top of the cliff was to form a bridgehead to cover our landing beach for the eventual re-embarkation. The training for this started with a simple drill allocating sub-section positions with the aim of 'every man Jack' knowing how he fitted in and who would be on his right and left etc. Our MO was also to land on Group 1 beach and set up his Regimental Aid Post within the bridgehead on the cliff top. Because of the limited time available for the whole operation we were all told that it would be impossible to evacuate the more seriously outlying casualties, whilst the walking wounded had to make their own way back to Group 1 beach, and strict instructions were issued to the effect that no officer or man would fall out to attend to casualties, because they were the responsibilities of the medical orderlies who were allotted to Groups 1 and 2. These seemingly harsh orders were necessary to ensure that the momentum of the operation was maintained and everyone knowingly accepted the need. Talking of casualties, during the training, officers and NCOs were often ruled out as casualties and their subordinates had to take over. It is a hallmark of sound and realistic planning to ensure that such measures are taken during training. For Cauldron it was an insurance policy that paid a dividend when two officers of the assaulting 'F' Troop were killed prior to the assault on the battery.

No stretchers were to be taken ashore, but there were some aboard the LCAs. With typical ingenuity this apparent shortcoming was overcome on the day by using some doors taken from the Battery office as stretchers! It was on an improvised stretcher that Pat Porteous was carried down to the beach after being badly wounded in the fierce hand-to-hand fighting in the final assault on the Battery, and it was for his gallant part in that action that Pat was awarded the Victoria Cross.

The main task of Group 1 as the 'fire' element was to get to the woods in front of Hess Battery as quickly as possible and take up good fire positions, but not to open fire until ordered to do so.

Given that we could now fire accurately, the key to the success of the Group 1 task was, therefore, to concentrate on the following three factors in training. Firstly, plenty of practice in judging distance so that the sights of the rifles and Brens were accurately set; secondly, the practice of good, clear and concise fire orders – with strict compliance – and thirdly, firm control of this fire.

Meanwhile the snipers needed to perfect their fieldcraft, moving and crawling to good firing positions without being seen or heard. They trained under a Section Sergeant, Hughie Lindley, but were expected to operate singly and independently in action. This obviously meant that, besides being marksmen, only confident, trustworthy and reliable men could be selected for this task.

Our Commando mortars, the 2-inch and 3-inch, were an integral part of the armoury of Group 1 and in the event these high-trajectory weapons played an important part in the firefight on the day.

The 2-inch was our own Troop weapon and, as TSM, I was responsible for it in action. Luckily, my team of two on this weapon were great chaps. 'Jock' Dale as Number 1 on the weapon carried the useful 'bit of piping' and was armed with a .45 Colt automatic as his personal weapon, whilst

Pte Horne, as his Number 2, carried the bombs, twelve in all. Carried in two carriers, one in each hand, they consisted of ten HE (High Explosive) and two smoke bombs. These two characters were so different, inasmuch as Dale was a little Glaswegian with sharp features whilst Horne was a lot taller, came from a rural background in Staffordshire and had a ruddy complexion and features to match. But they were great mates, bound together by a common 'love' – their 2-inch mortar. They were keen to excel in its use and during the build-up for Cauldron they were able to get nine out of ten bombs in a square measuring 10 yards by 10 yards at a range of 250 yards – that being about the maximum ideal range. With such a crude weapon, where accuracy depended on handling only, there being no sights as such, this was quite an achievement and one that was to account, in no small measure, for the success of the subsequent operation.

I will leave the reader to judge for himself how rewarding was the outcome of the mortar training by quoting from one of the many books containing accounts of No 4 Commando's action. It succinctly records the final effect of our mortar fire:

> Troop Sergeant-Major Dunning, and Privates Dale and Horne, set up their mortars at the edge of the wood. The first bomb fell short, but the second bomb landed in the centre of the battery, they kept the same angle and the third bomb landed on the cordite charges and ready ammunition lying beside the guns. There was a blinding flash, a mighty explosion and Hess Battery never fired again.

The guns had been silenced by the crew of our 2-inch mortar, nevertheless the crews of the guns continued to fight hard, as was expected and for which Group 2 had particularly trained in close-quarter and hand-to-hand fighting.

Normally for an operation we had four Brens in the Troop, but for our specific role in Group 1 it was decided to increase our firepower with the addition of two extra Brens. This meant nominating two more Bren pairs (Nos 1 and 2). As we had all recently qualified on the Bren on the Ranges in Ayrshire mentioned above, we had no problems in selecting suitable candidates for the two extra LMGs. The priority for the training of the Bren gunners, who were to operate under the control of two Section Sergeants – three Brens apiece – was to practice movement over beach, up cliffs, across obstacles, including barbed wire, and move rapidly at the double, but staying together as a team, so that when near to the target area they could quickly and quietly get into firing positions, unseen, overlooking the Battery. The sergeants had to control the movement, select the ultimate fire positions, give the crucial fire orders, then control and coordinate the subsequent fire according to the development of the battle. The Nos 2 on each gun had to practice the reloading of magazines in the field and the collection of spare ammunition from the riflemen of the Troop. Fortunately facilities in the Lulworth area afforded the right opportunities for this training and plenty of realistic field firing.

In the planning of the operation it was appreciated there was no likelihood of No 4 Commando being counter-attacked by German tanks, so on this score alone there was no apparent job for the Boys A/Tk men. However, aerial photographs had revealed an armoured-protected Flak tower located to the eastern flank of the Battery, mounted with a heavy machine gun which could undoubtedly be depressed to fire in the ground defence role and thus might make life for us in Group 1 a bit uncomfortable. So Lord Lovat decided that we would take along our A/Tk rifle, with its armour-piercing ammunition, to deal with this obvious threat. Although we had a very good chap, 'Barney' Davies, already allocated to this weapon, there was in 'D' Troop, not fully committed to this operation, the best shot in the Commando on this unpopular and cumbersome weapon, Gunner McDonough, a tough, lean and dour Scotsman of average height but as strong as a bull. So we, in 'C' Troop, 'borrowed' him for the job and 'Barney' became his No 2. It was a good arrangement, they got on well together and we had the insurance if anything should happen to McDonough, we had 'Barney', capable and well-trained, to step – quite literally – into the breach. They set to in their individual training which included the carrying of some 60 rounds of armour-piercing ammunition, quite a load.

They too had a successful day on 19 August, when McDonough, together with his 'pal' Davies, took up a series of positions from which they engaged the Flak tower; they had to move frequently because the pronounced muzzle flash, although there was a flash eliminator, could give away their position if they remained static. They put the crew on the Flak tower out of action, much to the relief of an RAF sortie, and also engaged some other emplacements. McDonough fired over 50 rounds, and that on a weapon, with its vicious kick, was in itself no mean feat. But it was the successful outcome of his accurate firing that morning that was recognised with a well-earned Military Medal.

One of the problems facing Group 1 was ferrying the heavy 3-inch mortar and its ammunition ashore. The 3-inch mortar team consisted of one officer and ten other ranks. Lieutenant Jock Ennis had attracted a lot of publicity following the raid on Hardelot earlier in the year when he went ashore in his carpet slippers, and was subsequently nicknamed 'Carpet Slippers'.

To overcome the problem of wet landings in deep water they had experimented with a wide range of floats and rafts. These included a notable trial whilst we were aboard the *Prince Albert* at Portland. It was conducted by Mills-Roberts who had managed to get a float made of joined tubular containers, capable, in theory anyway, of floating when filled with weapons and/or ammunition. The trial attracted a highly interested, but somewhat bemused, audience from the rest of the Commando who lined the deck to see the fun.

The container was ready on deck filled albeit not with the precious Commando mortar, but with a corresponding weight-load made up of spare rifles and some ammunition. After due briefing, the four Commando swimmers, who were to tow the container in the water, jumped overboard in preparation to receive it. To avoid being hit they swam clear of the anticipated dropping zone of the container, which was then duly launched over the side of the ship. Tension mounted as the container sped downwards. There was an impressive splash as it hit the water, but with a spectacular spread of bubbles it promptly sank, much to the dismay and consternation of Mills-Roberts. His reaction was immediate and typical. He loudly bawled out, as he could well do, to the stand-by swimmers: 'Dive down and rescue the bloody thing.'

No sooner had they started to do so when to the relief of Mills-Roberts the container, to a rousing and ribald cheer from all the spectators on board, broke the surface of the water and stayed afloat, enabling the swimmers to easily tow it away. However, after all this drama, the 'brainchild' was not used as the mortar team managed to get another seaworthy float with a greater carrying capacity.

The training for Group 2 conformed to their plan of action. They were to land in two waves on their own beach. The first wave, A Troop, would clear the beach and destroy any enemy there or covering it, so as to allow a clear and speedy exit of the landing beach for the main assault party, led by Lord Lovat, of B and F Troops. They had the important and major task of moving inland across country 'with all possible speed' to a pre-determined concentration area, in a wood, from whence they would make their final assault on the Battery. Having consolidated on the Battery, the demolition party, provided by F Troop, would destroy the six guns with prepared 'tailor-made' charges. On completion of the destruction of the Battery, B and F Troops would withdraw through Group 1 to re-embark.

Meanwhile A Troop, having cleared the opposition on the beach were to cut all telephone wires on the coast road and inland to deny the enemy their use, then to move on to a selected road junction to intercept and destroy any reinforcing reserves moving to assist the Battery. Finally, they too would withdraw through Group 1 to re-embark.

So much for the broad outlines of the operational plan for Group 2. Translated into priorities for training it meant that, firstly, all the Group had to be 'battle fit', especially B and F Troops who had the 'cross-country run' to contend with before their final assault. All in those two Troops remember the 'before breakfast' runs and cross-country runs in 'raiding order' as a part, an important priority part, of the build-up to concert pitch for the operation. As Lovat later wrote, his aim in training was to get us to that pitch where, 'Every soldier would meet the events of the day like a trained athlete off his mark to the crack of the starting pistol. We were playing for high stakes. All knew it. But I held the cutting edge.'

Whereas in Group 1 the main emphasis, as the fire element, was on the Brens, rifles, mortars, Boys anti-tank rifle and the cup dischargers, at a range of 150-200 yards, in Group 2 they were going to be involved in offensive action, fighting at close quarters. The emphasis was therefore different, with the Thompson sub-machine carbine, the Bren and the rifle (and bayonet) plus the .45 colt automatic, all fired from the hip as required in the assault role and when mopping up the enemy in the built-up area of the Battery. In addition there was a need to perfect the throwing of the 36 grenade plus a new phosphorous smoke grenade, which was to to be used in action for the first time.

Firing practice concentrated on improvised snap and opportunity targets simulating the conditions to be met in the assault/mopping up. No such organized targets or ranges existed for this type of training in the Lulworth area, so once again improvization became the name of the game. Many rehearsals were required to coordinate the assault on the Battery because it included the dash from cover to the wire perimeter, then breach it by blowing gaps before making the final bayonet charge. This charge had to be coordinated with the lifting of the fire of Group 1 and was to be done by means of Very light signals fired by Lord Lovat, just prior to the assault.

Although the use of rabbit-wire netting and wire cutters was reckoned to be adequate for dealing with the wire on Group 2 beach, Bangalore torpedoes were considered necessary to blow the gaps quickly in the Battery wire. The Tommy gunners of B and F Troops were detailed to relieve and help the men carrying the Bangalore torpedoes, so that they could keep up with the rest.

The demolition men earmarked for the destruction of the Battery's six guns all came from F Troop, six of them, one for each gun. With one exception, Cpl John Skerry, they were all sappers. It so happened that when the Commando was reorganized into six Troops, instead of ten, in late 1940-early 1941, a number of the original RE volunteers ended up in F Troop. These stalwarts included 'Jock' McKay, who had recently been commissioned, Bill Portman, who has already been mentioned and was to win the Military Medal for his part in the demolition of the guns, and Jack Lillicoe. All regular soldiers and experienced demolitionists, they had also been on visits to local coastal gun sites and were familiar with the layout and parts of the guns, specifically taking note of the vulnerable parts and discussing how best to immobilize and destroy them. With gunners in each Troop they didn't lack any advice on the subject.

With this knowledge plus a thorough briefing on the enemy guns to be tackled, they were able to prepare their charges beforehand, and even use a mock-up to practice on with some dummy charges. The actual charges, each weighing some 20 lb, together with the fuses and other bits and pieces for the job, were to be carried in rucksacks and all were made up whilst we were still at Weymouth, prior to leaving to embark on *Prince Albert*, and stored under the watchful eyes of Sgts Bill Portman and Jack Lillicoe in a tea-chest until issued out to the other four when we were on board. How well they had done their homework regarding shape and size of the charges was aptly confirmed by Jock McKay as they placed them into the breaches of the enemy guns: 'They fit like a glove, just like a glove,' he declared with obvious pride and satisfaction.

Once the plan was finalized it was gone over time and time again, at all levels. This was done both on the ground and on a first-class model which had been constructed, to scale, by a specialized unit of the RAF. As a result we were all fully briefed. 'Everyone fully in the picture' was a constant aim in the Commandos, be it on a simple exercise or for an operation.

One aspect which is worth recalling is the detailed drill Captain Dawson had worked out for the phased withdrawal of 'C' Troop, who were to cover the withdrawal of the rest and provide protection on the beach until all had re-embarked. Like the other 'drills' this was progressively practised, firstly as a verbal outline together with a sketch plan, then as non-tactical movement over the ground without arms, next with arms, finally in full equipment and using smoke generators as part of the dress rehearsals. The basic principle behind this plan was to leapfrog the forward sections back to the bridgehead party on the cliff top, where they, in turn, would thin out to the beach below passing through the defenders there to re-embark. The beach defence being the last to leave. The plan depended on the extensive use of smoke – to deny the enemy observation of our movement and re-embarkation. In the final stages of the withdrawal we were to depend heavily on the use of the bulky No 18 smoke generators which were taken ashore by the beachhead party.

So far no mention has been made of the training regarding the communications to be used on the operation. As far as the Commando were concerned we were to keep wireless silence during the run-in to the beaches. Once ashore we had three means of communicating: wireless, Very light signals and runners. Generally speaking there wasn't any special training required on these accounts once the wireless operators had been allocated from the Commando Signals Section to the two Groups and everyone knew what the coloured Very light signals meant.

We did, however, have some outside personnel attached to us for the operation and they included a small detachment of specialist signallers from the 'Phantom' Signals Section, mentioned earlier in connection with David Niven. It is gratifying to record the comments made by Captain Sedgewick, in charge of the 'Phantom' signallers, on their training. In his final report after the operation he wrote: 'Morale was high before setting out . . . due to association with the Commandos, whose fighting morale was high and whose training was objective.'

During the final couple of days before the raid all the finishing touches were put to the preparations for the operation and Prince Albert sailed back to Southampton, whilst we returned to civilian billets once more in Weymouth, before joining the ship.

Even at this stage, although thoroughly briefed on the 'exercise', we still did not know the actual location of the raid. It wasn't until Lord Louis Mountbatten came on board to give us one of his stimulating pep talks that we knew for certain that the 'job' was on and where we were going. The die had then been cast. Lord Louis left us in no doubt that we had a vital role and we must destroy the Battery. He was confident that we would – and so were we.

After he left I spent a few quiet moments, alone on the deck of Prince Albert, which was tied up alongside Berth 103 of Southampton Docks, and reflected, because for me it was portentous to be here about to go on this venture for only about 1 1/2 miles away outside the Docks gates was my widowed mother completely unaware of my nearness or the operation I was about to embark upon. I took a long look in the direction of our house and home, took a deep breath, sighed and rushed off to join the rest of C

Troop on our mess deck. All the hard, but purposeful, training of the past three weeks was behind us. Within a few hours, by dawn on the morrow, it would all be put to the test.

Now all that remained was to carry out those last-minute pre-raid rituals already mentioned in connection with the preparations for the St Nazaire Raid: snatch a couple of hours sleep, have 'breakfast' at just after 0130 hours and dress ready for action. We wore denims and woollen cap comforters instead of steel helmets; most wore SV rubber-soled boots although some of Group 2 wore PT shoes, but everyone wore his deflated Mae West under his equipment.

Unlike No 2 Commando on their St Nazaire Raid, we had only a short journey on a midsummer's night so we didn't need to wear much in the way of top clothing, although we had gas capes to shelter us from any spray. We were to leave these capes in the LCAs prior to going 'down the ramps'. Once dressed ready for the fray, we synchronized watches, the password 'Monkey' and countersign, 'Nuts', were given to all and then off we went, almost automatically, in single file along those familiar gangways and up the stairs as we had done so many times during the past couple of weeks, out into the darkness and along the deck to our boat stations, there to clamber and struggle aboard the landing crafts in complete and disciplined silence to our allotted seats to await the lowering, then 'Splash!', and away to the beaches – and the Battery at Varengeville in occupied France. Once we were on our way we inflated our Mae Wests.

There, just at dawn, we started to put the aggregate of all our training, not just that of the recent days, to the real test. And it worked. Even better than we had hoped. The operation went off like a well-rehearsed exercise. We had anticipated casualties, indeed we were prepared and had made provision for them. Sadly they did occur, but they neither deterred us nor interfered with our progress and the successful completion of our task.

Mention has already been made of the fact that the action by No 4 Commando was the only success achieved by those who landed on Jubilee, and naturally we were justly proud of that success. Nevertheless in the midst of all the euphoria that was showered on the unit, we knew that although we part owed that success to sound planning and leadership, the major factor was purposeful training, with perfection as the ultimate aim.

This realization understandably gave everyone added confidence and morale rose even higher, albeit there could not be – nor was there – any room for that arch enemy of success, namely, complacency.

Indeed after a few days' leave the whole Commando was back in Troon and training once again, but not before we had a grand parade and inspection by Brigadier Laycock who read out various congratulatory messages, including one from King George VI. Arguably for most of us on that parade the highlight was wearing the famous green beret for the first time. We in No 4 on that day, 5 September 1942, were probably the first Commando to wear it. And if we were not – and we'd like to think that we were – we must have been a 'good second'.

CHAPTER VIII

Small Canoes and Thick Jungles – SBS and Burma

James Ladd, the historian of the Royal Marines, pays a handsome tribute, in the preface of SBS – the Invisible Raiders, to the Army Commandos who, under Roger Courtney, founded the Special Boat Section (SBS).

Although later in the Second World War other special canoe units were formed under the auspices of Combined Operations for certain specialized tasks and operations, e.g. the Combined Operations Pilotage Parties (COPPs) and the Royal Marines Boom Patrol Detachment (RMBPD), the concept of clandestine canoe landings launched from submarines and/or surface craft was instigated by Courtney in Scotland in 1940.

The story of his SBS is well recorded in various books, but none better than that written by Roger's younger brother, G.B. Courtney – SBS in World War Two. 'Gruf' Courtney was actually recruited by 'big brother', Roger, to serve in 2 SBS when it was being formed, after the successes of 1 SBS, in 1942. 'Gruf' had previously served in the West African Frontier Force, but 'the rocky hills of Palestine and a tendency to be overweight had contributed to fallen arches and route marches in West Africa finished them off,' he wrote and so he was posted to a Holding Battalion in England. Happily for him Roger came to his rescue with the offer of action and excitement with his SBS, because he reckoned 'Gruf' could fight the war on his bottom in a canoe irrespective of the state of his feet.

But before outlining some of the features of SBS training, a word or two about its founder.

Roger Courtney was 38 years old when he volunteered in 1940 for the Commandos, he had already had a most varied and adventurous life. Besides being a professional hunter and gold prospector in East Africa, he had served as a sergeant in the Palestine police and paddled down the river Nile 'with a sack of potatoes and an elephant spear, which was all he owned at the time'. In short he was an adventurer, a wild man, but had that magnetism and cheerful courage that enabled him to become an inspiring and tremendous leader of men in war. Furthermore, he had the

determination and resolution to pursue ideas and aims regardless of set-
backs and frustrations, be they from natural circumstances or from his
superiors in the services. He lived hard in peace and war, and was to die
soon after the War at the early age of 47 years working for Desert Locust
Control in East Africa.

How he came to sell his concept of clandestine raiding in canoes is a
lovely wartime story and is typical of the man. It was while his Commando
was at Inveraray undergoing amphibious training from the assault ship
Glengyle in the autumn of 1940, training similar to that described in
Chapter IV.

Previous to this spell of training Courtney had already voiced his theory
of using canoes, launched from submarines, for raiding. Indeed, it is most
likely that he joined the Commandos with the idea of propounding this
concept, and by the time his Commando arrived at Inveraray he had
already persuaded his CO to let him experiment with a canoe.

So when the 'boss' of the Commandos, Sir Roger Keyes, visited the
lochside town to watch No 8 undergoing training Roger Courtney boldly
took the opportunity, with the blessing of his CO, to present his theory to
Keyes. In fact, Courtney not only outlined his ideas but typically issued a
challenge, in that he and his partner canoeist would attack the Glengyle at
night and then make good their escape without being detected; in
addition they would bring back evidence of their nocturnal visit. The
challenge was accepted by the Admiral.

Courtney duly carried out his 'raid' which was highly successful. He
reached the ship unseen and unheard, left marks (representing limpet
mines) on the hull; Courtney even got on board, climbing hand over hand
up the anchor chain, and managed to take the covers of two Oerlikon
guns, plus their breech blocks, as evidence.

Sir Roger was impressed but not quite convinced, so he in turn issued a
counter challenge, namely Courtney should carry out a further canoe
attack on a submarine depot ship. In this exercise 'raid' Courtney and
partner managed to successfully attack the ship, leaving chalk marks above
the waterline, but trying to board the ship to exploit this success they were
detected and captured.

Notwithstanding Sir Roger conceded that these two mock attacks had
clearly illustrated the potential effectiveness of canoeists and granted
Courtney permission, with his blessing, to form one Folboat Section of
Commando canoeists. It was later envisaged that each Commando would
have a similar section, or even a Troop of canoeists, but with the
exception of 101 Troop (No 6 Commando) this was never realized.

Late 1940 saw the birth of 101 Troop and the Special Boat Section who were to carry out small raids and attacks on enemy shipping using canoes. This early photo shows the first type of canoe used and also reveals the absence of any special clothing for the canoeists. (Photograph by courtesy of the Imperial War Museum.)

And so in the autumn of 1940 the SBS was born and started training in the windswept and often hostile waters of the Clyde and sea waters off the Isle of Arran. Initially, Courtney had to base his training and the development of techniques solely on his peacetime experiences and his limited military knowledge. There were no manuals or experienced instructors on this type of clandestine amphibious raiding to guide Courtney. It was yet again the case of a Commando volunteer pioneering, guided by his own vision and fuelled by determination.

Courtney's first canoes were not really suitable for war. They were recreational canoes manufactured by the Folboat Company, constructed of rubberized canvas on a wooden frame, capable of a good speed in calm waters but not strong enough for combating rough water and swells, neither were they capable of accommodating the weapons, navigational aids and stores required for raiding. Nevertheless, they were the only ones available. So pressed into service they were given the official title of Cockle Mark 1*. Because of this the canoes are referred to – often confusing the reader – by either of the following names: 'Folboat' or

'Cockle'. The later name, of course, gave rise to the popular cognomen, 'Cockleshell Heroes', for those who carried out the famous Bordeaux Raid in 1942.

The navigational aids consisted of an aircraft compass and 'makeshift' arrangements for charts, maps and a parallel rule. Whilst the weapons, magazines and grenades were stowed on the floor or held between the legs of the paddler.

As a result of training experiences, an improved canoe, the Cockle Mark 1** was built and supplied, and was so successful it remained the main operational canoe for the rest of the War.

Notwithstanding the SBS did experiment with and subsequently use, both in training and operations, other small surface and submersible craft. Prominent among these were the motor-powered Mark VI canoe, the 18-foot Dory, the 20-foot Surf Boat, the ubiquitous rubber inflatables, the Motor Submersible Canoe (fondly nicknamed 'Sleeping Beauty') and the Welman Submersible, the latter two being favoured for attacking harboured enemy vessels with limpet charges. In addition the SBS also took opportunities to adapt and use local craft wherever applicable, notably in the Far East. So much for the canoes and other small craft.

Nowadays, in an age of 'wet suits' and other sophisticated sub-aqua clothing and equipment it seems inconceivable that Courtney and his pioneer canoeists braved those wintry conditions off the west coast of Scotland in just their standard-issue battledress blouses and trousers, issued woollen underclothing, army boots or plimsoles and the woollen stockingette 'cap comforter'. They had no special clothing. Attempts were made to coat the BD with heavy greases, but this did not prove satisfactory. Later in 1941/42 'Tropal' clothing of blue, kapok-filled blouses and trousers was introduced and the kapok lining provided a degree of buoyancy when the canoeists took to the water – for any reason.

Of course, when in the Mediterranean and in the Far East, where it was warmer, the ordinary tropical khaki drill clothing could suffice, although there were plenty of times when warmer clothing was needed. Eric Newby, the famous travel writer served in the SBS in the Middle East in the Second World War. Of his training there he recalls: 'Learning to sink ships involved swimming at night in the Bitter Lakes (in Egypt) – which certainly lived up to their name in the depths of winter – covered with grease and wearing long woollen naval issue underwear...'

Footwear was a problem suffered by all the Commandos on amphibious operations. The standard ammunition boots were hardly suitable for boating of any kind, and although plimsoles were better in canoes and on board larger craft, they squelched when full of water and were unsuitable for long marches on landing. Experiments were carried out in the winter of 1940 with rope-soled boots and these were quite useful for the SBS, but not so for the rest of the Commandos. The SBS also used a type of rubberized lace-up calf-length boot, which was quite light yet robust. From 1942 onwards the SBS also had available the SV (Soulier-Vebrun) Boot. Robust and comfortable to wear, this multi-purpose boot was ideal for most Commando roles. It has stood the test of time and appropriately is still known as the 'Commando' boot.

Captain Jimmy Foot who joined the SBS after their first tour in the Middle East recalls his recruitment and initial training. He volunteered for the Commandos, not specifically for the SBS, but when he attended the interview board Roger Courtney was one of its members. He asked Jim if he had any experience in small boats and, true to form, whether he had been in the Boy Scouts.

Jim had done some sailing pre-war on the Dorset coast and so was able to answer in the affirmative. But he hadn't been a Boy Scout, albeit, told Courtney he had played lots of 'Cowboys and Indians' on the iron-age camp, Maiden Castle, near Dorchester, as a lad and this had involved a lot of cunning fieldcraft tactics!

Courtney was satisfied and Jim was in. This was before all new entries for the Commandos had to pass the Achnacarry course, so he joined SBS direct when they were then based in the Ardrossan-Saltcoats area on the Ayrshire coast of west Scotland. As was normal the SBS were billeted in civilian accommodation and received the usual subsistence allowances like the rest of the other Commando units.

By this time the SBS and 101 Troop had been on operations, the SBS in the Mediterranean and 101 Troop raiding on the French coast.

By the end of 1941, however, with the principles of clandestine operations carried out by the SBS well and truly established, Roger Courtney returned to the UK from the Middle East to form a second SBS unit, No 2 SBS. This was raised by absorbing the personnel of 101 Troop, calling for specialist volunteers from the other Commandos and the recruiting of likely new volunteers, such as Jimmy Foot.

Among the volunteers from existing Commandos were a couple of my old mates from the earliest days of No 4 at Weymouth. Trooper M, Smithson was in our original F Troop and had taken part in the first Lofoten Raid, and Cpl Charles King, a strong, upright Guardsman, who had been on the Dieppe Raid. It was ironic to think that Smithson, who came from the Royal Tank Regiment, having been taught to fight from within the solid protective shell of a tank, should set off, after his SBS training, to fight the Japs from within the flimsy confines of a rubberized canvas canoe.

In the spring of 1942 the training of No 2 SBS started with this mixture of 'old and new hands'. Fortunately, as the manning of their main little craft, the canoe, only required a crew of two, the pattern was easily and logically solved by pairing one experienced canoeist with a novice.

Jimmy was paired with Sgt Hutchison, an original volunteer in No 6 Commando and a member of 101 Troop. 'Jock' Hutchison, therefore, became Foot's instructor and mentor, although he was subordinate in rank.

Courtney's training philosophy was simple and forthright. The first priority was first-class seamanship and handling of the canoe. This necessitated paddling the canoe in all kinds of seas, building up the physical and mental stamina to carry out long paddles, navigation in the dark, and mastering the tricky business of transferring from the parent craft (submarine or surface craft) at sea in the dark to the canoe, and subsequently getting back on board.

And finally training for operations, be they a demolition attack on a vessel or a land target, the 'snatch' of an enemy prisoner, a beach reconnaissance, and the landing or bringing back of an agent.

With all this in mind, the main part of the SBS recruit's initial training was spent in paddling canoes. Initially, the 'paddles' were carried out in daylight, then at night, building up to 'paddles' of as much as eight hours in the sea. The rest of the training was given over to specific subjects relevant to the particular role of SBS. Weapon training was limited to personal small arms. Understandably, physical training excluded marches, emphasis being on upper body, shoulder and arm strengthening exercises and agility; also important was instruction on navigation, panorama sketching, beach reconnaissances, signalling, the use of explosives and 'living off the land'.

The initial training concluded with a final 'bender', designed to test the canoe pairs in all aspects of the SBS role, lasting up to 72 hours. It usually involved a night paddle, a landing and concealment of canoe, a 'lay-up' by day, then a night recce or an exercise mission, return to canoe and paddle off to the pick-up point. To add realism to the exercise the Home Guard or other regular troops were alerted to be on the lookout for the SBS raiders.

At the end of their basic SBS training some canoe teams (including Foot and his No 2) were sent to the Submarine Flotilla Base, HMS Forth, in the Holy Loch by Dunoon. Here they were housed on the Depot Ship for subsequent attachment to one of the flotilla's submarines for more advanced training.

Taking their canoes and handling them to the launch position on the exterior casing of the sub was tricky and required much practice and patience, as 'Gruf' Courtney describes:

> Getting into and out of a folboat from the forecasting of a trimmed-down submarine . . . with a sea running required no mean agility and a cool head. The painter (the line from the bow of a canoe) and the stern line would be in the hands of two naval ratings. It was important that they allow the canoe to float free with the swell. If the lines were drawn tight, it would capsize. Care was also taken not to allow it to ride too near the foreplanes in case it was swept under them and smashed. It took nice judgement to step into the centre of a canoe as it surged against the casing and to collapse oneself onto the bottom before one fell overboard. Then grasp the paddles and away clear before settling down for a long haul to the beach.

One of the major problems on the final run-in to land was the danger of capsizing in surf. It needed special training and also it was essential to have a practised drill to get upright and on board if the canoe did capsize. Surf was to be a problem experienced by Jimmy Foot and his comrades when they took the American General Mark Clark and his party ashore for a secret meeting near Algiers, prior to Operation Torch, in October 1942.

One of the practices developed to aid navigation during the paddle-in from a submarine to the landing beach was the making of a periscope sketch. During daylight, whilst the submarine was lying off the selected beach prior to the raid, the SBS canoeists would examine the shoreline through the periscope from as near inshore as was safe. A panorama sketch in silhouette of the terrain, noting the outstanding features, was made and then committed to memory for use that night. The beauty of this sketch was that, being made from sea level, i.e. through the periscope, it afforded a like picture as would be seen by the canoeists in their low-lying craft. Such sketching was a basic, but unusual aspect, part of SBS training undertaken during the attachments to a submarine flotilla.

On landing the drill taught during training was to carry the canoe immediately to cover, previously selected, camouflage and hide it, making sure it was facing out to sea and with the paddles ready for a rapid getaway. The question of ensuring a suitable onshore hiding place was a vital part of the outline plan for any mission and a great influencing factor on the choice of landing beach.

The seaward withdrawal after a landing was a testing time, fraught with anxieties and obvious dangers from both the enemy onshore and their surface craft offshore. But it wasn't just the risks from the enemy the SBS had to face. Although the commanders and crews of the submarines and surface craft supporting the SBS would – and did – take, what Courtney describes as, 'appalling risks to pick us up after an operation', all had to accept the fact that the SBS raiders were regarded as expendable. The safety of the submarine and its crew was more important.

Initially, in the early days, communications between the canoeists and the pick-up were rudimentary and consisted of nothing more than shaded (red or blue) flashes or some morse code signals from a hand torch, the only directional navigating aid being a compass bearing on an ordinary army prismatic compass.

However, methods of communicating and homing improved so that the SBS eventually had reciprocal homing devices that, as Gruf put it, allowed 'Mother' to appear out of the mist to pick them up.

One fundamental and obvious aspect of SBS training not yet mentioned was, of course, swimming. Potential volunteers for the SBS were expected to be able to swim (on front and/or back) for a mile, clothed, wearing equipment plus a weapon, albeit wearing an inflatable Mae West. They were tested during the early days of training. Swimming was in the sea and in local swimming baths. Initially, personal weapons included rifles but these were soon found unsuitable and too clumsy and were replaced with TSMGs and Colts. Later some Lugers were issued.

After their training with submarines on the Clyde, Jimmy Foot and the others in No 2 SBS travelled south to Hillhead on the Hampshire coast for continuation training on the Solent. This new base was also conveniently near HMS *Dolphin*, the submarine base at Gosport. (Today the Submarine Museum and HMS *Alliance* – a Second World War sub – are in Gosport and here one can see items connected with the wartime exploits of the SBS.)

Being located in the Hillhead area – permanently alerted to the possibility of enemy intrusions – the SBS had plenty of opportunities to test their skills and techniques against regular and Home Guard defence units and also to carry out realistic exercises across the Solent on the Isle of Wight.

However, one important sea condition lacking on the Solent was surf, so to rectify this deficiency detachments were dispatched to the Padstow area in Cornwall, where 'good' surf abounds. There, under the watchful and demanding eye of a Merchant Navy officer, an expert on 'surf', they underwent advanced training in navigation and night exercises contending with surf and Atlantic rollers. As it happened they also had to contend with another trial, winter weather, for it was December and not an ideal time to capsize in the sea.

Most of the post-war publicity and stories of the SBS's exploits in the Second World War tend to be focussed on their operations in Europe and the Middle East and it is not widely appreciated that they were much involved in the Far East, as were other Commandos.

It was not until early 1944 that units of Commandos arrived in the Far East, although individual Commando Officers and NCOs had previously been posted to special units, including the Chindits, to help with training and also to take part in the long-range penetration operations initiated by General Orde Wingate.

I well remember two such volunteers who went from No 4 – both distinguished themselves in jungle operations. Of Lieutenant Geoffrey Lockett, Seaforth Highlanders, the following description aptly fits the subaltern I knew in D Troop, 'the toothless kilted wonder — sometimes he had teeth and sometimes he hadn't ... he was always taking snuff'. In fact, in No 4 we gave him the nickname of 'snuff-shunter' and his moustache was frequently speckled with it. The other, Sgt 'Jock' Blain, was an original volunteer for No 4, a fine and capable regular NCO. He became frustrated with all the cancelled operations during the closing months of 1940 and, when we were incarcerated on the Isle of Arran over that Christmas, 'employed a wily stratagem' to board the ferry at Lamlash and go AWOL on the mainland. He returned to Arran a few days later in a rowing boat he had 'borrowed'. Given the option of facing a court martial or accepting the CO's judgement, he chose the latter. Reduced to the ranks, he begged to stay in No 4, promising to be 'a good boy'. His request was granted; such was his ability and worth as a senior NCO and weapon training instructor, he quickly won back his three lost stripes.

These two Commandos were not the only ones to help Wingate with the training of his Chindits – there were others and all went with him on his initial long-range penetration raid into Burma.

Blain became 'Mad Mike' Calvert's company sergeant major; his bravery and marksmanship won him the DCM; later he was commissioned and promoted to Major to command a special reconnaissance unit. Lockett also fought in that campaign with distinction winning the Military Cross and promotion to Major.

The first Chindit expedition was – in spite of casualties and suffering – a considered success, not so much for strategic reasons, but because it proved beyond doubt that Allied forces – regardless of their backgrounds, and even if they lacked previous battle experience – were capable of destroying the myth that the Jap was an invincible, super, jungle fighter.

Although training for irregular warfare in the jungle had been initiated by Wingate with the help of Commando officers and NCOs, no UK-raised Commandos saw action in the Far East until the dispatch of No 3 Commando Brigade (Nos 1, 5, 42 (RM) and 44 (RM) Commandos) to India over the period December 1943/January 1944.

It is therefore interesting to follow the training for jungle warfare as experienced by one of these Commandos, to wit No 1. It was typical of all four.

This Commando was in Winchester towards the end of 1943 when the call came for the overseas posting; some months earlier they had returned from North Africa where they had fought with distinction in the Tunisian campaign of 1942-3.

In expressing his gratitude to the Commando when they left that theatre of war, General Eisenhower, in a personal letter to the CO, Lieutenant Colonel Trevor, wrote, inter-alia:

> You and the men whom you command have been identified with the Tunisian campaign since the very day on which the initial landings were made. Since then you have been engaged actively on the most difficult mountainous terrain of the entire front.
>
> As the time draws near for your departure from this theatre, it is a real pleasure for me to express to you and your gallant men commendations for a job well done. You have exemplified those rugged, self-reliant qualities which the entire world associates with the very name 'Commando'.

That last sentence says it all, but the unit paid a high price in losses and as a result when it arrived back in this country was much depleted. In his book, *Commando Diary*, Tag Barnes MM, a veteran of No 1, recalls those days in Winchester as a period of the three 'R's – reinforcements, re-equipping and retraining.

The training at Winchester followed the normal Commando programme: early morning runs and PT, intensive weapon training, unarmed combat sessions, field firing, 48-hour exercises, night training, and being near to the sea they took the opportunity to do some canoeing on the river Itchen and Southampton Water. The later activities were incorporated into overnight exercises. Some of the Commando managed to get away to North Wales for training under the watchful and experienced eye of the Everest mountaineer, Frank Smythe where they tackled several climbs on Tryfan and other mountains of Snowdonia.

Colonel Ken Trevor remembers that having been detailed for the Far East they were, fortuitously, able to do a spot of appropriate 'jungle style' training in the nearby New Forest, but it was short-lived as they were soon on their way on the long sea voyage to India. En route they spent some thirty-six days at a desert camp near Alexandria in Egypt. This unplanned sojourn was entirely due to their troopship, *Ranchi*, being bombed in the Mediterranean and having to be repaired before they could continue. At this desert camp training consisted, mainly, of marches and other physical activities, including plenty of sport.

The Commando eventually left Egypt in January 1944 and just over a fortnight later arrived in Bombay. Their initial jungle training was in the area around Belgaum in Central India, which boasted some of the thickest forest in the sub-continent, ideal for this type of training.

What is clear from the personal accounts of those in No 1 is that the basic requirement for their training was one of adapting to the climate, terrain and the inherent problems of health.

Vic Ralph, a trainee in my Haydon Commando at Achnacarry, who joined No 1 to see action in Burma, wrote: 'Regarding our training in the Far East, it was really only adapting what we had learned at Achnacarry and onward, and acclimatising to the conditions none of us had previously experienced.'

'Know your enemy' too was a vital factor in the initial training, so lectures on the Jap and his methods were prominent in the initial stages. It was a prerequisite to appreciate that even after mastering the testing environment of the jungle there was still a formidable enemy to destroy.

As for the jungle, Tag Barnes writes:

> The jungle was exactly as one had seen it on films at the cinema, except the high tree canopy proved to be so dense it blotted out most of the sun's rays, thus creating a twilight effect throughout the day. However, the rest was all there, the towering trees hanging in vines, the whistling and screeching of birds and animals, day and night, the monsoon beetles whined through the trees in their thousands.

There was only one way to master these conditions, namely, living and training both day and night in the densest parts – and for days at a time.

Because of the obvious nature of the jungle and the Japanese tactics it was essential to appreciate the need to dig protective and weapon pits – nothing else would ensure survival. Again Tag Barnes emphasizes this basic need:

> When training began properly it consisted first of digging weapon pits and

trenches, morning, noon and night, appearing to be a mindless occupation, but was apparently something that would need to be done regularly once we got into action. It was hard work toiling in the oppressive heat ever present in the closed-in atmosphere that existed under the trees. We often had to 'stand-to' in our weapon pits while another troop would try to penetrate our defences, and the exercise would be repeated with our troop playing the attacking role.

All the slit trenches were made for two men, sleeping at the bottom and with overhead cover for protection against grenades and shrapnel. Under these conditions the troops had to depend on mess-tin cooking.

Digging-in was never easy as Henry Brown recalls, 'it was pretty nigh impossible to dig-in due to the awful mangrove roots which defied our efforts with just entrenching tools'.

During their training in India the Commandos devised a standard drill for the taking up of a defensive position wherein good and quickly dug slit trenches were a fundamental factor. It was essential to site them to provide all-round defence. In so doing the Japs were denied any opportunity to outflank the defences or infiltrate the Commando position. This defensive layout was appropriately known as a 'Commando Box'; although it was not always of four straight sides.

Ken Trevor describes a typical 'Commando Box', but this time forming a circle:

The concentrated camouflaged defensive circle was about 100 to 150 yards in diameter, depending on the thickness of the jungle or the type of terrain. The fighting (rifle) Troops occupied the perimeter, the arcs of fire of the subsections were so co-ordinated as to overlap. In the centre was located the Reserve Troop and the Headquarters. It was set up by Troop officers pacing out and using a compass to form the defensive circles.

As he reports, the 'Box' had many obvious defensive advantages but 'the unpleasant thing was that a section, or sub-section, could receive the full weight of a Jap attack. This is what happened at Kangaw on Hill 170 when Lieut George Knowland won his Victoria Cross.'

Tag Barnes remembers an alternative layout based on the same principles of all round defence with close mutual fire support from well-dug pits. This time it was triangular in shape with only three rifle Troops occupying the three sides. At each point of the triangle was sited one of the Commandos' Vickers machine guns; spaced around the three (short) sides were, in all, fifteen Bren guns, twenty-seven Tommy guns, six EY rifles (they ejected Mills grenades) plus the rifles. Incidentally, No 1 still retained the US Garand automatic rifles they had been issued with for the North African landings, and the firepower of these weapons greatly enhanced that of the 'Box'.

Vic Ralph aptly comments: 'The Commando Box was really based on the old infantry square, providing all round protection with all groups near enough to be in close contact – hearing and seeing – with their neighbours.'

The Commando spent many hours under all types of weather and terrain conditions preparing such positions and then rehearsing the 'Stand-to' so that on their first excursion into action, when they had finished preparing their defensive 'Box', prayers were offered that the enemy would pay a visit during the night to test the whole layout. Each day at dawn and dusk everyone 'stood-to' in their position, whilst during the night one man in each pit or small group would, in turn, be 'on stag' – listening and watching.

Allied to the 'Box' defence were warning devices, obstacles and booby traps.

In the absence of more sophisticated booby traps the Commando prepared 'Panjis'. Lengths of bamboo were cut and sharpened to a point at each end. Stuck into the ground at a slope, or concealed in a camouflage trench on approaches they served as a nasty deterrent.

Frequently, however, both in training and action the odd wild animal would set off the 'alarms'. Within seconds all were alerted – with fingers on triggers or grenades at the ready. Such false alarms, however, were not only frustrating but resulted in lost hours' of sleep and rest.

Another important feature of the training was compass marching, with the faithful standard prismatic compass. Although this was no novelty, it was more laborious and irksome in the jungle when a pathway would invariably have to be cut through the dense undergrowth.

Not all the time was spent in jungle training for the Commandos did have welcome opportunities to carry out some amphibious training at 'a horrible place' called Cocanada near the coast on the Bay of Bengal.

There, living conditions were terrible; although the camp looked idyllic there were serious health problems. Malaria and dysentery were rife, in addition there were skin disorders. Learning to combat these health and hygiene problems was a vital and important factor in the training. Fortunately for the Commandos, by the time they had arrived medical resources for fighting these diseases and ailments had greatly improved and normally they received a daily ration of the three necessary tablets, namely, anti-malaria (mepacrine), vitamin 'C' and salt.

'The mepacrine tablets,' writes Henry Brown, 'were a boon against the dreaded malaria – in fact many of us after a month or so were almost as yellow as the tablets, but they did the trick.'

After the campaign in Burma, Lord Mountbatten, Supreme Allied Commander in South-East Asia, was able to proclaim that he was able to count malaria as an ally because his troops, with their tablets to combat the disease, were able to fight and move in mosquito-infested areas, whereas the Japs were not.

However, in spite of these shortcomings training round Cocanada continued unabated – assault landings, attacks on mock pillboxes and defences, extended exercises involving long inland marches by day, and by night, usually drenched to the skin by teeming rain accompanied by violent storms.

It was whilst No 1 was training in Cocanada that they heard the news of the Normandy invasion and of the landings of their comrades in the two Commando Brigades there. As they listened they wondered, after six months training in India, when they would be called to put it all to the test in Burma.

They had worked hard adapting to the new set of operational conditions, and reckoned they were now ready for any type of operation in this theatre of war.

Finally, after a mixture of smaller operations, the whole brigade took part in the Arakan campaign where their heroic stand on Hill 170 at Kangaw was a decisive factor in that campaign and their action is reckoned to have hastened the end of the fighting there by several weeks.

It was a fitting and gratifying climax to months of demanding jungle training and once again the opinion was expressed, this time by 'Tag' Barnes, that 'the mind and body exercises endured (during this training) were often more gruelling than the real thing . . .'

CHAPTER IX

Snow, Mountains and Surf

A little-known Commando training unit was responsible during its wartime lifespan, 1942 to 1945, for diverse programmes of training and preparing Commandos for operations in snow, mountains, cliff assaults rocky landings and the handling of small craft and canoes for coastal raids. Such were the versatile roles of a small unit of instructors which began its life as the Commando Snow and Mountain Warfare Training Camp (CSMWTC) in the mid-winter of 1942. It has continued to exist ever since, although under different ownership. Today, some fifty-eight years after its founding it has a dual training and operational role – as ultimately did its original predecessor, an unusual combination for a training establishment – as the Brigade Patrol Troop of 3 Royal Marines Commando Brigade, still specializing in snow and mountain warfare and also in cliff assaults.

The first of the major changes in the role of the original CSMWTC came when the emphasis on 'snow' was dropped from training – and the title – and the unit moved from Braemar in Scotland to Llanwryst in North Wales to become the Commando Mountain Warfare Training Camp (CMWTC) concentrating on mountain warfare, mountaineering and rock climbing.

Then came a further and final change of emphasis – occasioned by strategic planning – and a move from the mountains of North Wales to the rocky coastline of Cornwall. In spite of a different role the CMWTC title was retained, apparently for security reasons . . .

Specialized operations in mountainous terrain and cliff assaults had been visualized from the onset as suitable subjects to include in Commando training, but for several reasons these topics did not enjoy a high priority during 1940 and early 1941, although there were exceptions.

One of the exceptions was No 5 Commando where, thanks to an enthusiast of rock climbing, a 'climbing Troop' had been designated. In this case as so often happened – it was due to the specific Troop Leader, Captain Geoffrey Rees-Jones, who was also a pre-war Welsh international rugby player. Fortunately No 5 Commando was based in Falmouth, not far

163

from the excellent climbing opportunities on the Lands End peninsula. Rees-Jones soon had his Troop climbing, and such was their prowess that later some of his men became instructors at CMWTC whilst he, himself, ultimately became CO.

During 1941, however, due to a policy switch at HQ Combined Operations from small-scale to large-scale raids and the consequent whole-Commando involvement in training exercises, there were very few opportunities for further Troop training in rock climbing. Nevertheless, in September 1941, after No 4 Commando was taken off a proposed large-scale operation in the Canaries, opportunities returned for more specialized Troop training.

I had just taken over as TSM of C Troop when Captain Robert Dawson, our Troop Leader, persuaded Lord Lovat to allow our Troop to go mountaineering and rock climbing in Snowdonia, with a view to us becoming the Commando's specialist Climbing Troop.

Robert loved the mountains and had some pre-war experience of mountaineering, although it didn't amount to much. Prior to the large-scale exercises mentioned above he had managed to send some of our NCOs on climbing courses informally organized in the Glencoe area and on the Isle of Skye. As a result, at the time of our departure for training in Snowdonia, we did have four 'qualified' climbing instructors, Sgts Langlands, McCarthy, Lindley and Bend. The latter had also been to Iceland on an excellent snow-warfare course and had become, among related subjects, an expert on building igloos.

In North Wales we based ourselves in the slate-village of Bethesda. Finding billets, with the aid of 'Sergeant Jones – Police', was no problem. We also took over a couple of empty shops for Troop Headquarters and Stores.

The first task was to adapt our ordinary boots for climbing, so they were, under Sgt McCarthy's supervision, studded with tricounis and clinkers on apses, borrowed from the village cobbler. Hemp ropes, spring clips and other climbing paraphernalia joined our stores of weapons, ammunition and other items in one of the vacated shops.

With preliminaries completed we set off for Tryfan, a recognized climbers' mountain which towers above Lake Ogwin in the Nant Ffancon pass, about 5 miles from Bethesda. On the rocks at the foot of Tryfan, unencumbered with equipment and weapons, we started our 'scrabbling and bouldering' and were introduced to the techniques of climbing with ropes, in teams of three. It was a pleasant prelude to the more serious climbing that followed.

C Troop climbing in North Wales

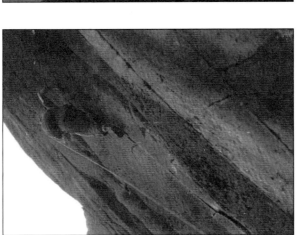

Left, No 1 of a team of three climbers leads the way on the Idwal slabs Centre, abseiling on Mt Tryfan. Right, L/Cpl Shearing, No 3 climber, crossing over to the Belle Vue Terrace, some 1,500 feet up, on Mt Tryfan.

Tackling 'moderate' climbs – as defined in the *Climbers' Club of Great Britain Guide to Wales* (1937 edition) – followed. All the climbing was supervised by Sgt Geoff Langlands, a short, wiry and bespectacled 'academic' wartime soldier, who had been a schoolteacher in Bristol before the War. Geoff was a natural climber and after a couple of years in No 4 Commando later left for a commission in the Indian Army and subsequently, after the War, stayed in Pakistan dividing his time between teaching at Atchison College and climbing mountains.

Initially as we had only four qualified climbing instructors, actual instruction on the rock face was limited, because each instructor could only cope with just three trainees. Consequently we had to organize a rota system, so those not actually rock climbing spent their days mountaineering/fell walking on such scenic routes as Pen-y-Pass, Crib Goch, Carnedds Llewellyn and Dafydd and ascents along different routes up to the summit of Snowdon. On these expeditions we usually wore Battle Order, took all our Troop weapons and invariably did some field firing or practical map-reading.

My first real climb was on the Holly Tree Route on Tryfan which rated in the guide book as a 'moderate' climb. With the aid of a modern guide book I was recently able to recall that first climb. It started with some fairly easy climbing – rated 'hardly more than a scramble' – before more difficult climbing on two exposed slabs to reach the famous holly tree itself; then followed two tricky pitches until (with a feeling of satisfaction, plus a sigh of relief) a further easy scramble to reach the summit.

Before tackling such a climb we were taught the use of the appropriate knots for climbing roped together. As a drill we climbed in teams of three, using hemp ropes (nylon ropes had yet to make their debut) and always, with only one man climbing at a time, the pay-out or run-out of rope varied according to the 'pitch' of the climb from 20 to 40 feet. The 'waist line' and a couple of spring clip karabiners was almost the sum total of our climbing equipment; we had none of the modern luxuries of harnesses, racks, and bags of chalk.

Within a couple of days we were all familiar with the jargon of climbers with 'traverses, belays, cracks, buttresses, walls, chocks, overhangs and chimneys' rolling off our tongues as though we had been climbing all our lives.

Although I had done a lot of mountain walking, often along steep precipitous tracks, I was surprised to discover that I would not make a natural climber and leader. I didn't like clinging to the rock face, like a fly, with exposures of hundreds of feet below me. Nevertheless, in spite of not aiming to be a leader I was quite happy to be number 2 or 3 in the team. Such was the confidence I had in the leaders and the rest of the teams. This mutual confidence was, of course, a basic and fundamental factor for successful climbing.

This personal discovery became apparent climbing with Sgt McCarthy on Tryfan's 'Milestone Buttress'. Albeit, I managed to conceal my innermost feelings as I followed Mac's patient instructions. A tough, hard-bitten 'Scouse', he might have guessed how I felt, and could have extracted 'the urine out of me', especially as I was his Sergeant Major, but he didn't. And to this day I don't know if he did have any inkling how I was feeling or not. In any event we all had our moments of apprehension on those climbs, but pride prevented us from disclosing them.

Some of the chaps took to climbing quickly and readily, and were soon capable of being further trained as leaders on the easier climbs. They included one or two surprises, such as 'Taffy' Andrews, a perky fresh-faced youngster with curly sand-coloured hair from a valley in South Wales. Nimble footed and as agile as a mountain goat, he rapidly developed into a first-class climber and leader; because of this newly found ability he was promoted to junior NCO. There is no doubt in my mind that his continued responsible role in the Troop had its beginning in Snowdonia. It is worthwhile mentioning that frequently in climbing the leader was junior to others in the team, and as such gave the orders for the climb. This was universally accepted by all ranks and never presented any problems.

Joe Martin was another whose true capabilities came to light in Snowdonia. Of medium height with fine facial features, he hailed from a tin-mining area in Cornwall. Although devoid of climbing experiences or indeed mining, he soon became another of the Troop's star performers. Steady, cautious but capable, Joe exuded confidence as he mastered a tricky pitch. Then after securing his belay, he called up No 2 with clear reassuring directions in his calm and softly-spoken Cornish drawl, 'Move your left foot along to that crack there . . . about eighteen inches to the left . . . Yes, that's it . . . good . . . now, your right hand up to that chock stone just above your head . . . OK' and so on until with a final little haul, No 2 was alongside, the slack rope taken in, a new belay made, and all was set to call up No 3.

It was interesting to note in the historical notes of the post-war editions of the *Climber's Guide to North Wales* mention of our climbing activities. It comes in a reference to the late 1930s: 'then a quiet descended on the Cwm until the War broke out and mountain troops started training here.

Then the noise of mock battles echoed between rock bastions and hollows. The clank of nailed boots as Commandos toughened up, but their scrape on the easy and hard climbs fined down the holds . . . until hard rubber soled boots were introduced.'

So there we have it. The reference to the hard rubber soles obviously relates to the Soulier Vebrun (SV) boots we were issued with from 1942 onwards. They were excellent all-purpose boots, good for silent approaches on metalled roads as well as for rock and cliff climbing and coping with those wet slippery boat decks.

When Troops were detached from their Commando Headquarters and base – such as our three weeks' sojourn at Bethesda – they were burdened with some extra administrative chores including organizing transport and billets, arrangements for weekly pay and ration cards, medical cover and secure storage of weapons, ammunition etc. The Troop Leader was granted, under the relevant legal authority contained in King's Regulations, modified powers of a Commanding Officer regarding punishments and fines. He was also appointed as an 'Imprest Holder', which meant he was authorized to draw cash, from a nominated local bank, to make the weekly payments to his men and also for the purchase of other necessary items and services. All these extra chores required a suitable person, within the Troop, be appointed to assist the Troop Leader. Fortunately, this never presented any problems because within the ranks of all Troops, there was someone adequately qualified in previous civilian life to take such administration in his stride without detriment to overall training. It was yet another example of the self-sufficiency of even the smallest units in training which helped to stimulate initiative and resourcefulness in the Commandos.

In the early days of the Commandos we all suffered from a lack of suitable clothing. When slogging uphill in the mountains we sweated profusely and as a result our normal army woollen vests and shirts got soaked with perspiration, consequently on reaching the summit or halting to take up defensive positions or to bivouac we had soaking wet underclothing which soon became not just wet but very cold especially in the already cold temperatures. This obvious shortcoming had been reported to the 'powers-that-be' by the instructors at Lochailort, where among their numbers were reputed Arctic explorers and mountaineers of great experience. But in those days the wheels of change ground very slowly and it wasn't until 1942 that new and suitable clothing began to filter through.

In spite of the Commandos' successes in the Lofoten and Vaagso raids, no similar large raids in Norway followed, but there were some smaller ones on Norwegian objectives in 1942, carried out by mixed forces from No 12 Commando and Norwegian Commandos operating under the command of Captain F.W. Fynn from a base at Lerwick in the Shetlands. These raids were judged successful enough to extend their scope and as a result it was decided to regularize Fynn's raiders; they became 'North Force', he was promoted to Major and, importantly from the training side, a Commando Training camp (centre) was to be established in the Scottish Highlands, based in the Cairngorms, to train reinforcements for North Force, and also train other Commandos to operate in the snow and mountains under sub-zero conditions.

In December 1942 the Commando Snow and Mountain Warfare Training Camp (CSMWTC) was set up with its base in Braemar. A team of experienced mountaineers and Arctic explorers, including some officers and NCOs already in Commandos, was recruited.

The Commandant, then serving in the RAF with the rank of Squadron Leader, was the famous mountaineer Frank Smythe, and his Chief Instructor was Major John Hunt (KRRC), a regular officer who had experience in alpine-style climbing before the Second World War in the Karakoram and the Himalayan mountains. After the War he was to become world-famous as the leader of the first expedition to conquer Everest – Lord Hunt of Everest.

In his book, *Life is Meeting*, John Hunt describes the relationship between Smythe and himself:

> Frank and I got on well together... we made an effective partnership. He was a gentle, most unwarlike character, whose main contribution to the work at the Centre was to impart his deep, poetic love of the mountains to the tough, high-spirited wearers of the Green Beret. His achievements won him respect, the more so because of his slight physique. I was able to supply the element of military pragmatism to the exercises, which tended to be rather aimless mountain walks which Frank enjoyed so much.
>
> With the support of an able and enthusiastic staff I put the Commando units, which were sent to us, through a rigorous programme of all the permutations of action in all weathers and seasons, both on foot and on ski, in the testing vastness of the Cairngorms. The Troops moaned a little about the amount of plodding through the endless heather-clad slopes to reach the high tops. Some wit planted notices along the road up the river Dee announcing 'You're in the Khad country'.

Let me explain: 'Khad', pronounced 'Cud', was an Urdu word, meaning mountainous or hilly country. It was adopted by the British Army in India, with a strong undertone of disdain for plodding over such terrain, and this slang word was used universally throughout the Army. In Commandos we referred to cross-country marching as 'Cud-bashing' in the same way as the modern-day RM Commandos refer to 'Yomping'.

John Hunt continues:

> But at the end of each period of six weeks, which included a spell of rock-climbing in North Wales, they were good movers over difficult ground, inured to the vagaries of weather and cold temperatures, knowledgeable about Arctic rations and mountain equipment, superbly fit; their leaders skilled in navigation through dense mist and driving snow. Above all they had their baptism of that most demoralising element, the wind. I have experienced winds in the Arctic and the Himalayas, I know of nothing worse than being caught in a blizzard on the peaks and plateaux of the Cairngorms. On one occasion, climbing up the track towards Loch Etchachan carrying skis and heavy packs, I saw Frank Smythe, who was just ahead of me, lifted off his feet by a violent gust and deposited several yards away in a small burn [stream]. These troops [Commandos] would have been a match for the crack German Gebirgstruppen and Italian Alpini [the special mountain-trained troops of the Axis forces].

John Hunt also expressed the view that, although this training enhanced the wide range of fighting skills of the Commandos, it was a pity that they and the 52nd Division, which was trained extensively in Speyside for mountain warfare, were not used in Italy for this purpose.

Having established the CSMWTC base in Braemar, where adequate civilian billets were available and suitable buildings had been requisitioned for administrative needs and indoor lectures and instruction, the Commando intakes went off into the surrounding mountains for three to five days at a time for individual and collective training.

To meet the basic demands of training in the hostile terrain and also to combat the low temperatures and biting winds at high altitude the Commandos were issued with the best equipment then available, including windproof overgarments of smocks, with hoods, and trousers, Arctic mittens and, of course, string vests. Tinned and dried foods together with small portable primus stoves were issued to all before the exercises; cooking in two-man tents was on the 'Me and My Pal' basis. The preparation of hot food was testing, even in daylight, when howling winds, snow, sleet or hail were competing to aggravate the situation.

Generally training was on a Troop basis. From Braemar each Troop would trek off into the mountains to establish its own base camp and from thence carry out various activities: rock climbing, some skiing, navigation/map-reading, section tactics and field firing. All equipment, weapons and ammunition had to be man-packed and carried in rucksacks. However, there was one dispensation allowed on the marches: the luxury of small quantities of 'regulation' dark chocolate, similar to the famous Kendal Mint Cake, or dried fruit to sustain energy and help stamina.

There was also another unusual procedure, namely, the normal drill of stopping soon after each start on a climb, take off the smocks and remove sweaters, pullovers or shirts, pack these discarded items, put the smocks back on, and continue the slog uphill. In this way undue sweating and dampening of the underclothes was avoided. Of course, when halts were called the process was reversed and the dry undergarments put on once more. This simple, but often irksome, drill prevented having to endure cold, wet underclothes; instead one had dry, warm clothes to face the cold temperatures and winds at higher altitudes. And those who went to the Cairngorms in June found some of the peaks – and there were several over 4,000 feet – still snow-capped. So they were glad to have taken the basic precautions.

One of the most exhilarating, yet somewhat irritating, features of mountaineering was 'scree jumping'. Having sweated and struggled to reach the summit of a peak, say 3,000 feet or more up, and thinking to oneself, 'Thank God, that's over,' it could be frustrating to be told almost immediately, 'Right, that's it. Down we go, scree jumping.' And off we would go like Olympic skiers, non-tactical, to have a bit of excitement.

It was a wild, yet controlled charge downhill. Once the momentum got going feet hardly touched the ground, leaping from one foothold to the next at speed, arms outstretched, weapons slung across our bodies. Invariably mini-landslides of rocks and stones cascaded down, but unless they were serious, the downhill rush went on. If and when it was too dangerous the cry of 'Rock' went up and – in theory – everyone stopped. Normally all went well, and we were down in a matter of exciting minutes whereas the ascent had been long and toilsome.

Three full Commandos, Nos 1, 4 and 12, underwent training at CSMWTC, but then the decision was taken not to train any more Commandos specifically for this role, but to train the Lovat Scouts as a Mountain Battalion.

This regiment was a Territorial Army (TA) unit which had been raised by Lord Lovat's father and which he commanded with distinction during the Boer War; it was often called the 'last of the clan regiments'. Because

Sgt Amos (No 12 Commando) spent his 21st birthday, April 1943, undergoing snow and mountain warfare training in the Cairngorms, Scotland. He is seen here in the special clothing then issued for the purpose and behind him is his two-man tent.

Lord Lovat's name is synonymous with the Commandos it has frequently and mistakenly been assumed that the Lovat Scouts were a Commando unit. This was not so.

Following the decision to 'lend' the CSMWTC to the War Office for the training of the Lovat Scouts there were several changes. First came a change in the title; the 'Snow' was dropped and the unit became known for the rest of the War as Commando Mountain Warfare Training Centre (CMWTC); there was also a change in command, Geoffrey Rees-Jones, ex-No 5 and as already mentioned an original Commando volunteer, was promoted to Major and took charge. Frank Smythe, his main task of setting up the unit duly completed, left for duties elsewhere. John Hunt was promoted and sent to Italy to command a battalion of his regiment.

The third and final change was that of location – to train the Lovat Scouts the whole unit 'packed its bags' and left for Snowdonia to establish its base in Llanwryst, quite near to where we, in 'C' Troop, had established ourselves a year earlier.

Following the conclusion of training the Scouts, the staff of CMWTC returned to the task of training Commandos once more. With a requirement for cliff-climbing assaults visualized in the overall plan for Operation 'Overlord' it was decided that three RM Commandos would undertake such training under the aegis of CMWTC.

To carry out this new role the unit had to move from Wales to the rocky sea cliffs near the Cornish fishing village of St Ives. Thus December 1943 saw the unit established in that attractive town, the staff and trainees being accommodated in civilian billets whilst suitable buildings were requisitioned for administrative purposes and stores.

RM Commandos daily climbed at either Bosigran, Porthcurno, Porthgwarra, Sennon or Logan Rock. The programme was progressive, building up from simple climbs to a tactical Troop climb by night.

Having mentioned the climbing areas used by CMWTC it is pertinent to record that after the War the local authorities decided that the most-used climbing ridge, Bosigran, should officially be renamed 'Commando Ridge' so that posterity should remember its part in the training of Commandos in the Second World War. So in 1946 an engraved granite plaque was set into the rocks there. The legendary Commando cliff-climber Joe Barry was responsible for its installation. Joe started his Commando career in No 12 before becoming a specialist climber and NCO. instructor. He took part in small-scale raids on the French coast before joining the staff of CMWTC as a sergeant; towards the end of the War he was commissioned and as Captain 'Joe' Barry, continued to instruct RM Commandos for many years afterwards, earning a well-deserved MBE for his services. His son, John, ultimately, followed in the footsteps of his father to become a RM Commando, then CO of the Commando Mountain and Arctic Warfare Cadre (1973-6), and more recently a famous mountaineer who has tackled many of the world's great peaks including Everest.

In one of his books, John Barry recalls that long after the War, in 1984, he accompanied his father to the scene of one of his wartime raids, near St Pierre Porte in Normandy, where in a pre-D-Day clandestine raid, Joe and his climbing comrades had been thwarted by a final pitch of smooth chalk, so negating the raid. Joe revisited the scene because he had felt cheated of success and the disappointment had so played on his mind he wanted to

Cliff climbing on Bosigran Ridge, near St Ives, Cornwall, This was a much-used training area for trainees of the CMWTC, so-much-so that after the War the local authority officially had it renamed 'Commando Ridge'.

find out the exact nature of the hazard they had encountered on that nocturnal climb some forty years earlier. He discovered that given the equipment later developed, say a small, light, hand-thrown grapnel to which a line would have been attached, they would almost certainly have made that final defying pitch on the abortive wartime raid.

During the training of Nos 45, 46 and 47 RM Commandos for their cliff assault roles on D-Day many experiments were carried out to develop climbing aids. One, the 'Schumally' rocket was used to carry a grapnel head, onto which a length of climbing rope was attached. The grapnel having been hoisted over the cliff-top edge by the rocket, fastened itself into the ground and was anchored by those at the foot of the cliff by pulling on the end of the rope. Thus secured the Commandos were able to

The Death Slide – a typical Commando innovation in military training was always popular – here it was used in training for a quick descent from the cliff top at Kynance Cove, Cornwall, to the beach below.

tackle the cliff face. Initially, these rockets were not reliable and although they were not available for D-Day, sufficient progress ensured their use afterwards.

Another weird contraption was the attempt to adapt a London Fire Brigade extending ladder for use on an amphibian. Had this succeeded it would possibly have been of tremendous use to the US Rangers at Pointe de Hoc, but unfortunately it was not to be.

By April 1944 all three RM Commandos had completed their training in Cornwall and returned to the Isle of Wight to finish their preparations for D-Day; several of the St Ives instructors went with them to provide specialist advice and help on the chalk cliffs of the Island. As it happened it was decided that these instructors be integrated into the RM

Commandos for the invasion and all duly embarked in the landing craft for Normandy, but just prior to the actual operation there was a big disappointment when it was announced that the objective for No 46 – a coastal defence battery – had already been put out of action by the RAF. Notwithstanding, the task of destroying another coastal battery by No 47 was to go ahead, and they set sail on the eve of D-Day to carry out their allotted mission, but a short while before they were due to attack their assault was also called off, for once again splendid work by the RAF had made their task redundant.

However, the RM Commandos were employed on other tasks in Normandy, and that is another story, but the interesting thing is that although CMWTC personnel were ordered to return to England several of them re-enacted the 'Nelson touch' and went ashore to fight with their RM Commando comrades, until they reluctantly did have to obey a further order to return to St Ives.

From D-Day onwards the CMWTC had an extended role as a planning, training and experimental centre for different types of small-scale Commando operations employing a variety of small boats including dories, canoes, inflatable dinghies and surf boats. The most favoured craft, however, was the 18' dory, already referred to in Chapter IV. During this period Major 'Jim' Fraser took over command and the unit became increasingly involved in developing techniques for landings under all sorts of sea conditions and landing on all types of coast lines, including mud and through surf. These last two hazards became pre-eminent towards the end of the campaign in Europe when attention was being focussed on potential operations in the Far East.

During 1944-5 intakes from all the Commandos including the Dutch, Belgian, Norwegian and French from No 10 (1A) attended courses in St Ives and as a result, these were extensive and varied, some tailor-made to suit specific training for potential operations. Consequently by the end of 1944 CMWTC was able to offer instruction for operations ranging from small reconnaissances in inflatable dinghies or canoes through surf to a full Troop rocky landing to establish a bridgehead by night and then withdrawing, the use of mechanical methods and rockets for surmounting cliffs and the use of various homing devices, such as the 'S' phone, for direction-finding back to a parent ship. It was a full and comprehensive range of instruction – and a far different one from that of the CSMWTC at Braemar!

Fortunately the region of St Ives offered plenty of scope and suitable locations for training activities; those for rock climbing have already been mentioned, whilst both the major beaches at St Ives offered testing surf conditions.

Throughout the NW Europe campaign members of CMWTC were also engaged on operations with the British Liberation Army, either with the Commandos there or on separate 'recces'. In fact, every single instructor – officers and NCOs – carried out at least one such operation, a unique achievement for a training centre ostensibly based in England. These operations – all in small boats, carried out initially on the coast of France and later in the Scheldt, on the Dutch rivers and canals, and finally on the Rhine and Elbe crossings – were extremely hazardous and several members of CMWTC received awards and commendations for gallantry on them; although tragically there were casualties too.

CMWTC was the sole army Commando unit to survive disbandment in 1946. I was Adjutant at St Ives at the time and under the leadership of Major Norman Easton MC, we fought hard and long for the survival of the unit in peacetime, eventually succeeding in ensuring its future as a training centre within the post-war Royal Marine Commando organization. Many of the army instructors (including Joe Barry) stayed on, seconded to the Royal Marines, to hand over their expertise and knowledge to our successors.

One of the most hazardous training exercises ever devised and carried out by any Commando was Operation Brandyball by No 4 Commando on the Lands End peninsula in June 1943.

The object of this exercise was to carry out a mock seaborne raid on an 'enemy' objective, some few hundred yards inland, that was protected from such an assault by 300-feet-high precipitous cliffs that rose vertically from the sea-washed rocks below. The plan was for the assaulting Commandos to land from Goatley boats directly onto these rocks, and once ashore for the first wave to climb the cliffs and establish a bridgehead on the top of the cliffs thereby enabling the rest of the Commando to follow up, using ropes and hauling equipment for the heavy weapons, then to pass through to attack and destroy the enemy target. The success of the whole exercise depended wholly on the rocky landing and cliff climb going according to plan.

In the light of operations being planned at the time such a raid could be envisaged in the context of Operation Overlord. Indeed, there was a marked similarity between the exercise 'Brandyball' and the ultimate D-Day task of the US Rangers at Pointe du Hoc in Normandy, already mentioned. However, the writer has no knowledge of any connection between this exercise and the bloody and costly operation at Pointe du Hoc.

Commanding No 4 at this time was Robert Dawson who, as always, was keen to test and exploit the climbing skills of his Commandos to gain tactical surprise. Exercise Brandyball provided the opportunity to demonstrate to a collection of senior Allied Commanders, including 'Monty', and their staffs, the skills and capabilities of highly trained and adventurous troops and their potential employment for such daring missions.

The cliffs selected for the exercise were the 'Brandys' near Zennor in Cornwall, where just inland the buildings of an old tin mine afforded a suitable and realistic target to attack and destroy. Accordingly the Commando, organized into three Troops plus the Heavy Weapons Troop, moved to the St Ives area and immediately began training as though for a proper operation. Tank landing craft were made available to convey the Commandos and their Goatley boats from St Ives to the 'Brandys'. During the next four days intensive cliff climbing, boat handling and landings onto the rocks formed much of the basic training. Then followed trips to sea in the LCTs and launching the Goatleys from these craft about 200 to 300 yards from the coast. This in itself was a tricky affair, launching the boats over the lowered ramps in the Atlantic swell.

Each boat carried up to twelve men, plus a coxswain and kedgeman. It was a full load, especially as all were fully armed and some carried not only climbing ropes etc., but token explosives to simulate the demolitions.

On nearing the rocks the kedgeman was to throw out the kedge and by paying out the line control the final run-in to the rocks. At the rocks themselves, where slabs and ledges were the landing places, he would hold the line taut, allowing the Goatley to rise or fall just a few inches from the rocks and near enough for one man at a time to jump ashore as the boat started its downward fall. It was a hairy start to an even more hairy rock climb.

The actual demonstration was scheduled for 7 June, with a dress rehearsal fixed, coincidentally, for 6 June. Little did those men of No 4 know that a year later, to the day, they would be assaulting the beaches of Normandy on D-Day.

Not all the landings on the final rehearsal were successful. There were some nasty incidents, a boat overturned in the swell and men missed their footholds leaping onto the rocks. As a result not a few ended up 'in the drink'.

Many brave rescues were made as every effort was made to help and save floundering comrades in the surging sea. All were rescued except two. Prominent among the rescuers were two sergeants, Eric ('Nobby') Clarke and Sid Meddings – both deserved medals for their efforts.

The rehearsal was called off and the remaining craft returned to the waiting LCT before making back to St Ives to consider whether to carry on with the demonstration on the morrow. There the Colonel, in effect, let his men decide, by – as had happened before St Nazaire and elsewhere – allowing any man, without any fear of reprisal or defamation, to opt out. Not a single man moved out of line to decline this challenge of nature. They were confident they could do it – and, probably, what is more, they wanted to show the 'Brass Hats' what the Commandos could do!

Next day conditions were about the same, and although there were some mishaps and spills, the demonstration was an unqualified success. The assembled VIP gathering, some of whom were even reluctant to witness landings from the cliff-top edge, were all greatly impressed. Montgomery was, reputedly, so moved as to call No 4 'all proper chaps', a fitting accolade from the lips of the austere general. The expression so amused all in the Commando that it soon became a unit catch phrase.

'Brandyball' was described by one spectator as 'one of the most startling examples of Special Forces' training.' A few of those involved readily asserted it was certainly more dangerous than some of their later operations against the enemy. It was the type of training that prompted the experienced SBS raider, Roger Courtney, to once admit, 'I was to have greater frights in training than I ever had in war.'

Also there to witness and record this historic training episode were official Army and RAF film crews, and as a result Exercise Brandyball, preserved as a film, now resides in the film archives of the Imperial War Museum.

To sum up on this exercise one can do no better than to quote from No 4 Commando War Diary: 'Brandyball was carried out with great success, in spite of the coast being wild and exposed . . . cliff approaches which were thought inaccessible were overcome.' Succinct and concise, albeit a success that cost those two lives.

During the preparations for D-Day there was an obvious need to collect up-to-date information on the beach defences and the immediate hinterland of not only the invasion beaches, but also, to raid those in the Pas de Calais area as part of the elaborate deception plan.

To help in these operations, although parties were sent from Nos 4 and 10 Commandos in particular, another special little 'ad hoc' Commando force, 'Forfar', was formed. In its numbers were experienced climbers more versed on granite than chalk, so to rectify this shortcoming, the force was based on the Isle of Wight, in the Freshwater area, where chalk cliffs, like those in Northern France, abound.

There, in addition to their training on the cliffs, they also tried out various climbing aids without success, so it was decided they should train for parachute descents on the hinterland missions and plan to withdraw to the cliff tops, and rope down to embark on waiting dories. The technique worked well enough in training to justify such methods operationally.

Parachuting presented no problems for the Commandos. Although it was not part of their basic training, many did qualify as paratroops, especially in the small specialists groups as SBS, SSRF and those little 'ad hoc' groups such as Forfar Force. Furthermore as the reader will discover in the next chapter, in more detail, Commandos were Britain's first paratroops.

CHAPTER IX

Parachuting Pioneers

It is not generally appreciated, nor even known, that Britain's first parachute unit was a Commando, the original No 2 Commando, formed along with the other original Commandos in July 1940.

Churchill had called for a force of 5,000 paratroops, but this was scaled down to 500 and just a single Commando was earmarked for the role; the other Commandos being earmarked for amphibious operations, although being prepared to parachute was a condition for all the first volunteers.

Up to this time Britain, unlike Germany, USA and Russia, had no airborne forces, nor were there any established facilities to start training. No 2 had, therefore, to start from scratch. It was a daunting challenge for any unit, literally 'a leap into the dark'.

Ironically RAF chiefs had declared their belief that there was no requirement for Allied airborne forces in any future campaign, nevertheless they were ordered to be responsible for the training of Churchill's paratroops, so when volunteers for No 2 began to arrive in the Ringway (Manchester) area some preparations had been initiated at the small peacetime airport nominated as the centre for future parachute and glider training. It transpired to be a wise and satisfactory choice.

A small headquarters of RAF and Army personnel had been set up, with a First World War flying ace, Flight Lieutenant L. Strange DSO MC DFC (he had been a Lieutenant Colonel in the old Royal Flying Corps) appointed as CO of the new 'Central Landing Centre'. Alongside him, in charge of the military side of the training, was Major Rock RE.

In many ways the total unpreparedness for airborne operations was worse than those already described for the seaborne operations. Indeed the predicament facing the would-be paratroopers was aptly summed up by an RAF officer involved in the new venture, when he wrote:

> There are real difficulties in this parachuting business. We are trying to do what we have never been able to do hitherto, namely to introduce a completely new arm (parachutists) into the service at about five minutes notice, and with totally inadequate resources and personnel. Little, if any,

practical experience is possessed in England of any of these problems and it will be necessary to cover in six months the ground the Germans have covered in six years.

Notwithstanding, a nucleus of potential parachute jump instructors from both the RAF and the Army (APTC) had been recruited and, even though they lacked any erstwhile experience and had no manuals or special equipment, they were keen, enthusiastic and willing to make a start on this exciting new venture.

The little knowledge of parachuting possessed by these potential instructors was limited to the RAF personnel, recruited from RAF Hendon, where pre-war trainee pilots received some instruction on emergency parachuting just in case they had to 'bale out'. As a result they knew something of the behaviour of 'chutes in flight and they were well versed in the drying of used 'chutes, packing and maintenance.

These instructors and their charges, No 2 Commando, were therefore to be the 'guinea pigs', who would lead the way to military parachuting, and progress would only come by the painful process of trial and error. That is exactly how it all started at Ringway in 1940.

Although some studies were made of the paratroops of Germany and Russia, the first methods of parachuting at Ringway were based on the peacetime techniques of stuntmen for films and those who gave demonstrations at pre-war air displays.

As a result the 'pull-off' method was first tried; briefly it was based on the peacetime jumper climbing out onto the wing of a biplane, hanging on to the struts with one hand whilst pulling his ripcord with the other hand and allowing the canopy to develop in the slipstream until there was sufficient drag to pull the parachutist off and away.

Obviously this spectacular method, ideal for stunts and displays, was simply not practical for military uses, nevertheless the pioneers had no other alternative at the onset than to see if this 'pull-off' method, accepted in principle, could be adapted for use on RAF planes.

The plane first chosen and available for the initial trials was the Whitley bomber and it was decided to open up the rear gunner's turret, instal a little platform and use that for the 'pull-off'. Crude and frightening as it was, it enabled a start to be made by both the RAF and army 'jump' instructors-to-be.

Meanwhile from 9 July troops for No 2 started to assemble in Knutsford, adjacent to Ringway airfield and the nearby proposed dropping zone (DZ) at Tatton Park.

Like the other Commandos, then forming up in their seaside locations,

The first parachute jumps by No 2 Commando were from rear of a Whitley bomber, the rear turret having been removed, as seen here, where the 'jumper' is adopting the 'pull-off' position. (Photograph by courtesy of the Imperial War Museum.)

No 2 were also responsible for their own administration and accommodation in civilian billets.

Although earmarked as the parachute Commando, the manner in which the volunteers were selected for No 2 was exactly the same and identical to that of the other Commandos, namely by Troop Leaders in a single interview – no medical examination and no physical or weapon skill tests. As one volunteer recorded, the main credentials were enthusiasm and the burning zeal 'to have a go at "Jerry" plus the "guts" to have a go at parachuting'.

Lieutenant Colonel Jackson, Royal Tank Regiment, was appointed as the first CO and his Commando was organized on the same lines as the others and armed with similar weapons.

Members of No 2 Commando undergoing training on the 'hole exit' technique from a suspended mock-up of a Whitley bomber at Ringway. (Photograph by courtesy of the Imperial Museum.)

The only difference between No 2 and the others was how they would arrive on enemy-held territory to 'hit and run' – No 2 from the air, the rest from the sea.

Four days after their arrival in Knutsford the parachute jump instructors put on a demonstration at Tatton Park for No 2 Commando, on 13 July, and then without any further delays the para training started – lectures, PT exercises designed to ensure smooth and accident-free landings, practice of aircraft procedures and drills for movement in the plane.

Then came the day – they didn't have to wait long – for the men of No 2 to make their first jumps which were all predominately with the 'pull-off' method. All the volunteers were put through this initiation and having made the first jump were declared 'acceptable for parachute training', but a few found this introduction to jumping the most frightening thing that ever happened to them!

Captain Martin Lindsay, a pre-war Arctic explorer and one of the original instructors at STC Lochailort, having volunteered for the Commandos and been made a Troop Leader in No 2 dramatically described his first descent, at Ringway, in Julian Thompson's book *Ready for Anything*:

> We climbed into the aircraft and sat on the floor of the fuselage. The engines roared and we took off. I noticed how moist the palms of my hands were, I wished I didn't always feel slightly sick in an aircraft.
>
> It seemed an age, but it cannot have been more than ten minutes when the instructor (dispatcher) beckoned to me. The Germans had a chucker-out for the encouragement of nervous recruits. Flight Sergeant Brereton, six foot two inches, would have made a good Absetzer. I began to make my way down the fuselage towards him, screwing up to do so. I crawled on hands and knees into the rear-gunner's turret, the back of which had been removed. I tried not to overbalance and fall out, nor to look at the landscape speeding across below me as I turned to face forward again.
>
> I now found myself on a small platform about a foot square, at the very back of the plane, hanging on like grim death to the bar under which I had such difficulty in crawling. The two rudders were a few feet away on either side of me; behind was nothing whatsoever. As soon as I raised myself to full height, I found I was to all purposes outside the plane, the slipstream of air in my face almost blowing me off. I quickly huddled up, my head bent down and pressed into the capricious bosom of the Flight Sergeant.
>
> I was about to make a 'pull off', opening my parachute which would not pull me off until fully developed – a procedure which was calculated to fill me with such confidence that I should be only too ready to leap smartly out of the aircraft on all subsequent occasions.
>
> The little (warning/dispatch) light at the side changed from yellow to red. I was undeniably frightened, though at the same time filled with a fearful joy. The light changed from red to green and down fell his (Brereton's) hand. I put my right hand across the D-ring in front of my left side and pulled sharply. A pause of nearly a second and then a jerk on each shoulder. I was whisked off backwards and swung through nearly 180 degrees, beneath the canopy and up the other side. But I was quite oblivious to all this. I had something akin to a blackout. At any rate, the first thing I was conscious of after the jerk on my shoulders was to find myself, perhaps four seconds later, sitting up in my harness and floating down to earth.
>
> I looked up and there was the silken canopy billowing in the air currents. I looked down, reflecting that this was certainly the second greatest thrill in a man's life. Suddenly, I realized that the ground was coming up very rapidly.

Before I knew what had happened I was sprawling on the ground, having taken a bump but not hurt. As I got to my feet, a feeling of exhilaration began to fill me.

Well, that says it all, a fair description of a first jump in those infant days of military parachuting, and although kinder methods of exit from the aircraft, techniques for controlling the descent through the air and for landing, were developed those emotive impressions held good for most of us on our first jump. Unforgettable but . . .

Clearly this method was far from ideal. The next step in development was an exit through a hole in the bottom of the Whitley's fuselage. This, however, had its fair share of nastiness too. A much-preferred exit was another alternative provided by jumping from the side doorway of the Bombay aircraft.

The hole-in-the-floor exit from the Whitley allowed the jumper to have his ripcord pulled for him by means of connecting it to a static line fixed to a strong point on the frame of the aircraft.

Exits from the 'hole' in the floor required much practice on a mock-up fuselage of a Whitley. One of the inherent nasty aspects of this method of exit was the likely risk of hitting one's face on the opposite side of the hole, which was quite small. A painful experience, it was bemusedly – except for the victim – known as 'bell-ringing'.

During August, after some 135 descents, the first fatal accident occurred when Driver Evans (RASC) of No 2 became entangled in the rigging lines of his parachute and plummeted to his death.

This death brought jumping to a temporary halt whilst investigations were held into the problems of twisting in the rigging lines following the exits. One of the main problems was resolving the way the 'chute canopy developed subsequent to the pull on the static line. After experiments with dummies (instead of live men from No 2) and in collaboration with the manufacturers of the parachutes, a new combination parachute was decided upon – the X-type parachute, packed in a 'G parachute' bag. This radically altered the development of the canopy following the exit and was most successful, thus allowing the parachute training to continue.

By 21 September some 340-odd other ranks of No 2 Commando had parachuted, but the wastage rate had been discouraging inasmuch as there had been two fatal accidents, twenty badly injured or declared medically unfit to carry on, whilst thirty of the original volunteers had refused to jump and had been RTU'd.

On the bright side those who had jumped – an average of two descents per man – were now keen to carry on and their enthusiasm is reflected that by the end of the year the original volunteers of No 2 Commando had made some 2,000 descents and were, like their seaborne comrades, now based on the Isle of Arran, keen and eager for action, although with hindsight, not really ready.

November was an important month for No 2 Commando – all men had completed at least three jumps, that being the prescribed number to merit recognition as a qualified parachutist, although at that time it did not qualify them for any extra-duty pay. Like all other Commandos they did not receive any such increments. Later, of course, when all parachutists were part of Airborne Forces, and not Commandos, they did – after qualifying as parachutists – receive an extra payment of 2 shillings (10p) per day. I might add that we in Commandos who had qualified at Ringway as trained parachutists and returned to serve with 'green berets' likewise received this extra 'para' pay too.

Also in that month two other important events affected the future of No 2 Commando. Firstly, its title was changed to 11th Special Air Service Battalion and unlike the other Commandos, who were at the same time also retitled as 'Special Service Battalions', for a while, before reverting back to Commandos once more, and a new No 2 Commando, under Lieutenant Colonel Newman was subsequently formed.

The other event was when No 2 gave the very first demonstration of an air drop by British paratroops with B Troop jumping on Salisbury Plain and after landing at once setting about seizing exercise objectives. It was watched by a number of high-ranking British and Allied 'top brass'.

Hilary St George Saunders recalls an amusing story of how the Troop Leader, Cleasby-Thompson, having cleared the DZ after the drop, commandeered a large limousine and in it surprised the exercise bridge guard at nearby Shrewton. It was not until later in the day that he discovered that the car belonged to one of the more distinguished of the spectators, HRH Prince Olaf of Norway. It was a nice piece of Commando initiative, typical of the heady 1940 days.

Throughout the winter the newly fledged paratroops continued to live in civilian billets in the Knutsford area and Ringway became established as the Parachute School. There, new equipment, installed in hangars, helped to improve landing techniques. Whilst away from Ringway the men of the unit, remembering that parachuting was but the means of getting to battle, not the means of fighting the battle, concentrated on training in physical fitness, weapon training and field firing, demolitions, cross-country and the like in the same way as the other Commando units.

New pieces of equipment and clothing were designed and tested. One of the most successful items was the distinctive airborne smock. Like the other Commandos the parachutists continued to wear their own regimental headdress and cap badges until the red (maroon) beret was issued and worn during the North Africa campaign in 1942. It was then that the Germans christened their airborne enemies – out of respect and with regard – the 'Red Devils'.

This part of the story, in the context of 'Commando training', really ends here, except to add that the men that took part in Britain's first airborne operation on the Tragino Aqueduct in Italy in February 1941, under the banner of 11th Special Air Service Battalion, were, in fact, members of the original No 2 Commando, including such outstanding leaders as 'Tag' Pritchard and Tony Deane-Drummond.

Hilary St George Saunders makes a fitting tribute in his book *Red Beret* to the important role of No 2 Commando in the birth and development of Britain's parachute and airborne forces with these words:

> The patience, hardihood and steadfastness of those who had joined No 2 Commando in the early days were to be rewarded – not perhaps in the conventional manner with medals and promotions – but with something more precious, the sight of other men, volunteers like themselves, who, seeing their example felt the same urge and were eager to face the same risks for the same rewards.

The links between the Parachute Regiment and the Commandos during the War were strong and cordial, none more so than when they fought alongside each other in Normandy. Furthermore, after the War when the Army Commandos were disbanded many officers and other ranks swapped their green berets for red ones. Off-hand, I can think of Colonel ('Mad') Jack Churchill DSO MC, Dennis O'Flaherty DSO, David Style MC, Knyvet Carr MC, Gordon Pollock MC, and 'Paddy' Byrne DCM, who in the post-war years, after the disbandment of the Army Commandos served either as regulars or TA volunteers in Airborne Forces.

But, back to those war years – from 1941 onwards Commandos attended courses at Ringway, qualified as parachutists and as such not a few were involved in raids and operations. In several instances a whole Troop in a Commando did the course; my old 'C' Troop in No 4 was one such example. These courses, even if the qualified Commandos did not parachute into action, did, nevertheless, afford exciting, exacting and excellent training.

The training procedures and techniques had moved on tremendously since those pioneer days of 1940 and there had been many changes – a considerable number attributable to the influence and drive of Wing Commander Newnham who took over command in July 1941. I reckon that Newnham was to Ringway as was Vaughan to Achnacarry – the driving force to success. Both were experienced veterans of the First World War, both had clear aims and the determination to make the respective special training centres the finest in the world, and they succeeded.

In both cases one of the main factors contributing to their success was their ability to ensure that their instructors were not only experts in their field, but had the right psychological approach to obtain the maximum effort from the trainees, and by personal example, setting the highest standards, then obtaining results through patient, understanding and cheerful instruction. Both Commandants refused to tolerate bullying, bluff or 'bullshit' from their instructors.

Newnham was instrumental in changing the nature of the first descent from an aircraft jump to one from a balloon. Anxious to find out what a balloon jump was like he made a descent himself and this convinced him that previous objections to its use were purely psychological, and ballooning offered many advantages for the 'first-timer'.

I went on the course whilst at the Holding Operation Commando (HOC) at Wrexham after leaving Achnacarry and whilst waiting for a posting to an operational Commando overseas. I had always wanted to parachute and this was my chance.

The course started with lectures and films on the background of parachuting, the types of aircraft in use and the jargon and terms used.

The latter included such obvious and easily understood words as twists, oscillations and slipstream but also ones that needed an explanation, like the dreaded 'Roman Candle' – a descent when the 'chute completely failed to develop and the hapless jumper plunged helpless to the ground below. But, hopeless as this situation may seem, cases were recorded whereby maintenance of the correct landing position and the para-roll reduced the risks of a fatal outcome.

It has to be remembered that during the War there was no issue of a reserve (emergency) 'chute – this was a 'luxury' of the post-war years.

We practised the all-important 'para-roll' ad nauseam – feet and legs together, elbows well tucked into the sides and hands (as on the lift webs) in front of the face, head slightly forward, then into the roll – feet, shins, hips and roll, keeping the elbows into the side. Sgt Instructor Woods was strict but patient as on and on we practised, under his beady eye, until he was satisfied – and he took some satisfying!

Then off to the swings which enabled us, suspended in a harness, to practice drills to correct any malfunctions during descents, such as twists, oscillations and collision action. One ingenious piece of equipment was the 'Fan' which allowed one to make a controlled descent, inside a hangar, from a 30-foot platform on to a padded mat and go into the famous para-roll to make a 'nice safe landing'.

We practised the drills for emplaning, movement in the plane, hooking up to the static line, 'Action stations', 'Stand-by-the-door', and finally, 'No 1 Go, Two Go'. All on the mock fuselages.

Although highly disciplined, throughout the course there was always time for a laugh and joke, not infrequently at someone's misfortune, but that was always accepted anyway. Typically one distinguished airborne officer has commented: 'The Parachute School has always been a sort of well-disciplined, dedicated funfair.'

Like thousands before there came the time for the testing first jump. In the main, dawn or dusk were favoured for first jumps, times when the winds were usually at their lowest. A very early breakfast, or at least a cup of tea and a fag, then mustered by Woods to draw our 'chutes, wondering if the WAAFs had packed them correctly, but glad we didn't have the nerve-racking trial of packing our own, as did many of No 2 Commando during the early period – July and August 1940 .

Our first jump was from the balloon – an unforgettable experience.

We were to jump in pairs. Our dispatcher called forward the first pair. It was an accepted rule that the senior rank, officer or NCO, was No 1 in the stick (a stick being the term used for an aircraft (or balloon) load of paratroops to drop on any one run over the DZ).

As a captain at the time I was the senior rank in Woods' squad, so had the dubious honour of making the first jump. With my No 2 following we entered the basket, nodded to our dispatcher and seconds later the winch paid out the restraining cables of the balloon and with an eerie, soft, swishing sound we floated upwards, swaying slightly in the early morning breeze. We (Nos 1 and 2) checked each other's packs and hooked up, ready at the end of the ascent to step forward to the opened doorway at the cage. At about 600 feet the balloon came to rest, the swaying increased noticeably, but not dangerously. Then came the moment of decision – 'No 1 stand by the door.' All our ground training was about to be put to the test. I moved to the opened space, looking straight ahead, one-hand on each of the outsides of the opening, legs braced for that vital step forward into space.

I didn't have to wait long for the order. It was short, sharp and compelling, accompanied by a sudden firm tap on my right shoulder, 'Go!'

Instinctively and immediately I went. A good exit, feet together, hands to the side, a perfect position of attention. Too concerned to get this right position, I didn't think of anything else as I fell silently almost unnoticingly into empty space. Just as I began to wonder, it happened. A strong tug on my shoulder and sudden jerk halted my speeding fall. Looking up with relief, there was my lovely canopy fully developed . . . 'Thank God!'

I had barely started to go through the routine drill of in-flight checks before I heard the instructor's voice from down on the DZ, 'OK, No 1 . . . that's it . . . pull a bit on your back-lift webs . . . not too much . . . gently does it . . . now get ready to land . . . feet together.'

In next to no time at all I was putting all that training on those para-rolls into practice. And it was all over – my first parachute jump. It had been fun . . .

After that there was no looking back. Another balloon jump, then on to aircraft jumps from Dakotas, five from these splendid transport planes before the final night descent from a balloon, all on the DZ at Tatton Park. These jumps, eight in all, were the required number to qualify as a paratroop, be awarded our 'Para wings', and the 'two bob' a day 'Para pay'.

Unhappily, my final jump of the course ended in a disaster. Late in the dark night and silent descent my 'chute developed considerable oscillation. Trying to correct this misfunction by pulling hard on my back-lift webs, my legs and feet came up. Unfortunately, I didn't know, because it was so dark and I couldn't see the sole ground light, that I was near to the ground. Too near, with my feet and legs still up, I hadn't the correct landing position – and to make matters worse I was drifting in backwards.

With a mighty thump I landed on the base of my spine.

There I lay, conscious but helpless. I couldn't move, I couldn't shout. I was paralysed. For some minutes – it seemed ages – I just lay there, helpless and speechless. I heard voices shouting, 'Number One, where are you?' Then I must have passed out, for the next thing I remember was being in the 'blood wagon' – the ambulance – on my way to the hospital. I had fractured my spine . . .

It took a long time to mend. I spent that spring encased in plaster from neck to crutch; by the time I was liberated from that encasement and had undertaken remedial training the war in Europe was over. But there was still the Japs, and I was posted to CMWTC at St Ives as Adjutant. That wasn't the end of my parachuting days, for some years later I finished off my service in the Army as a company commander in the 2nd Battalion,

The Parachute Regiment, chasing EOKA terrorists in Cyprus and also taking part in the Suez Operation of 1956.

By that time military parachuting had made much progress in every way from the primitive pioneering jumps made by the men of the original No 2 Commando in that summer of 1940, when they blazed the trail to become the founding fathers of The Parachute Regiment.

CHAPTER XI

And Finally . . .

One of the aspects of training not yet dealt with in any detail so far is that of street fighting and house-clearing, nor has any specific mention been made of the training of the original Intelligence and Medical sections or the latter-day additions of the Signals and MT sections. This final chapter affords an opportunity to make good these omissions.

Like several other subjects of warfare, that of street fighting and house-clearance had received scant attention during the inter-war years. Fairbairn and Sykes directed some attention to this subject on their courses at Lochailort, but even so this subject was not fully developed until after the daring daylight raid on the Norwegian town of Vaagso by No 3 Commando in December 1941.

That raid was the first Commando experience of sustained street fighting and house-clearance. Although the raid was a pronounced success, practically all the casualties – seventeen killed and fifty-three wounded – were suffered in the ferocious fighting amongst the quayside warehouses and the houses that flanked the single main street of the port. The raid emphasized the need for more thought and training on this subject. There were important lessons learnt from this operation and these were reflected in subsequent training.

Firstly, there was the need to have more simple rehearsed drills to deal specifically with different situations such as movement between houses or across open spaces and roads, and forcing entrances into buildings, with or without explosives, and from either ground level or from roofs. These drills would ensure immediate reactions to situations and circumstances with everyone knowing their role and what was expected of them.

Moving 'split-arse' in these situations was the aim. And this became another good reason for battle fitness. As a result drills were devised for such movements with covering fire and/or smoke. A new set of urban obstacles had to be tackled – climbing walls and gaining access to upper floors and roofs using not only the issued toggle ropes, but also learning to improvise other aids from nearby materials.

Next came the need to reassess the type of weapons that dominated this type of action and the firing practices required. Obviously the short-range automatic weapons came into their own, but rifles and Brens fired quickly and accurately from the hip were equally effective. The Vaagso experiences emphasized the need to practice these methods with live ammunition at targets in realistic settings – in real houses and streets. But where?

Ironically, Hitler's Luftwaffe provided the answer. In many major cities and towns there were residential areas which had been laid to waste by bombing during the Blitz. Areas were cleared and the houses quickly requisitioned and made available for street fighting training.

An instance of where No 2 used just such an area in a blitzed area of Plymouth, prior to their raid on St Nazaire, has already been cited. The Commandos, wherever they were, took opportunities to use such areas. I remember one in Southampton, down by the river at Woolston, alongside the bombed aircraft factory of Supermarine where the pre-war Schneider Trophy 'S6' seaplane, the forerunner of the Spitfire, was built, which we used in 1942.

There we practised house-clearing using live ammunition and grenades, plus token explosive charges and devices to blast holes in walls through which to lob grenades – a technique known as 'mouse-holing'.

Improvised snap targets, body silhouettes or head and shoulders, were sited in rooms and corridors, wherever possible some were connected to ropes and pulleys, so that they could 'pop' up for a second or two to further the speed of the firer's reaction.

Various methods for mouse-holing were employed, such as a 'pole-charge' made with guncotton slabs, primer and detonator, tied to a wooden length so that the resultant hole would be conveniently sized to crawl through. Four No 75 (Hawkins) grenades were similarly used to make a pole-charge. In training we often used 'sticky' anti-tank grenades in lieu of pole-charges, with, I might add, not a lot of success.

No 3 had made much use of flame to set fire to the wooden houses used by the Germans at Vaagso and although this element of destruction was advocated in action it was seldom employed in training except by flame-throwers on selected ranges where adequate safety measures could be enforced. Nevertheless, we did prepare for a raid in spring 1942 where we were to use flame-throwers on an enemy house on the coast of Holland. We were issued with the Lifebuoy man-pack flame-throwers and three or four chaps were selected to train on them. The flame-thrower was carried on the back, in the same fashion as a rucksack, and, fully laden with fuel, weighed about 60 lb. From the pack came a hose, with a nozzle, and this was aimed at the target. The extreme range of the ignited flame was about 30 yards, but the duration of the fuel was less than a minute.

In the event this potential raid was cancelled, the flame-throwers withdrawn and I, personally, did not come across them again in the Commandos. They certainly were not included as weapons at Achnacarry. I understand, however, that they were used to attack German strongpoints in No 2 Commando Brigade's assault on Lake Comacchio in Italy in April 1945.

One of the major problems in house-clearing was that the enemy naturally favoured taking up defensive positions on the higher floors of buildings and the ideal way to tackle this was to clear from the roof down. This was, inevitably, difficult; nevertheless where there were terrace houses roof-top movement was possible. It afforded some exciting and daunting training.

Having gained entry it was often a matter of 'mouse-holing' towards the rooms occupied by the 'enemy'. Grenades and bursts of automatic fire followed the mouse-holing. In the early stages of practising these drills thunderflashes and other less dangerous pyrotechnics were used and even 'blanks' for the rifles.

Only blanks and thunderflashes were used whenever street fighting and house-clearing exercises were carried out against other troops and, in particular, the Home Guard, who had a vital role to play in the defence of towns etc.

It so happened, contrary to what has been subsequently portrayed in *Dad's Army*, many of the Home Guard units responsible for urban defences were extremely well prepared and well briefed. This was in no small measure due to the influence and writings on the subject by Tom Wintringham, who had fought in the Spanish Civil War and was an accepted authority on urban warfare and tactics. Our exercises against these HG units were of mutual value.

As outlined earlier when the Commandos were formed, provision was made to include both a Medical and an Intelligence Section on the establishment of each Commando Headquarters, and personnel for these sections were all volunteers.

The original Commanding Officers recruited and chose their own Medical Officers (MOs) from RAMC volunteers. Our first MO in No 4 was recruited after Dunkirk, where he had been in a Field Ambulance.

In turn 'Doc' Wood selected his own section of RAMC medical

orderlies, most of whom had already served with him, so they were already halfway to becoming a team.

All the 'medics' had to partake in the general training. Doc Wood, tall, lean and an ex-Police Surgeon, readily took to all of the physical side of the training. Furthermore, he and his orderlies were all armed, first with Webley pistols, then later with .45 Colt automatics.

Being thus armed they could not, in action, qualify for the rights of protection under the terms of the Geneva Convention for those attending to the wounded. It was argued that as they accompanied the Commandos in action and were bound to be in the 'thick of it', they would need to defend themselves. One could not guarantee that the enemy, in the heat of battle, would refrain from firing at anyone alongside raiding Commandos. Accordingly all, without exception, took more than a casual interest in weapon training and jumped at the chance to join in the firing of Troop weapons on the ranges.

Some of them became good shots and frequently wanted to get into the battle by firing at any enemy snipers who might be interfering with their attending to the wounded. There was the case of Sam Cory, the MO of No 3, who on one raid whilst attending to the wounded in the beachhead was being sniped. He was, and I quote, 'seen several times, first attending to his wounded, then seizing their rifles to get a few shots at the enemy'.

Apart from the daily routine duties of treating those (often referred to as the 'lame and the lazy') attending Sick Parades and leading his section on other training and exercises, the MO ran courses of advanced medical treatment for his orderlies, teaching them to carry out treatment normally accepted as being the province of only Medical Officers and also preparing them to give First Aid lectures and instruction to the Troops to which they were attached for training and exercises.

It was normal for the same orderly to be attached to a Troop so that he became a member of that Troop, getting to know them and they, in turn, accepting him. Great bonds of mutual respect and trust were established, as was evident at Dieppe, when several of F Troop were so badly wounded they had to be left behind. Their orderly, Joe Pasquale, unselfishly and bravely opted to stay behind with them, tending to their wounds until all were captured by the Germans. Joe spent the rest of the War as a POW, but his on-the-spot care during that fateful morning helped to save some of his comrades.

No better example of the courageous and devoted service of the Commando medical orderlies can be related than that of Lance Corporal H.E. Harden (RAMC), attached to No 45 RM Commando, who for his unselfish valour under enemy fire, during an operation in North-West Europe in 1945, was awarded a posthumous VC.

From the onset, in 1940, all ranks in the Commandos received instruction in First Aid and Hygiene. Naturally there was an emphasis on the treatment of wounds and shock, the use of splints (including rifles) for fractures and the emergency treatment for burns. Instruction on Hygiene included lectures and demonstrations appertaining to water and insect-borne diseases, venereal diseases, and the taking of preventative measures. A little course of six sessions was part of the curriculum at Achnacarry.

So much for the medics, now to take a quick look at the Intelligence set-up within the Commandos and some aspects of their particular training.

The Intelligence ('I') Section was the smallest sub-unit in a Commando and normally consisted of an officer, usually a lieutenant, although there were times when his responsibilities warranted promotion to captain, a sergeant, a corporal and four privates. The section came under the direct command of the CO and was part of Commando HQ.

Frequently, additional personnel were attached to the 'I' section for specific operations, usually coming from No 10 (Inter-Allied) Commando. For detailed information of the extraordinary exploits of the multi-national Commandos of No 10 one should read Ian Dear's *Ten Commando*.

The basic job of any 'I' staff, at all levels, is to 'collect, collate and disseminate' intelligence information to the commanders to enable them to be successful in battle. It covers a wide field of activities. However, at the unit level, the main tasks include the responsibility for all maps required for operational and training purposes and making enlargements from them, preparing and maintaining the 'battle maps', i.e. showing the locations of friendly and enemy forces, the interpretation of air photographs and the making of scale models for operations, the issue of codes and passwords, the decoding of messages, the maintenance of the unit 'War Diary' – a record of the important details of the daily activities of the unit during training and in action; all these diaries have been kept at the Public Record Office at Kew for permanent reference (I did refer to some when preparing this book) – instructing the unit on recognition of enemy uniforms, badges of rank, equipment, weapons, aircraft etc., the interrogation of prisoners, and advising the CO on all security matters within the unit.

Practically all these tasks were common to all fighting units, and training courses were provided at centres run by the Intelligence Corps and Inter-Services establishments. The IO and his NCOs attended these courses and also special briefings at Combined Operations HQ in London.

Here it is pertinent to break away from the narrative to point out that the Commandos were probably the first combat units to take advantage of the then latest developments of oblique air photographs and how this came about is told in some detail by Major General Tom Churchill (brother of Jack Churchill) in his book, *Commando Crusade*. Tom Churchill was an expert on the interpretation of air photographs on the Intelligence staff at Home Forces from 1940 to 1942, and as such provided the air photographs and helped Commando 'I' sections in their interpretations for several operations including the St Nazaire Raid. This contact ultimately led Tom to join the Commandos and he became the Commander of 2 Commando Brigade in Italy and the Adriatic, after the Battle of Salerno in 1943.

All 'I' Sections had their 'personalities'. In No 4 we had a couple of outstanding IOs, Lieutenant Tony Smith, who on promotion to Brigade IO was followed by Captain Ken Wright, who had been an instructor at one of the Intelligence Training Centres. Among the NCOs were Brian Sellers, a brilliant draughtsman, who at the end of the war in Europe designed No 4 Commando's Roll of Honour, featured on the Commemorative Display Plaque at Weymouth; Brian Mullen, a talented artist, whose tiny body contained a brave and stout heart, but was sadly killed on the beach of Normandy on D-Day; and Ken Phillot, a man of many parts.

Security was a vital subject for all units and, indeed, all folk living in these islands during the War. At the time of the threatened German invasion with its inherent problems and dangers of spies and 'Fifth Columnists' everyone, service personnel and civilians alike, were constantly warned of the dangers of 'careless talk'. Posters appeared everywhere warning that 'Careless Talk Costs Lives' and advising all to 'Be Like Dad, Keep Mum' and that 'Even Walls have Ears'.

The problems of security were particularly important to the Commandos whose clandestine operations could be jeopardized by information leaking back to the enemy, and it was one of the roles of the 'I' Section to keep security within the Commando under surveillance. Being expert on the various ways security could be breached or compromised and, appreciating the unorthodox methods employed by the Commandos when tackling problems – be it in training or in action – the 'I' Sections were occasionally asked by higher authority to check or test security elsewhere, other than within their own unit.

Ken Phillot was engaged in several of these security checks and his experiences make amusing reading. In one well-planned effort Ken and another from the Commando 'I' section, 'conned' an overnight stay in a unit Headquarters, and during the small 'wee' hours were able to take some classified documents from an unlocked office before making off next day. On another occasion Ken and one other dressed in German uniforms, less the swastika badges, were sent on a walkabout in a nearby Scottish port to see what the reaction would be. It was revealing. Although they caused a certain amount of interest from some servicemen, a policeman, a courting couple and other civilians, it was several hours before anyone was sufficiently suspicious to actually get them arrested and interrogated by the Military Police. This, in spite of them visiting an ice-rink, riding on a bus, having a drink in a pub, walking down the main road in daylight and strolling inside the dock gates.

Searching for valuable intelligence information was an important feature of 'I' training, but there was seldom any scope to put it to the test during training, except when chances arose like that just illustrated. On raids and other operations it was so important that ultimately a special unit for this role was set up, namely 30 Assault Unit, which started its life as No 30 Commando. Its most notable work was achieved working ahead of the Allied lines in France and Germany to secure plans and information after the invasion in 1944. There seems no doubt that the training and exploits of these specialists greatly influenced the literary creation of Fleming's famous hero, 'Bond 007', because Ian Fleming was involved with its operations.

Finally, a good example of an 'I' Section's success on a raid is recorded in Durnford-Slater's account of the Vaagso Raid. He wrote: 'Before any German-occupied building was blown up, a member of the intelligence section searched through it for documents. This precaution paid off beautifully when we found the master code for the whole of the German Navy. For many weeks to come, as a result of this priceless discovery, the Admiralty in London was able to freely decipher German naval signals.'

Some idea of how the lack of any unit transport within the Commandos was overcome in the early days by the use of private cars, requisitioned trucks and coaches, use of cycles, and putting the onus to get to the training areas and other venues on the individuals concerned, has already been dealt with.

When it came to exercises against other troops and the Home Guard, without transport for rapid deployment, we were invariably disadvantaged and had to rely on our ingenuity to offset this handicap. Fortunately we had plenty of men with loads of practical experience with all types of motor transport and tanks, not only as drivers but also as mechanics. They had the 'know-how' and skill to start and take away so-called 'immobilized vehicles' and use them for our own purpose – much to the chagrin of their owners, whether they were service or civilian.

On many occasions when we acted as 'enemy' in training exercises to test regular and Home Guard units defending vulnerable points and installations we made ourselves mobile by acquiring 'opportunity' vehicles in this way. We claimed that it was fair game and what any invading German paratroops would have done in the the same circumstances.

We were encouraged to look out for any chance of getting vehicles in this way during exercises, and we quickly earned a reputation for doing so. However, although this reduced our chances it did sharpen the awareness of those whose job it was to be on guard and vigilant. More importantly, it provided an apprenticeship for those Commandos who were sent to the Mediterranean in 1941 and 1942 without transport. They knew the only way they would get much-needed transport was to 'beg, borrow or steal'. And that they did.

One typical example is recorded on No 6 Commando exploits in North Africa, when, following the landings in Tunisia, they were employed as line infantry, unfortunately without support weapons or any transport. After recalling the tragic results of having no support weapons of any sort, one commentator reported: 'Nor did they have much transport – officially. They had to win what they could: a Christmas present here of a staff car and three trucks; there, several vehicles swiped from the roadside before the official recovery vehicles could get to them for repairs.'

By early 1943 the situation had changed a little for the better. The issue of heavy weapons necessitated some light load-carrying vehicles and these were forthcoming in the form of jeeps and trailers.

There was no problem of finding drivers from within the Commandos. Some volunteers for the job thought it might mean the 'cushy' opting out of marches, assault courses, cross-country runs and the like, but were mistaken; like their comrades in the Orderly Room and others in Headquarters they had to partake in all the active training. Indeed, some of the drivers in No 4 got an extra rude shock when as part of the Commando's training for mountain warfare in the Cairngorms in 1943 they were sent on a course with the 52nd Infantry Division (who had been designated and trained as 'the Mountain Division') for training as 'muleteers' in the Highlands of Scotland. They returned with a mixture of memories of tortuous treks up and along mountain trails and great regard for those stubborn but surefooted and hard-working creatures – the mules.

Prior to the issue of jeeps various trials and tests were carried out to 'man-pack' heavy loads of ammunition, mainly as a requirement for some possible operations in which, after landing, the Commandos had to advance with all speed, attack, secure the objectives and then hold them against enemy counter-attacks. Without support weapons this was no mean task and meant they would have to rely and depend on their own small arms fire – plus plenty of ammunition.

During 1941 we started to train for this type of operation carrying heavy loads on 8- to 10-mile speed marches. We tried using hand carts for load carrying, but in the end more reliance was placed on 'pack mules'. These were volunteers within every Troop who carried excessive loads of ammunition in extra basic pouches; a typical load was 1,000 rounds of .45 ammunition.

'Tanky' Byrne was one such volunteer. Ruddy faced, strong as an ox, from the Border country, his knees visibly buckled as his heavy load was lifted up by his 'Pal' onto his broad shoulders. I can still see him on those killing speed marches, his sweating face, strained yet set with grim determination. Yet he never flagged or faltered. But at the end of these marches, as he dumped his load down on the ground, the verbal torrent of expletives gave vent to his feelings and relief.

For all that, the arduous and burdensome efforts of Tanky and his fellow pack mules were of no avail. The planning for this operation simply fizzled out and died. And for once we weren't sorry.

When we formed up at Weymouth in 1940 our signalling resources were basic and limited to the needs of those within the Troop itself. They consisted of verbal and written messages, the standard infantry hand and rifle signals, coloured Very light signals and various bird-sound signals. In our original F Troop we also practised semaphore with flags and tried to master the morse code using a hand torch to beam the 'dot-dashes'. It was all very amateurish!

The standard infantry hand and weapon signals were useful, although their use was subject to daylight and good visibility. All ranks were trained in the use of these simple signals, the main hand signals being 'Close on me' and 'Close on me at the double'.

The firing of coloured flares had a limited, but useful operational and training value, usually restricted to use when contact with the enemy (real or 'exercise') had been made. These coloured signals fired from the bulky Very light pistol consisted of three colours, white, red and green. Prearranged signals were used, to coordinate fire plans and tactical movements. They were easy and quick to implement and could be seen and acted upon by troops over a fairly large unit area. In training and especially on field firing exercises, the red signal was almost exclusively used on its own and meant 'Cease all firing'. It was a vital safety measure.

Initially in training we experimented with a variety of sound signals, indeed, it is amusing to read in our original 'F' Troop diary the account that followed our very first night exercises held on 25 and 26 July 1940 (only three and four days after our formation). The relevant sentence reads: 'We found the "nightingale" – bird imitation – signal was not a success as one could only use it in woods, but the "owl" signal worked very well.' On the whole little use was made of this type of signal thereafter.

Although many original COs had high hopes of every man in a Commando being able to use semaphore and morse code – see Colonel Newman's formidable list of training subjects, item 10, in Chapter III it was not possible because of higher priorities in the training syllabus.

However, a big step forward in the means of communication came when all the Commandos were concentrated on the west coast of Scotland and on the Isle of Arran in the winter of 1940. Plans were then afoot for a particular large-scale Commando operation, 'Workshop' – the capture of Pantellaria, a small island off Sicily, by a large force of four full Commandos. And it was rightly projected that this operation would need the proper means of communication and signals, both within the force and from force HQ to its higher command, for control and coordination. So in the first instance a Brigade Signals Troop should be formed.

Captain John Leahy (later Colonel) was given the task of raising this Troop on Arran. This significant measure was subsequently followed within a few months by the addition of a Signals Section in every Commando.

The personnel for these sections were recruited from within each Commando. Where necessary officers and NCOs were sent on courses of instruction at Lochailort or other signals training centres so that they could instruct and train the signallers and wireless operators within each Commando.

The Signals Section, commanded by a Lieutenant, often from the Royal Corps of Signals, consisted of up to a total of twenty NCOs and men and it was part of the Commando HQ, signallers being, as with the other specialists, detached to the fighting Troops as required for training and operations; again it was customary to attach the same signallers to the same Troops to promote that vital factor of 'team spirit'.

Although the main means of communication was voice on the wireless sets, the signallers were instructed in morse, semaphore and the use of the heliograph – although there wasn't much need for the latter two – and the laying of line telephones, the tracing and repair of line faults and the operation of a field exchange.

In the earlier days, following the issue of wireless sets, training focussed on the man-pack Nos 18 and 38, the ranges of which depended largely on the 'lie of the land' – where there were obstacles such as mountains, forests and buildings, the range was curtailed, and atmospheric interruption distorted reception. Bearing this in mind the maximum range of the two-man No 18 was up to 5 miles (voice) and 8 miles (continuous wave morse), whilst the much smaller and lighter one-man No 38 was up to an optimistic 4 miles.

The No 18, which weighed some 35 lb, plus batteries etc., was mounted on a frame and carried on the back of No 1, whilst his partner on the set operated it from his 'oppo's' back.

In addition to the normal problems of a regimental signaller those in the Commandos had to be able to keep up with the rest of the Troop, be it on a speed march, 'bashing cross country', rock climbing or in hazardous wetshod and rocky landings. It wasn't easy and to this extent their physical fitness and agility had to be not just as good as their Troop comrades, but even better. However, life was easier for the signallers operating the lighter No 38 set, which was small enough to be conveniently carried on the chest and operated from that position without any trouble. These signallers only needed the occasional helping hand.

As opposed to unit signallers in other regiments those in Commandos had to contend with waterproofing problems; after many experiments to solve this problem specially designed canvas waterproof bags were provided. They were so efficient that they kept the sets dry even after several hours of total submersion – which is more than can be said for their operators who frequently had to wade ashore through icy-cold, shoulder-high sea water or stumble through equally cold and fast-flowing rivers in Scotland carrying their previous equipment – and keeping up.

From the humble beginnings outlined here, by the end of the War the Commandos had the means – and were able – to call for supporting fire from artillery and tank units – plus air strikes. This was a long way off from those Weymouth days when we waved semaphore flags by day and experimented with bird calls on night exercises.

By 1943 practically all the innovations and new techniques developed in training by the Commandos from 1940 onwards for raiding and other operations, whether landing from the sea or by air, had been absorbed into various schemes of training by the rest of the Allied armies. Whereas in 1940 the phrase 'Commando Training' was unheard, unknown and meant nothing, by 1943 it was accepted and respected – by friend and foe alike – as the ultimate in the training of Special Service troops.

The aim of this training was simple and unequivocal: to produce an elite force of high morale, dedicated and prepared to carry out any military task asked of it. Fundamental to this aim was the basic training of the individual covering a wide range of military skills, but equally important was the development of such attributes as self-confidence, self-reliance and mental stamina.

Individualism was not sufficient in itself. Much of the success of the Commandos can be ascribed to their 'spirit'. This important factor was the end-product of various ingredients. Foremost of these was the fact that all the army Commandos were volunteers and could be RTU'd. Secondly, in the demanding and realistic training it was possible to test the leadership of the officers and senior NCOs, so that mutual respect could be built up between all ranks. And thirdly, in every Commando there was tremendous teamwork. This spread from the 'grass roots', with 'Me and My Pal', upwards through the Sections and Troops to embrace the whole Commando.

It was the combination of all these factors and attributes, fostered and developed during the training described that enabled the Commandos to succeed in action, so that by 1943, in their green berets, they had won an enviable and worldwide acknowledged status of military elitists.

But further, it is also imperative to appreciate that the sum product of this training extended far beyond the success of Commando operations. From mid-1941 onwards the offensive style and methods of this training became increasingly accepted, after some initial open and hostile opposition, copied and adopted by all the Allied land forces. It helped to raise morale and inculcated that resolute offensive spirit that was needed to beat the hitherto successful enemies in the Middle East, Europe and the Far East. This contribution, inspired by the then new style of Commando Training, must never be overlooked.

All the Commandos were frequently and regularly requested to provide

And finally. . .high morale and confidence, the outcome of thorough and demanding training under sound leadership, is evident on the faces of 1 Troop, No 3 Commando, in this photograph taken at the Limehouse Street Fighting location, London, just prior to D-Day 1944.

officers and ORs to assist in the training of other units. One has only to peruse the War Diaries to find ample evidence, whilst small detachments from outside were attached to Commandos 'for Commando Training'. At Achnacarry we had a constant stream of visitors for this purpose.

Furthermore, Commandos were constantly asked to put on demonstrations on a wide range of subjects – from rock climbing to street fighting. One pertinent comment following a demonstration for a group of VIPs headed by General (later Field Marshal) Alexander after they had watched a landing exercise, is worth repeating. It reads, '(he) was impressed by the speed, silence and general sinister efficiency of the Commando troops . . . ' Such was the revolution in training effected and developed by the Commandos during their formative years 1940 to 1942, and which later stood the tests of all their battles right to the end of the Second World War.

The high standard of rugged and thorough training was part of the proud heritage which we in the wartime Commandos were able to pass on to our post-war successors, the Royal Marine Commandos, who likewise in their green berets have fought with equal distinction in Korea, Malaya, Suez, Borneo, Aden, the Falklands and elsewhere. They would be the first to admit of their training too – 'It Had To Be Tough'.

Bibliography

There have been many good books written about the exploits of the Commandos and their 'offshoots', including the SAS and SBS, in the Second World War. The following list provides a selection for further reading. I have referred to some in the narrative and where I have quoted from any book, I have given the source and the author's name in the text as explained in the Introduction.

Barnes, 'Tag', *Commando Diary*, Spellmount Ltd, 1991.
Bradford, Roy & Dillon, Martin, *Rogue Warrior of the SAS*, Arrow Books, 1987.
Byrne, J.V., *The General Salutes A Soldier*, Robert Hale Ltd, 1986.
Churchill, Thomas, *Commando Crusade*, William Kimber & Co Ltd, 1987.
Courtney, G.B., *SBS In World War 2*, Grafton Books, 1985.
Dear, Ian, *Ten Commando 1942-1945*, Leo Cooper Ltd, 1987.
Durnford-Slater, John, *Commando*, William Kimber & Co Ltd, 1953.
Fergusson, Bernard, *The Watery Maze*, Collins Co Ltd, 1961.
Gilchrist, Donald, *Castle Commando*, Oliver & Boyd Ltd, 1960.
Gilchrist, Donald, *Don't Cry For Me*, Robert Hale Ltd, 1982.
'J.E.A.', *Geoffrey – the Story of 'Apple'*, Blandford Press, 1946.
Hunt, Sir John, *Life is Meeting*, Hodder Ltd, 1978.
Keyes, Elizabeth, *Geoffrey Keyes*, George Newnes Ltd, 1956.
Ladd, James, *Commandos and Rangers in World War 2*, Macdonald and Jane's Publishing Ltd, 1978.
Lovat, Lord, *March Past*, Weidenfeld and Nicholson Ltd, 1978.
Mason, David, *Raid on St Nazaire*, Macdonald & Co, 1970.
Messenger, Charles, *The Commandos 1940-1946*, William Kimber, 1985.
McDougal, Murdoch, *Swiftly They Struck*, Grafton Books, 1989.
Millin, Piper Bill, *Invasion*, Book Guild Ltd, 1991.
Mills-Roberts, Derek, *Clash By Night*, William Kimber & Co Ltd, 1956.
Moulton, J.L., *Haste to the Battle*, Cassell & Co Ltd, 1963.
Neillands, Robin, *The Raiders*, George Weidenfeld & Nicholson Ltd, 1989.

Phillips, Lucas, *The Greatest Raid Of All*, William Heinemann, 1958.

Riley, J.P., *From Pole to Pole*, Bluntisham Books, 1989.

Saunders, Hilary St George, *The Green Beret*, Michael Joseph, 1949.

Saunders, Hilary St George, *The Red Beret*, Michael Joseph, 1950.

Seymour, William, *British Special Forces*, Grafton Books, 1986.

Thompson, Julian, *Ready For Anything*, George Weidenfeld & Nicholson, 1989.

Young, Peter, *Commando*, Ballantine Books (New York), 1969.

Young, Peter, *Storm From The Sea*, Greenhill Books, 1989.

Index

(The index is limited to cover the main characters, main places and other relevant factors contributing and involved in 'Commando Training'; ranks given are those achieved – where known.)

Abyssinia/Eritrea 17
Achnacarry 21, 68, 70, 79-82, 88, 97-125, 153, 159, 189, 195
Adriatic operations 15
Airborne Forces 18-19
Aircraft, see Dakota, Whitley
Alexander, F.M. 206
Alexandria, Egypt 159
Allen, Capt Ken 80-1, 110
Allowances, Commando daily subsistence 23-4, 36, 168
'Altmark' 61
Amphibians, landing vehicle tracked (LVT) 66
Andrews, L/Cpl 'Taffy' 167
Appleyard, Capt G. 19, 26-7, 67
Arakan 162
Ardrossan, Saltcoats area 153
Army Physical Corps (APTC) 42
Arran, Isle of 37, 58, 151, 157, 187, 202
Ayr 64, 131

Balchin, Capt Tim 123
Bangalore Torpedoes 92, 138, 144
Barnes, Sgt 'Tag' 158-60, 162
Barry, Capt Joe 173, 177
Barry, Capt RM, John 173
Battle of the Atlantic 126, 133
Battle of Britain 28, 44-5, 51
Battle Inoculation/Battle Training 77-84
Belgaum, India 159
Bellringer, Sgt 115
Bend, Sgt Frank 164
Ben Nevis 97, 122
Bethesda, N. Wales 92, 164, 168
Bicycles, mobile reserve 47-51
Billets, civilian 24-29
Bitter Lakes, Egypt 152
Bissell, Sgt 'Sonny' 111, 113, 115
Black, Capt Gerald 19
'Black Out', wartime 43
Blain, Sgt Jock 157
Blunden, L/Cpl 'Chalkie' 9
Bombay, India 159
Bonner, Capt RM 66
Boots, Soulier Vebrun (SV) 147, 153, 167
Boys, Anti-Tank Rifle 9, 41, 76, 110, 142, 144

Braemar, Scotland 163, 169-70
'Brandyball', cliff climbing exercise 177-9
Bren Light Machine Gun (LMG) 20, 31, 41, 73-4, 78, 82-3, 106, 110, 139, 141-2, 144, 160
Brett, Capt Gerald 18
British Expeditionary Force (BEF) 1, 14
British Liberation Army (BLA) 177
Brookes, Sgt Ernie 21
Brown, Henry 160, 162
Burma 14, 159, 162
Burntisland, Scotland 128, 131
Byrne, Sgt J.V. 109-110
Byrne, 'Tanky' 201

Cairngorms, Scotland 169, 200
Calvert, Brig, 'Mad Mike' 89-90, 157
Cameron, Sir Donald of Lochiel 97
Camouflage 118
Campbeltown HMS 127, 130, 131
Canadian Army Forces 134
Canary Islands 67
Canoes, see Folbots
Cardiff Docks 128, 129
Carr, Capt Knyvet 86-7, 188
Castelorrizo, Dodecanese 17, 56
Cator, Lt Col 'Kid' 17
Chapman, Lt Col Spencer 89
Chattaway, TSM, Lew 10, 21
Chindits 17, 89, 157
Churchill, Lt Col Jack 13-14, 69, 188
Churchill, Capt Randolph 11
Churchill, Major General Tom 198
Churchill, Winston 1, 2, 17, 22, 28, 34, 46-7, 55, 181
Clarke, General Mark 155
Clarke, Lt Col Dudley 2
Clarke, Sgt Eric 199
Cleasby-Thompson, Capt 187
Climbers' Club of Great Britain 166, 167
Climbing, see Chapter IX, also 103, 120-1
Clovelly, Devon 51
Clovis, Capt Jack 102
Cocanada, Bay of Bengal 161-2
'Cockles', canoes 152
Comacchio, Lake 13, 20, 66, 195
Combined Operations 12, 53, 60, 68, 119, 130, 135, 164, 198

Commandos
 No 1 – 1, 16, 128, 158-61, 171
 No 2 – (Para) (No 11 Special Air Service
  Bn) 18, 51, 181-8
 No 2 – 13, 15, 18, 34, 38, 127-35, 194
 No 3 – 10, 12-14, 33-4, 59, 128, 134, 193
 No 4 – 4-9, 16, 21, 27, 52, 59, 128, 134-48,
  154, 164-8, 171, 177-9, 188, 200
 No 5 – 26, 128, 158-162
 No 6 – 21, 150, 200
 No 7 – 11, 27
 No 8 – 10, 11, 12, 25, 150
 No 9 – 13, 19, 20, 128
 No 10 – (Inter-Allied) 39, 176, 179, 197
 No 11 – 11, 12, 27, 37
 No 12 – 18, 39, 128, 169, 171, 173
 No 30 (later retitled 30 Assault Unit) 199
 No 40 (RM) originally 'A' RM Cdo 125, 134
 No 41 (RM) 125
 No 42 (RM) 125, 158
 No 43 (RM) 125
 No 44 (RM) 125, 158
 No 45 (RM) 125, 174-5
 No 46 (RM) 125, 174-5
 No 47 (RM) 125, 174
 No 48 (RM) 106, 125, 196
 No 50 (Middle East) 16, 52-3
 No 51 (Middle East) 16-17, 39, 52
 No 52 (Middle East) 16, 39, 52
 101 Troop (No 6) 150, 153
Commando Basic Training Centre, see Achnacarry
Commando Snow Mountain Warfare Training Centre
 (CSMWTC) 163, 169-72
Commando Mountain Warfare Training Centre
 (CMWTC) 163, 172-91
Holding Operational Commando (HOC) 125, 189
Commando Memorial, Spean Bridge, Front Cover
Commando – organization (UK) 3-4, 30-1, 85, 202
Commando – organization (Middle East) 28, 31
Commando – volunteers/selection/types 3-22
Copland, Major Bill 131
Cory, Capt Sam 196
Courtney, Capt Roger 5, 11, 149-50, 179
Courtney, Capt 'Gruf' 149, 155
'Crack and Thump' Demonstration 118
Crete 17

Dakota, aircraft 191
Dale, Pte 'Jock' 140-1
Darby, Lt Col, US Rangers 28-9, 104
Davidson, S/Sgt 116-7, 118
Davies, Bdr 'Barney' 142
Dawson, Lt Col Robert 16, 82, 84, 136, 145, 178
D-Day 10, 21, 25
Dear, Ian, author 197
Demolitions 90-1, 111
Demonstration Squad (Pipe Band) CBTC 117
Dene-Drummond, Maj General Anthony 17-18
Dewing, Maj General R.H. 2, 3
Diary, Unit War Diary 179, 197, 206
Dieppe, Raid, training 73, 133-48
Dill, FM, Sir John 28
Dinghies 66, 152, 176
Donkin, Pte 9
Dories, powered craft 65, 119, 152, 176
Durnford-Slater, Brig John 12, 33-4, 113, 199

Durrant, Sgt Tom, VC 128

Easton, Major N.K. 177
Eisenhower, General 'Ike' 158
Ennis, Lieut 'Carpet Slippers' 142
Eurekas, landing craft 56-7
Evans, Dvr, RASC 186
Explosives, types and uses 90-1, 128, 133, 145, 194

Fairburn, Capt W.F. 89-90, 93-7, 193
Fairclough, Gdsm 20
Fergusson, Brig Bernard 55
Fieldcraft, compass, map-reading 14, 41, 89, 102,
 116-9, 161
Fifth Columnists 50
Finland 88-9
First Aid/Hygiene training 36, 196-7
Flame-throwers 194
Fleming, Ian 90, 199
Fleming, Capt Peter 90
Folbots, canoes 151-2, 176
Foot, Capt Jimmy 153-5
Forfar Force 179-80
Fox-Hunter, Capt (DLI) 17
Fraser, Major Jim 176
Free French Commandos, see No 10 Cdo)
Frickleton, CSMI 111, 115
Fynn, Lt Col 169

Garnett, Sgt ('Tich') Vic 4, 21
Geneifa, Egypt 52
Gilchrist, Capt Donald 79-80
Glencoe 164
Glengyle, HMS 55, 59-64, 150
Glenroy, HMS 55
Goatley, folding boats 64-5, 119, 177
'Goebels' Battery, Dieppe 134
Grenades 20, 26, 83, 84, 194, 195

Halliday, Sgt Jimmy 9
Hardelot (France) Raid 142
Harden, L/Cpl H.E., VC 196
Haydon, Brig J.C. 105, 111
Hayes, Capt Graham 19
Heaynes, TSM, Les 21
Herbert, Lieut George 101
'Hess' Battery, Dieppe 135-6
Hill 170, Kaungdaw 20, 160, 162
Hillhead, Hampshire 156
Hilton-Jones, Capt Brian 39
Hitler's Directive – re Commandos captured 19
Holmes, Capt Bobby 90
Home Guard 1, 44, 67, 92, 154, 156, 195, 199-200
Horne, Pte 141
Houghton, Capt J.B.T. 19
Hunt, Brig John (later Lord Hunt of Everest fame)
 169-70, 172
Hunter, Col T, VC 66
Hutchison, Sgt 'Jock' 154

Imperial War Museum 95
Independent Companies 2, 13, 33
Inter-Services Training & Development Centre
 (ISTDC) 54-5
Invasion, Britain
 fears of 43
 scare 197-8

INDEX

Inveraray 61, 63, 68
Isle of Wight 156, 157, 180

Jackson Lt Col 183
James, RSM 115
Jungle 159

Keigwin, Capt Jim, RM 119
Kemp, Major Peter 89
Kennett, Sgt Ken 21
Keyes, Lt Col Geoffrey, VC 11, 36-7, 105
Keyes, Admiral Sir Roger 34, 53, 105, 150
King George V 148
King, Cpl C. 153
Kirkwall, Orkneys 67-8
Knowland, Lieut George, VC 20, 160
Knutsford, 182, 184, 187

Ladd, James, author 149
Lamlash, Arran 157
Landing Craft Assault (LCA) 55, 61-3, 138-9
Landing Craft Tank (LCT) 58
Langlands, Sgt G. 164, 166
Lassen, Capt Anders, VC 20, 36
Laycock, Maj General 'Bob' 5, 10-12, 109, 148
Layforce 11-12, 17, 61
Leach, 'Spider', CSM 120
Leahy, Col John 202
Legard, Lt Col, CPD 4, 6-7, 59
Lindley, Sgt Hugh 21, 140, 164
Lindsay, Capt Martin 185-6
Lister, Lt Col, Dudley 10, 27
Llanwryst, N. Wales 163, 173
Local Defence Volunteers (LDV), see Home Guard
Lochailort (STC) 70, 88-97, 129, 168, 185, 193, 202
Lochs, Arkaig and Lochy 97
Lockett, Major Geoffrey 157
Lofoten Islands 75, 168
Logs, use for PT 75, 168
Londonderry 39
Lovat, Brig, Lord 34, 83, 87, 89-90, 107, 135, 136, 142, 144
Lovat Scouts 171-2
Lulworth, Dorset 135, 136, 142
Lympstone, Devon 125

'Mae Wests' 58-9 147
'Maid of Honour' 19, 20, 66-7
Major, Sgt Frank 21
Malaria 161
Mann, L/Cpl 'Dickie' 139
Marching, route, cross-country and speed marches 35-40, 106-8, 201
March-Phillips, Major 'Gus' 19, 26-7, 66-7
Martin, L/Cpl Joe 167
Martin, Major 'Slinger' 10
Mayne, Lt Col Paddy 12, 37
McCarthy, Sgt 164, 167
McClelland, Sgt A. 116, 118
McDonough, L/Bdr 142
McDougal, Lieut Murdoch 9
McKay, Lieut 'Jock' 145
McVeigh, Sgt 9
'Me and My Pal' 48, 72-3, 108
Meddings, Sgt Sid 179
Medical sections 30, 139, 193, 195-7

Messenger, Charles, author 2, 28, 52
Millen, Piper Bill 117
'Milling', form of boxing 123-4
Mills, Sir William (re Mills grenades) 84
Mills-Roberts, Brig Derek 66, 135-6, 143
Montgomery, FM, Sir Bernard 179
Montgomery, Capt R. 129, 131
Moon, CSM, 'Ossie', 108-9
Morris, RSM, 'Jumbo' 21
Mortars, 2-in/3-in 20, 30, 76-7, 87, 110, 140, 143
Motor Transport (MT) 30, 47, 85, 193, 199-201
Moulton, Lt Col Jim 106
Mountbatten, Lord Louis 12, 127, 133, 146, 162
Mullen, Cpl Brian 198
Munn, Lieut 57
Murphy, Capt 'Spud' 110

NAAFI (Canteen) 99
Nash, Capt Bill 120
Neillands, Robin, author 107
Newby, Lieut Eric 152
New Forest 159
Newman, Lt Col Charles, VC 13, 34-6, 38, 127, 133
Newmarket 26
Newnham, Wing Commander 189
Niven, David 95
Normandy 16, 68, 162, 198
North Africa 11, 52
North Force 169
Norway 8, 89, 169

O'Brien, Sgt 20
O'Flaherty, Brig Dennis 18, 187
Olaf, Prince of Norway 187
Operations – Codenames
   'Cauldron' 135-6, 140
   'Chariot' 131-2
   'Cromwell' 47
   'Jubilee' 134, 147
   'Musketoon' 19
   'Overlord' 68, 87
   'Pilgrim' 67
   'Rutter' 134
   'Sea Lion' 1, 51
   'Torch' 155
   'Workshop' 202
Opposed Landing, Achnacarry 79-82

Padstow, Cornwall 156
Pantellaria, Island of 202
Parachuting, training 181-91
Parachute Regiment 188, 191-2
Paratroops (UK) 5, 181-92
Paratroops (other countries) 181, 182
Pascale, L/Cpl Joe 196
Pedder, Lt Col P. 37
Pennington, Lieut H. 128
'Phantom' Signals 95, 146
Phillot, Sgt Ken 21, 198-9
Phillips, Lucas, author 129
Physical training 42-3, 111, 113-5, 138, 154
PIAT, Projector Infantry Anti-Tank 76, 110
Pike, Sgt 'Spike' 9, 120
Pistols, Smith & Wesson, Colt .45 26, 41, 140, 144, 156
Plymouth 131

Pointe du Hoc, Normand 177
Poole, Dorset 19, 67
Porteous, Col Pat, VC 140
Portman, TSM, Bill 21 129-31, 145
Prince Albert, HMS 138, 144, 145
Pritchard, Major 'Tag' 188
Pritchard, Capt W. 128, 131
Public Records Office, Kew 197

Quiberville, Dieppe 138

Radio/Telephone/Wireless, see Signals/Signals
  Section
Ralph, Vic 159
Ranges, firing and practices 77-9
Ration cards and rationing 23-4, 36, 107
'Red Devils' 188
Red Sea 52
Rees-Jones, Major Geoffrey 163, 172
Return to Unit (RTU) 6, 24, 104
Rhine and Elbe River crossings 177
Rhodes, Island of 11
Ridgeway Hill, Dorset 48-50
Rifles, SMLE, No 4, Snipers and EY 10, 31, 41, 42,
  69, 70-1, 74, 77, 106, 108, 110, 117, 139, 144, 156,
  160, 195
Ringway 181, 182, 187
Rock, Major (RE) 181
Rockets, climbing aids, see Schumally
Roderick, Capt John 131, 132
Rommel's HQ, raid on 37
Ropes, climbing and rope-ways (i.e. 'Death Slide',
  Tarzan Course, etc) 111, 113-5
Royal Air Force 145, 181
Royal Navy, see Glengyle, Prince Albert
Ryder, Commander 'Red', VC 127

Saunders, Hilary St George, author 187, 188
Scapa Flow 75
Schumally rockets 174
Scilly Isles 132
Scots Guards, 5th Bn ski-troops 88-9
Sedgewick, Capt 146
Sellers, Sgt 198
Shanghai Police 89
Signals 30, 156, 201-2
Signals section 146, 202-4
Skerry, Sgt John 21, 145
Skye, Isle of 164
Slapton Sands, Devon 54
Small Arms School, Hythe 77
Small Scale Raiding Force (SSRF) 19, 20, 26, 66-7
Smith, Capt Tony 198
Smithson, Tpr M. 153
Smythe, Sqn Ldr Frank 158, 172
Snowdonia, N. Wales 158, 164
Southampton 130, 146, 158, 194
Special Air Service (SAS) 8, 11-12, 109, 120
Special Air Service Bn (original No 2 Cdo) 34, 187-8
Special Boat Section (SBS) 5, 8, 11-12, 149-57, 180
Special Service Bns (SS Bns) 31-2, 187
Sports and Games 42-3
St Ives, Cornwall 173-8
St Nazaire Raid, training for 13, 18, 126-33, 147, 194
Sten Machine Carbine (Sten) 76
Stirling, Lt Col 'Bill' 89

Stirling, Lt Col David 12, 44
Strange, Flt Lieut 181
Street Fighting 122, 131, 191-5
Sturges, Maj General R. 105
Style, Capt David 187
Submarines 5, 154-5
Swimming 4, 41, 57, 58, 59, 156
Sykes, Capt 89-90, 93-7, 193
Syllabus training 35-6, 102

Tatton Park 182, 184
Tenby, S. Wales 136
Territorial Army (TA) 2, 8, 13, 171
Terry, Sgt 11, 109
Thompson, Julian, author 185
Thorneycroft, Shipbuilders 55
Todd, Brig Ronnie 13
Toggle ropes 112, 114, 115
Tragino Aqueduct, Italy 188
Trevor, Lt Col Ken 16, 158-60
Troon 58, 83, 135, 136, 148
Tryfan, mountain, N. Wales 158, 164, 166
TSMC, Tommy Gun, Thompson Sub Machine
  Carbine 9, 20, 41, 74, 75, 76, 82, 83, 106, 111,
  144, 156, 160
Tunisian campaign 158

U Boats 126
Ulster Monarch, HMS 123
Unarmed Combat 35, 93-7, 116
US Rangers 28-9, 104, 105, 175, 177

Vaagso Raid 13, 14, 19, 168, 193-4
Varengeville, Dieppe 135, 147
Vasterival, Dieppe 138
Vaughan, Lt Col Charles 10, 21, 97, 100-1, 103,
  104-5, 111-2, 124, 189
Very light signals 81, 144, 146, 201, 202
Vickers MMG (Medium Machine Gun) 85-7

Wallbridge, Capt Wally 70-1, 110
Waugh, Evelyn 11
Weapons, Commando, see Bren LMG, Grenades,
  Mortars, Pistols, PIAT, Rifles, Sten, TSMC,
  Vickers MMG, also Chapter V in toto
Weapons, Enemy, use of 111, 160
Weapons, US, use of 111, 156
Webb, Capt Gordon 18
Welman, submersible 152
Weymouth 6, 21, 38, 41, 44, 51, 135, 136, 198, 201
Wheeler, Lieut George 132
Whitley aircraft 182, 186
Winchester 158
Wingate, Maj General Orde 17, 157, 158
Wintringham, Tom 195
Wireless sets, see Signals/Signals section
Woodcock, RSM, 'Timber' 21
Woodiwiss, Cpl 132
Woodward, Sgt 21
Wright, Capt Ken 198

Young, Brig Peter 5, 13, 31, 79
Young, Capt L.C. 4, 6, 8, 58
Young, Lt Col G. 16-17

Zennor, Cornwall 178